Biological Science

Teachers' Guide to the Laboratory Guides

Volume I
Maintenance of the organism
Organisms and populations

14 082605 X

Nuffield Advanced Science

Advanced Biological Science

Organizers

P. J. Kelly, Centre for Science Education, Chelsea College, University of London

W. H. Dowdeswell, School of Education, University of Bath: formerly Winchester College

Development team

J. A. Barker, Centre for Science Education, Chelsea College, University of London: formerly Borough Road College

B. J. Bull

L. C. Comber

J. F. Eggleston, School of Education, University of Leicester

W. H. Freeman, Chislehurst and Sidcup Grammar School for Boys

P. J. Fry, Brentwood College of Education: formerly Westcliff High School for Boys

J. H. Gray, Department of Education, University of Keele: formerly Manchester Grammar School

R. E. Lister, Institute of Education, University of London: formerly Wolverhampton Grammar School

B. S. Mowl, Centre for Science Education, Chelsea College, University of London: formerly Churchfields Comprehensive School

M. K. Sands, Department of Education, University of Nottingham: formerly King Edward VI Camp Hill School for Girls, Birmingham

C. F. Stoneman, Department of Education, University of York: formerly Dulwich College

B. J. K. Tricker, Victoria College, Jersey: formerly Eton College

K. O. Turner, Department of Education, University of Cambridge: formerly Hinckley Grammar School

Biological Science

Teachers' Guide to the Laboratory Guides

Volume I

Maintenance of the organism

Organisms and populations

Nuffield Advanced Science

Published for the Nuffield Foundation by Penguin Books

Penguin Books Ltd, Harmondsworth, Middlesex, England
Penguin Books Inc., 3300 Clipper Mill Road, Baltimore, Md 21211, U.S.A.
Penguin Books Ltd, Ringwood, Victoria, Australia

Designed by Ivan and Robin Dodd
Illustrations designed and produced by Penguin Education

Filmset in Monophoto Ionic by Oliver Burridge Filmsetting Ltd, Crawley and made and printed in Great Britain by Butler and Tanner Ltd, Frome.

Contents

Foreword

Sixth form courses in Britain have received more than their fair share of blessing and cursing in the last twenty years: blessing, because their demands, their compass, and their teachers are often of a standard which in other countries would be found in the first year of a longer university course than ours: cursing, because this same fact sets a heavy cloud of university expectation on their horizon (with awkward results for those who finish their education at the age of 18) and limits severely the number of subjects that can be studied in the sixth form.

So advanced work, suitable for students between the ages of 16 and 18, is at the centre of discussions on the curriculum. It need not, of course, be in a 'sixth form' at all, but in an educational institution other than a school. In any case, the emphasis on the requirements of those who will not go to a university or other institute of higher education is increasing, and will probably continue to do so; and the need is for courses which are satisfying and intellectually exciting in themselves – not for courses which are simply passports to further study.

Advanced Science Courses are therefore both an interesting and a difficult venture. Yet fresh work on Advanced science teaching was obviously needed if new approaches to the subject (with all the implications that these have for pupils' interest in learning science and adults' interest in teaching it) were not to fail in their effect. The Trustees of the Nuffield Foundation therefore agreed to support teams, on the same model as had been followed in their other science projects, to produce Advanced courses in Physical Science, in Physics, in Chemistry, and in Biological Science. It was realized that the task would be an immense one, partly because of the Universities' special interest in the approach and content of these courses, partly because the growing size of sixth forms underlined the point that Advanced work was not *solely* a preparation for a degree course, and partly because the blending of Physics and Chemistry in a single Advanced Physical Science course was bound to produce problems. Yet, in spite of these pressures, the emphasis here, as in the other Nuffield Science courses, is on learning rather than on being taught, on understanding rather than amassing information, on finding out rather than on being told: this emphasis is central to all worthwhile attempts at curriculum renewal.

If these Advanced courses meet with the success and appreciation which I believe they deserve, then the credit will belong to a large number of people, in the teams and the consultative committees, in schools and universities, in authorities and councils and associations and boards: once again it has been the Foundation's privilege to provide a point at which the imaginative and helpful efforts of many could come together.

Brian Young
Director of the Nuffield Foundation

General Editor of *Teachers' guide 1*:
W. H. Dowdeswell

Editor, *Maintenance of the organism*
C. F. Stoneman

Contributors:
C. F. Stoneman
W. H. Freeman
Margaret K. Sands

Editor, *Organisms and populations*
John H. Gray

Contributors:
John H. Gray
John A. Barker
L. C. Comber
W. H. Dowdeswell

Preface

The materials produced by the Nuffield Advanced Biological Science Project do not represent a rigid syllabus. They have been devised after careful evaluation of the results of extensive school trials so they can be used in a variety of ways related to the different circumstances found in schools and the varied abilities, backgrounds, and aspirations of students.

The work has three major objectives:
To develop in students the intellectual and practical abilities which are fundamental to the understanding of biological science.
To introduce students to a body of biological knowledge relevant to modern requirements, through investigating living things and studying the work of scientists. In doing so, students will consider the processes of research and the implications of science for society.
To develop in students the facility for independent study, especially how to learn through critical evaluation rather than memorizing by rote.

These aims have been central not only to the design of the publications and other materials but also to the complementary examinations that have been prepared.

Abilities

It is intended to develop abilities in the following kinds of work which are assumed to provide the basis for learning biological science:
1 Acquiring a knowledge of living things and an understanding of the techniques used to study them.
2 Making observations and asking relevant questions about them.
3 Analysing biological data and synthesizing it into conclusions and principles.
4 Handling quantitative information and assessing error and degree of significance.
5 Critical judgment of hypothetical statements in the light of their origin and application.
6 Making use of acquired knowledge for identifying and investigating problems with unfamiliar materials.
7 Evaluating the implications of biological knowledge for human society.
8 Communicating biological knowledge both coherently and with relevance.

Subject matter

The subject matter covers four units, each of approximately 90 periods (of 40 minutes) of class work and parallel homework or preparation. The units can be taken in various sequences and there are opportunities for a flexible treatment within each unit. The outlines of the units are as follows:

Maintenance of the organism
Interaction and exchange between organisms and their environment
Gas exchange systems
Transport inside organisms
Transport media
Digestion and absorption
Enzymes and organisms
Photosynthesis
Metabolism and the environment

The developing organism
Sexual reproduction
Early development
Cell development and differentiation
The nature of genetic material
Gene action
Development and the internal environment
Development and the external environment

Organisms and populations
Variation in a community
Inheritance and the origin of variation
The cell nucleus and inheritance
Population genetics and selection
Population dynamics
Organisms and their physical environment
Organisms and their biotic environment
The community as an ecosystem
Evolution and the origin of species

Control and co-ordination in organisms
The organism and water
The cell and water
Control by the organism
Stimuli and their influence
Nerves and movement
Structure and function: the nervous system
Social behaviour

We have attempted to provide a comprehensive, balanced, and integrated coverage of the main fields of biological science, both pure and applied (including biological technology). Where it is relevant, we have considered aspects of the physical sciences and mathematics in a biological context. Also, under a number of topics, we consider the nature of biological investigation and the social implications of the subject.

The units cover all levels of biological organization, that is, molecular levels, cellular levels, organ and tissue, organism and population. However, the focus of each is on the whole organism. They also illustrate many of the major themes or concepts of biology, such as variety and adaptation; structure in relation to function; organisms in relation to their environment; the similarity of many processes of physiology and behaviour; the genetic and evolutionary continuity of life; matter and energy cycles; homeostasis; development and the uniqueness of the individual.

We hope that students will also be encouraged to appreciate the aesthetic and humanitarian aspects of the subject, although this is clearly something for which the teacher must be primarily responsible.

We suggest that investigations should play a major part in the work. These can involve either practical work or investigations based on secondhand data, mainly in the form of excerpts from published literature, the results of experiments carried out by the project, or visual aids.

The practical work is described in the *Laboratory guides*, non-practical work in the *Study guide*.

The work in the *Laboratory guides* and *Study guide* is complementary and, in some cases, alternative. This makes it possible for students to do practical and non-practical work in varying proportions. At the same time, through the use of cross-references, questions, and bibliographies (which mention the specially prepared Topic Reviews), it is possible to make discussion, reading, demonstration, and written work an integral part of the investigations.

The work in the *Laboratory guides* and *Study guide* is of three types. *Preliminary work* aims to cover possible deficiencies in the students' background and provides reinforcement material for the less able student. *Main work* is within the capacity of the majority of A-level students. The amount of practical work has been carefully limited to fit into a reasonable allowance of time. *Extension work* contains broader and more rigorous treatments of some of the main work. It is intended for the more able and advanced student and gives him a range of exercises to choose from.

The materials have been devised so that they can be used for work with a class or small group or by individual students. However, we recommend that students should be encouraged gradually to rely more and more on their own resources. This is particularly important for Extension work and for projects. The latter are small-scale, open-ended, individual investigations described in the *Projects book*.

In short, this is not a specialized course, nor is it harnessed only to the needs of future biologists. It is an attempt to provide a way of presenting biological science as an interesting and important subject, relevant to scientist and non-scientist alike. We also hope that it will help those who undertake it to cultivate the abilities and attitudes which are necessary if they are to understand and evaluate the contribution that biological science makes to our society.

Using the Laboratory Guides

Each chapter in the *Laboratory guide* provides a coherent treatment of a series of biological topics based on practical investigations. Although the chapters are arranged in a logical order this is not intended to be prescriptive; other arrangements are possible.

Only the *Teachers' guide* makes a distinction between preliminary and main work. Extension work follows immediately after those chapters to which it is most closely related.

The investigations are enumerated by a decimal system. Before each, there is a short introductory section; each is arranged under two headings:
Procedure – The instructions for carrying out the investigations.
Questions – These provide a guide for analysing the results and also indicate the direction and purpose of the investigation.

A student should be familiar with both the procedure and questions before embarking on an investigation.

Preliminary and main investigations have been carefully designed to provide reliable results. Those in the Extension work are more open-ended and rely much more for their success on students' initiative.

The investigations are not simply intended to enable students to acquire knowledge of a biological topic. Other aspects are equally important and include experience of working personally with biological materials, of critically analysing their observations and techniques, of developing the intellectual abilities concerned with investigation, and of understanding how questions about living things can be answered.

The practical work is also intended to introduce students to biological topics in a way which will lead them to discuss and read about these further, as well as perform further practical work. The questions and the bibliographies will assist these continued studies.

Each investigation is treated in this Teachers' Guide under five headings:
Associated materials – References to complementary work in the *Study guide* and to visual aids.
Principles – An outline of the aims of the investigation.
Teaching procedure – Suggested approaches, links with other work in the *Laboratory guide*, and possible difficulties.

Practical problems – This section is concerned with practical teaching problems. Details of equipment, organisms, chemicals, etc., are found in the *Laboratory book*.
Questions and answers – This section repeats the questions in the appropriate part of the *Laboratory guide* and gives outlines of the kind of answers to be expected, together with suggestions for discussion and other relevant notes. The 'Additional bibliography' at the end of each chapter is an extension of that in the *Laboratory guide*.

The same headings are used in the *Teachers' guide* to the *Study guide* (*Teachers' Guide III*) with the omission of 'Practical problems'.

Cross reference

1 The reference number and title of an investigation in the *Laboratory guide* are the same in the corresponding *Teachers' guide*.
2 The reference number and title of an investigation in the *Study guide* are also the same in the corresponding *Teachers' guide*.
3 Details of laboratory organization, organisms, recipes, and apparatus are listed alphabetically in the *Laboratory book*.
4 Cross references to related investigations in the *Study guide* and *Laboratory guide* are listed in an abbreviated form under 'Associated materials'. Two examples follow:
L(M) 3.1. This denotes Laboratory Guide *Maintenance of the organism*, Chapter 3, investigation
S(M) 3.1. This denotes *Study guide*, part entitled 'Maintenance of the organism', Chapter 3, investigation 1.
Similarly, 'Associated materials' uses the symbols:
(P) for *Organisms and populations*.
(D) for *The developing organism*.
(C) for *Control and co-ordination in organisms*.
As with (M) for *Maintenance of the organism*, this applies whether the letter denotes a *Laboratory guide* or a part of the *Study guide*.
6 E denotes Extension work in the *Laboratory guides*.
7 Topic reviews are included in the bibliographies of the *Laboratory guides* and the *Teachers' guide* for the *Study guide*.

Planning work

1 The lists of 'Associated materials' in the *Teachers' guides* are intended to provide an outline of the topics covered. It is important to work out a suitable balance between practical and non-practical work and to take care to see that adequate time is available. In the early stages it is best to confine planning to a programme of preliminary and main work.

2 Consult the *Laboratory book* for requirements for practical investigations, including the preparation of materials in advance and the timing of work.
3 Questions can be selected from both the *Study guide* and *Laboratory guides*. These can be used as a basis for reviewing the topics by discussion or writing when the investigations are completed.
4 Use the questions and the bibliographies to lead into a programme of further reading and, if appropriate, Extension work from either the *Study guide* or *Laboratory guides*, or from both. Sometimes the ideas arising from an investigation may be used to guide pupils into project work.
5 From time to time it will be necessary to review large sections of the work in order to show the interrelations between topics. This will also provide an opportunity to stress major themes or concepts such as variety and adaptation, and the influence of the environment on organisms. There are some aspects of a subject which do not purely concern that biological topic alone but many others. They will, nonetheless, require separate consideration from time to time. They include:
The processes of biological research.
The historical development of certain fields of research.
The economical and social implications of biology.
6 It will be necessary for students to revise when they are preparing for more difficult work, for example, when they are using preliminary work to prepare for main work or when a review of the latter serves as an introduction to Extension work.

The *Teachers' guide* to the *Study guide* provides suggestions for organizing reviews and revision. Material can be collected by using the references under 'Associated materials', the indexes, and the bibliographies. Some of the investigations in the *Study guide*, especially Extension work, will be found useful for reviewing. Questions in both the *Laboratory guides* and *Study guide* can also be used as a starting point for reviews.

Maintenance of the organism

Chapter 1

Interaction and exchange between organisms and their environment

Chapter review

The chapter is intended to draw attention to a small community of organisms and show that questions which arise from examining it, though apparently simple, are really exceedingly complex. The distribution of populations, as an example, is complicated by the interaction of organisms with their environment.

The sequence of topics is:

1 Distribution in a model or natural community.
2 Concentration of oxygen in pond water. (We measure this environmental factor to see if it has any bearing on distribution.)
3 Interaction between organisms and their environment. (We measure the changes in atmospheric composition brought about by insects, plants, and human beings, to illustrate the extent to which organisms can influence their environment.)
4 Variation of carbon dioxide in air.
5 The effect of gas changes on locusts' breathing. (We measure the repercussions of 3 and 4 upon the physiology of locusts.)
6 Human consumption of oxygen. (This is measured by spirometry.)

Assumptions

– That students know the terms 'environment' and 'species'. The environment can be regarded as the sum total of the conditions in which an organism exists. Part of it is composed of other living things (biotic environment) and part, such as oxygen and temperature, is physico-chemical. The concept of species is apt to be difficult but it can be regarded here merely as the smallest classificatory group. There is no need at this stage to introduce any ecological or genetic aspects. No detailed knowledge of classification is needed beyond the fact that the animal and plant kingdoms have been divided into large groups or phyla. Students need not know names such as Mollusca and Arthropoda in advance.

- Ability to use a hand lens and a microscope properly.
- That students know the chemical terms 'acid', 'alkali', and 'indicator', and have a general idea of chemical reaction. Previous experience of titration will be useful but not essential.

1.1 Distribution in a model or natural community (preliminary)

Principles

In any community, however small, populations are seldom distributed uniformly. The uneven distribution of organisms can form a useful starting point for biological investigation.

Teaching procedure

Associated materials
S(M) 1.5
S(P) 1.1
Key to pond organisms

Much will depend on whether students have undertaken this type of work before. Ideally there should be a small pond or community of equivalent size close to the school laboratory which students can use from time to time throughout their school life. In the laboratory itself, aquarium tanks or shallow plastic containers make excellent substitutes and act as a convenient source of living creatures once they have been stocked with a variety of pond organisms.

If there is enough space each pair of students may adopt one such tank and observe it each time the laboratory is used. Even a single tank is enough to provide for a small class working in limited surroundings.

The more involved the students become in the establishment and maintenance of these tanks, the better. If they are going to study this chapter at the beginning of an academic year, model communities should be set up in the previous term. If this is not possible, tanks set up three or four weeks in advance will serve quite well. If organisms are not abundant at the time when they are most needed, additional *Daphnia*, *Tubifex*, and *Elodea* may be obtained from an aquarist supplier. There is no need to imitate a natural balance when attempting to provide a community of living organisms, and, obviously, it is necessary to take particular care not to introduce potential predators.

Practical problems

The number of organisms it is appropriate to examine and identify depends on the previous experience of the class. Consider that one plant and one animal are an absolute minimum; if students wish to identify more, this should be encouraged provided that there is adequate time. The paramount aim is to see that organisms are nearly always localized to some extent – that is, that they are distributed unevenly – and to seek explanations. This enquiry is the key to the next investigation.

Students will be using the tanks later so these should not be dismantled when the work of this chapter is completed. If laboratory space is severely limited, the tanks can be taken to a shaded part of the grounds or to a flat roof. If they are protected from falling litter by wire netting, communities will survive indefinitely. Out of doors, plastic tanks are preferable to glass ones as they are unbreakable.

Questions and answers

Did you find that the two species you selected each had a characteristic distribution, occurring in some places and being absent from others?

a Almost certainly the answer will be 'yes'. Sometimes the dividing line between colonized and uncolonized localities is surprisingly clear cut; more often it is gradual.

Within the range of the two species, to what extent did their density vary?

b The answers to the question will vary, particularly if relatively few specimens are involved. This may be a good point at which to introduce the idea of sampling errors, where numbers are small.

Could you show a relationship between variations in distribution and abundance, and the mode of life of the organisms concerned?

c Possibly, in the case of herbivores such as pond snails, which often have quite marked food preferences. Light can have a marked effect on distribution and species inhabiting shady corners may well be different from those preferring sun.

1.2 Concentration of oxygen in pond water (preliminary)

Principles

This exercise should introduce students to the technique of sampling water from a pond or tank and carrying out a simple analysis of one component of the physical environment.

Teaching procedure

Associated materials
S(M) 1.1, 1.3, 1.4

The method adopted for determining oxygen should be matched to the previous experience of the students. If they have already used the Winkler method, there is no point in using the simpler one described in *Laboratory guide (M)*. Winkler's method involves a little more chemistry than the simple iron(II) sulphate reaction suggested. The point to be made is that oxygen concentration is one physical factor out of many, which can be determined easily. It is undesirable to let the practical details obscure the primary aim, which is to see if there is any correspondence between variation in one physical factor and the distribution of one or more populations in the community.

Practical problems

It is important to emphasize that students should take samples of pond water carefully. The return of indicator colour, after titration is completed, is a most useful teaching point as it brings home the fact that oxygen from the air dissolves readily in water. This is exceedingly relevant to the subject of animal distribution in aquatic habitats.

Questions and answers

What was the concentration of oxygen in the water sample that you tested?

a A wide range of results is possible, from about 30 per cent saturation near the mud to almost 100 per cent at the surface.

At the height of the summer when photosynthesis is proceeding actively and there is much green vegetation, the water may be super-saturated, i.e., contain bubbles of undissolved oxygen.

How far did successive estimates of samples from a particular locality vary? How do you account for any variations?

b Variations could be due to inconsistent sampling or poor technique in titration. There will always be some error; the question is how much can be tolerated – see L(M) 1.3.

Did the class results show any variation of dissolved oxygen in different localities? If so, can you suggest any hypotheses to explain them?

c If a pond is sampled during summer the results can be striking. The oxygen gradient in a tank will never be marked. Oxygen will tend to reach a maximum concentration near photosynthesizing green plants and a minimum on mud.

1.3 Interaction between organisms and their environment

Principles

The aim of this investigation is that students should find that organisms change the content of oxygen in the environment round them, and should gain some idea of the meaning of interaction as a two-way process. For practical reasons it is better to use larger animals than those found in model communities. Now we are using terrestrial organisms, we need to introduce a technique for measuring the content of oxygen in air.

Teaching procedure

Associated materials
S(M) 1.1, 1.2, 1.3, 1.4, 1.6, 1.7, 1.8

If possible, students should investigate further the question raised in *Laboratory guide (M)* concerning the fate of organisms in a sealed tank. Comparing this with a sealed bottle of plants, often used for indoor decoration, can be a useful way of comparing an aquatic environment with a terrestrial (gaseous) environment.

The programme of work is highly flexible; the basis proposed in *Laboratory guide (M)* is minimal. If the technique of gas analysis is new to students, it may be best to limit the range of experiments to this minimum. But if they find no problems in the techniques, the scope of the investigations can be widened. Students, of course, know that animals consume oxygen but they may be less sure how much is taken in. They may also be unsure of the atmospheric changes brought about by plants. Germinating seeds are atypical in this respect and are suggested as suitable material partly because they are easily obtained and prepared, and partly because they raise fundamental questions about the position of plants in general, as suppliers and consumers of oxygen.

Possible additions to the three samples of air proposed are:
1 A transparent container of green plants such as cress which have received continuous light for 24 hours.

2 A similar container of plants which have been kept in the dark for 24 hours.
3 A container of locusts kept at high temperature (25° C) for 24 hours.
4 A similar container of locusts kept at lower temperature (15° C) for the same time.

In all cases there should be as many organisms as possible in the containers without causing apparent distress to the insects, so that head space is reduced and the change in atmospheric composition is as great as possible in the period of 24 hours.

The proposed method of air analysis is concerned only with content of oxygen and carbon dioxide and depends on simple principles. Students can readily understand these, and they should realize that the technique is limited and does not result in a complete analysis of air.

The questions of experimental error and the consistency of results are almost bound to arise in practical work of this kind. The term 'standard deviation' is mentioned to students in passing. Whether or not this is the place to go more deeply into the subject depends on the students' previous experience and mathematical inclinations. The following example of calculations indicates how little effort need be involved:

Per cent oxygen in air obtained	*mean per cent*	*deviation from mean*	*square of deviation*	*mean of squares*	*square root of mean, i.e. standard deviation from the mean*
20·2		−0·9	0·81		$\sqrt{1{\cdot}34/3}$
21·8	21·1	+0·7	0·49	$\frac{1{\cdot}34}{3}$	$\sqrt{\frac{134}{3}}$ ±0·67
21·3		+0·2	0·04		

This is a good way of showing that merely to calculate a mean does little to show how reliable results obtained by a class or individual are. What we need to do is to establish the degree of divergence from the mean. Thus, in our example, having calculated the standard deviation we can re-write the mean as 21·1±0·67, i.e. the true mean lies within the range 21·77 to 20·43 per cent. A small standard deviation is an indication of consistent procedure and stable apparatus. It is no guarantee that the results are correct; the technique may be consistently inaccurate! This kind of consideration should be presented to students at this stage.

Practical problems

Capillary tubes of suitable bore are available from suppliers. These are bent into the shape of a J to make it easier to introduce a sample from air collected over water. If the sample is introduced from a syringe barrel, a straight capillary will be as good as a J tube. If a straight tube is too long for a sink, a measuring cylinder (500 cm^3) full of water will serve instead. A piece of Scalafix tape on the side of the cylinder makes it possible to measure the length of the bubble without withdrawing the tube from the water. Errors due to parallax must be avoided.

If the bubble is moved to and fro too quickly it may break into smaller ones. This is less common in straight tubes than in J tubes and in any case is usually put right by a little slow, careful shunting. Traces of oil or dirt in the capillary are sometimes to blame. Tubes should therefore be well cleaned with detergent before use.

Questions and answers

Compare the figures for oxygen and carbon dioxide obtained from air associated with locusts, germinating seeds, and human breath and from unaltered, laboratory air (control). Which set of results differs most from that obtained for laboratory air?

a The sample of human breath would be expected to show the greatest divergence from laboratory air. Much will depend on the relative amounts of respiring organisms and head space in the container.

Compared with normal, laboratory air, do the other samples show: an increase in oxygen and an increase in carbon dioxide, or an increase in oxygen with no change in the amount of carbon dioxide, or a decrease in oxygen with an increase in carbon dioxide, or a decrease in oxygen with no change in the amount of carbon dioxide? (As already mentioned, no decrease in carbon dioxide, compared with 0·03 per cent, can be measured by this method.)

b There is an increase in oxygen with an increase in the amount of carbon dioxide.

Was the answer to question (b) *expected? If so, for what reason or reasons?*

c That organisms consume oxygen is well known. It seems reasonable to suppose that this is replaced by another gas, carbon dioxide. The effect of plants upon the atmosphere round them may not be quite what was expected. No production of oxygen should occur unless the plants exhibit green coloration, and even if they do, the amount of light shining on them in the 24 hour period is a critical factor.

What further measurements would you have to make in order to find out the amount of change in the composition of air produced per unit of living organisms by locusts, germinating seeds, and human beings?

d It is necessary to know the amount of living material present in the containers. This may give rise to a discussion of fresh and dry weights. The volume of head space must be known though it is difficult to measure. If green plants are used, the amount of light must be known. Temperature plays an important part and should be considered when dealing with plants and insects. In the case of exhaled air from people, note the activity of the person giving the breath sample. This serves as a link with investigation L(M) 1.6.

1.4 Variation of carbon dioxide in air

Principles

The inadequacy of the capillary method for detecting the minute fraction of carbon dioxide (0·03 per cent) in normal air, emphasizes the need for alternative techniques in a scientific investigation.

Carbon dioxide forms a weak acid when dissolved in water; other gases of the air do not. Appropriate indicators change colour with changes in the concentration of carbon dioxide. Standard bicarbonate solution is used with the indicators to ensure stable colour in air of constant composition. The fact that carbon dioxide is determined by way of pH and not by a specific reaction, should be borne in mind.

Teaching procedure

Associated materials
S(M) 1.2, 1.4

The bicarbonate/indicator technique has wide applications and should not be restricted to the three examples, locust, seeds, and human breath, unless time is pressing. A useful way of revising is to set up additional corked tubes with organisms from the model community, such as pond weed and small animals, which will survive actually immersed in the bicarbonate/indicator. When pond weed or any green plant is used it is easy to observe the effect of illumination on the concentration of carbon dioxide.

Questions and answers

Assume that the changes in colour are due to carbon dioxide alone. Which of the test-tubes contains more carbon dioxide after one and a half hours and which contains more after twenty-four hours? Suggest a reason for this.

a The colour changes indicating increased carbon dioxide should correspond with the results obtained previously with the capillary tube method. Exhaled air changes bicarbonate/indicator to pale yellow. In each instance the amount of respiring tissue compared with the volume of the sample is the important consideration when comparing results.

Has the locust caused the same change in colour as the germinating seeds?

b If left long enough any respiring tissue will cause bicarbonate/indicator to turn pale yellow. This means that the concentration of carbon dioxide is high, but not necessarily the same in all cases. In a period of a few hours it is unlikely that locust and germinating seeds, in equivalent quantity, will produce the same colour change.

Is it reasonable to expect the same change in colour when equal amounts of bicarbonate/indicator are exposed to equal weights of living materials for equal periods?

c No. Equal weight of living material may imply equal quantities of living protoplasm but organisms may consist of varying amounts of non-living material such as skeleton. Even if this were not so, there is no reason to suppose that one gramme of animal protoplasm produces carbon dioxide at the same rate as one gramme of plant protoplasm.

What factors outside the test-tubes might influence the rate of carbon dioxide production by the organisms?

d Temperature. If green plant tissue is used, light is important.

How could you modify this technique so that it is more quantitative?

e By measuring the colour of the indicators by comparison with standards. This may be done visually or by means of a colorimeter. A graph showing equivalence between indicator colour, pH, and carbon dioxide concentration should be consulted.

1.5 The effect of gas changes on locusts' breathing

Principles

The concentration of carbon dioxide has marked effects on the breathing rate of insects and man. Students can discover that this is the primary factor when they put locusts into atmospheres of pure oxygen and mixtures of oxygen and carbon dioxide.

Teaching procedure

Associated materials
S(M) 1.4, 1.5, 1.7

This is an easy piece of practical work but it requires careful observation and some thought. The procedure may be extended to include the use of nitrogen if this is available; it is not essential. The argument runs thus. Exhaled air causes an increase in locust breathing rate. Is this due to low oxygen concentration or high carbon dioxide? If, instead of breath, we used a mixture of 96 per cent oxygen and 4 per cent carbon dioxide, this should decrease the breathing rate if it is governed by oxygen concentration but leave the rate unaffected if it is governed by carbon dioxide concentration. This kind of experiment provides an opportunity for students to make their own hypotheses and test them.

Questions and answers

What effect, if any, does exhaled air have on the frequency of the breathing movements of a locust?

a It increases the breathing rate.

Does this result support the hypothesis that the movements become faster as the concentration of oxygen becomes less?

b Yes; there is less oxygen in exhaled air than normal air. But there are several other differences between the two that might have an effect on breathing rate.

What conditions around the locust have been altered because you breathed into the syringe barrel? Do you have adequate means of knowing all the changed conditions?

c The oxygen concentration is less. The carbon dioxide concentration is greater. The concentration of water vapour is greater. The temperature is higher. These changes have been discovered either from the gas analysis of previous experiments or from direct observation (e.g. of the condensation of water droplets on the inside of the syringe barrel). There may be other changes (e.g. in nitrogen concentration) which we cannot know at this stage.

How can you modify stage (3) of the procedure in order to reduce the number of variable factors associated with exhaled air?

d We could pass breath through soda lime to remove carbon dioxide, and through calcium chloride to remove water, and cool it. This would reduce the number of variables. Alternatively, a mixture of oxygen (approximately 15 per cent) and nitrogen (85 per cent) could be made from pure sources. The results in either case should question the hypothesis.

Do the results of stage (6) of the procedure support the hypothesis or do they run counter to those of stage (3)?

e The hypothesis may still be open to consideration, depending on the experiments actually performed, but the idea that carbon dioxide plays or may play a significant part in controlling breathing rate should be apparent.

Formulate a hypothesis about the rate of breathing and the composition of the atmosphere, from your results.

f Breathing rate of resting locusts depends on the concentration of carbon dioxide in the air breathed. It is, perhaps, more important that the hypothesis is derived from the observed results than anything else. Attempts to guess the 'right' answer should be discouraged.

1.6 Human consumption of oxygen

Principles

We have been concerned in this chapter with changes in an environment brought about by organisms living in it. Qualitatively, the gas changes in the atmosphere are well known. To answer the question, 'How much oxygen do we take out of the air?', we use a spirometer. If this is filled with pure oxygen and the carbon dioxide produced by the subject absorbed, then we can determine the amount of oxygen consumed in a short period.

Teaching procedure

Associated materials
S(M) 1.4, 1.7

In investigations with human subjects, apparatus must be faultless; do not use home-made spirometers. The dimensions, particularly those affecting the volume of dead space, are critical.

Official guidance on experiments with pupils states that they should not undertake work with a spirometer unless the teacher is adequately trained in its use.

Give careful consideration to the selection of the subjects; medical histories should be known. The safest course may be for the teacher to be the only subject of such an investigation – always providing that he or she is physically fit. Point out to students the dangers of using spirometers when unsupervised, and explain the biological reasons.

It is necessary to use medical grade oxygen. Although industrial and laboratory cylinders are filled with pure oxygen, harmful dust may accumulate inside. Medical cylinders are checked against this hazard.

The instructions provided by manufacturers, with the spirometer, should be consulted and followed in detail.

This investigation measures the subject's uptake of oxygen in a five minute period. This is much shorter than the duration of 'environmental' change in locusts and seeds in L(M) 1.3.

Questions and answers

Would you expect the rate of consumption of oxygen, after exercise, to differ from the rate in a resting subject? Give reasons for your answer.

a Most students will expect a greater consumption of oxygen after exercise, because panting is a familiar phenomenon. But it should be pointed out that the subject, on both occasions, is sitting down and it is more reasonable to expect high consumption of oxygen during, not after, exercise. This could lead to an elementary discussion of oxygen debt.

Determine how much oxygen the resting subject consumed in five minutes and calculate how much he would consume, at the same rate, in twenty-four hours. Compare this with the amount of oxygen the locusts consumed in the earlier investigation (1.3).

b To compare the uptake of oxygen in two different animals, it is necessary to find the amount of organism present in each. If we know the weight (mass) of the organisms, the dead space volume, and the duration, it is possible to convert the results of the gas analysis into oxygen consumption expressed as $cm^3\ h^{-1}\ g^{-1}$. Though the weight of the human subject is the obvious quantity to find and use, the surface area of the body is found to be a more reliable datum when comparing the oxygen consumptions of different people.

Calculate the rate at which a subject consumes oxygen after vigorous exercise. Compare this result with the rate for a resting subject. Is the amount consumed after exercise greater than, the same as, or less than in a resting subject?

c The amount is greater after exercise than it is in a subject who has been resting for an hour.

Are the results of the two measurements (stages 6 and 7) strictly comparable? Are the conditions the same for both measurements? If not, state the factors which vary. What steps could be taken to overcome this variability?

d A subject who has just finished some vigorous exercise usually feels and appears hot. It may be argued that the breath on this occasion is hotter than previously and that this may affect measurements of gas volume. The temperature of the gas in the box should be measured on both occasions. If it differs considerably, the volume of oxygen consumed should be corrected. For example if 5000 cm^3 of oxygen at 27° C were consumed in 5 minutes but 'resting' consumptions of oxygen had been measured as 1000 cm^3 at 20° C, then the volume at the higher temperature could be reduced to one at 20° C thus:

At 20° C the volume 5000 cm^3 would be $5000 \times \frac{293}{300} = 4883\ cm^3$.

Alternatively, both volumes could be corrected to 0° C. It is important that students should realize that temperature can have a considerable effect on gas volume.

Additional bibliography

General reading

Macan, T. T. and Cooper, R. D. (1960) *A key to the British fresh- and brackish-water gastropods*. Freshwater Biological Association Scientific Publication No. 14.

Nuffield O-level Biology (1966) Text Year I *Introducing living things*. Longmans/Penguin. (Clear instructions are given on how a microscope should be used.)

References

Best, C. H., and Taylor, N. B. (1964) *The living body*. 4th edition. Chapman & Hall.

Bishop, O. N. (1966) *Statistics for biology*. Longmans, Green.

Bryant, J. J. (1967) *Biology teaching in schools involving experiment or demonstration with animals or with pupils*. Association for Science Education.

Dowdeswell, W. H. (1967) *Practical animal ecology*. 3rd edition. Methuen. (Estimation of oxygen and other physical factors. Statistical aspects.)

Eggleston, J. F. (1964) 'A note on the measurement of the oxygen content of an air sample.' *Sch. Sci. Rev.* **156**, 398.

Nuffield O-level Biology (1966) Text Year III *The maintenance of life*. Longmans/Penguin.

Chapter 2

Gas exchange systems

Chapter review

This chapter follows up lines of enquiry begun in the previous one, turning from the activities of living organisms to the structures responsible for them. Its aim is to seek an anatomical basis for the functions studied previously. Plants and animals breathe in the sense that they change the surrounding atmosphere. What parts of their bodies are responsible for gas exchange and how are they adapted for this function?

Microscopic study and dissection are introduced as essential techniques for dealing with such questions. These are seen as scientific investigations demanding observation, imagination, and the formation of hypotheses, not merely illustrations supporting statements in textbooks.

The sequence of topics is:

1 Gas exchange in leaves.
2 The breathing system of a locust.
3 The fine structure [histology] of the breathing system of a locust.
4 The breathing apparatus of mammals.
5 The fine structure [histology] of the lungs.
6 The capacity of the human lungs [spirometry].

Assumptions

For this chapter, there are hardly any facts which have to be known in advance. Even the carriage of dissolved gases by blood is not a necessary item of information at the outset. However, two concepts are important:

- The diffusion of gas and liquid molecules and the enormous difference between the rates of diffusion through air and water. Diffusion through water is about ten thousand times slower than through air.
- The diffusion of molecules through apparently solid barriers, such as cells.

Note: (*1*) The whole chapter is concerned with diffusion, though this is not stated explicitly in *Laboratory guide (M)*. (*2*) The terms 'respiration' and 'respiratory' are reserved for metabolic (chemical) activities. This chapter is concerned with 'breathing'.

2.1 Gas exchange in leaves (preliminary)

Principles

Leaves have a spongy mesophyll and contain much air. By choosing a leaf with stomata on one side only (e.g. *Impatiens balsamina*) we can, in a simple experiment, connect the escape of air with the distribution of stomata as seen under the microscope.

Teaching procedure

Associated materials
S(M) 2.2

Showing the escape of gas from a leaf is a common O-level experiment and students need not repeat it if they are already familiar with it.

The examination of leaf surfaces can be undertaken by three groups, each adapting a different method: stripping, impressions, and replicas. It should be stressed that the third method does not damage leaves and so a number of replicas can be made of one leaf over a period of time without detaching the leaf from its parent plant.

Ideally, microtome leaf sections of the same plant (*Impatiens*) should be available but failing this *Ligustrum* (privet) is a satisfactory substitute.

Laboratory guide (M) does not mention the guard cell mechanism or the fact that stomata open and close. This is of great importance but adequate studies of the process are lengthy. Students' previous knowledge and the teacher's discretion can decide whether to raise the subject at this stage in the work.

Practical problems

It will not be possible to see air emerging from leaves unless the water is very nearly boiling.

If other curing agents are used Silcoset 105 may take hours to set. With curing agent 'D' this process is rapid.

Questions and answers

(First set)

Do the bubbles come from the upper surface only,

a No.

from the lower surface only, or

b Yes.

from both surfaces? (The terms 'upper and 'lower' refer to the natural position of the leaf on the plant.)

c No.

(Second set)

Can you find holes (stomata) in the epidermis (see 1) or epidermal strip (see 2)?

a Yes.

Are stomata to be found in the upper epidermis only, the lower epidermis only, or both?

b Lower (abaxial) surface only.

Do these answers correspond to those to the previous set of questions?

c Yes; anatomical investigation agrees with experimental results.

How do the epidermis cells of Impatiens *differ from those shown in figure 7*, which is taken from the leaf of another kind of plant? Make a simple outline drawing to show about the same number of cells as in figure 7 but taken from your preparations.*

d A tracing from the micrograph might form a useful comparison beside the drawing of *Impatiens* epidermis.

You can see from figure 7 that the stoma itself may be easily confused with the larger depression which surrounds it. Measure the length and greatest width of an open stoma in your preparation.

e –

(Third set)

How many different kinds of cells, judging by their shape, can you find in the leaf section? Describe their shapes and positions briefly.

a Four or more; epidermal cells, palisade, and spongy mesophyll cells. Various vessels.

What is the distance d *(figure 8).*

b –

2.2 The breathing system of a locust

Principles

After studying the breathing movements of living locusts, the next step is to look inside the body for air passages.

Teaching procedure

Associated materials
S(M) 2.1, 2.3

It is appropriate to consult textbooks when problems of interpretation arise but it is possible to find out a good deal about the tracheal system of a locust without prior knowledge of internal anatomy.

The exercise provides an opportunity to outline the general principles of dissection. Students should identify the large organs (e.g. alimentary tract) in preparation for later work.

Questions and answers

Describe the different silver structures in the locust's body.

a In addition to many silver threads (tracheae) there are also conspicuous air sacs.

*Figure references in the questions refer, of course, to figures in the *Laboratory guide*.

List the internal parts of the body with tracheae leading to them. Examine for example the muscles and the ovaries or testes. (The ovaries are prominent yellow bodies; the testes are white, finger-like structures in the abdomen.)

b The point of the question is to bring home the fact that *all* the internal organs are supplied with tracheae.

Describe the general arrangement of tracheae and their relationship with the apertures or spiracles in each segment. This is a difficult task; to answer the question completely demands skilled dissection and much time. The relationship between tracheae and spiracles is fairly straightforward. Record your findings in diagrammatic form, that is, a plan which shows the relative positions but does not necessarily make the organs look like the real ones.

c This is a difficult task; students should not be allowed to spend too long trying to work out the system. (See figure 1.)

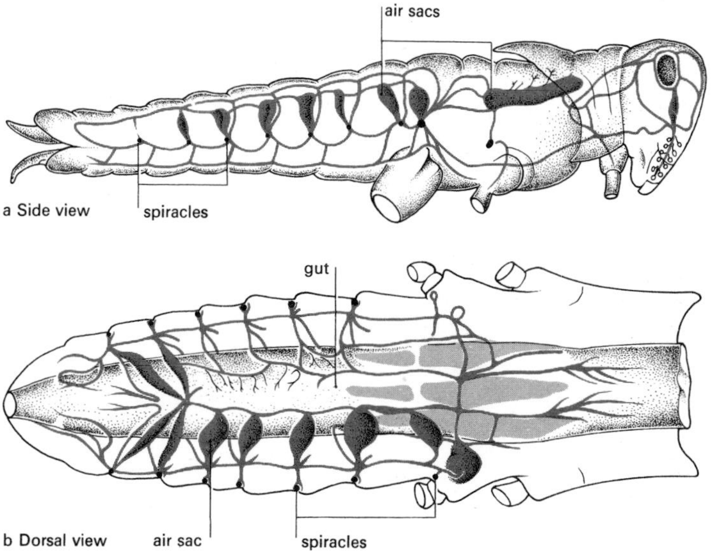

Figure 1
Dorsal view of the locust's tracheal system.

Is there any anatomical evidence to support the idea that locusts breathe through their mouths?

d No, but this does not rule out the possibility.

2.3 The fine structure of the breathing system of a locust

Principles

The thread-like tracheae permeating organs such as the gut wall are easily seen under a microscope. However, the smallest branches of these appear to end abruptly.

Students may conclude, rightly, that this is due to fluid in the tubes which obscures the terminations. *Laboratory guide (M)* does not mention tracheoles because these cannot be seen in temporary, unstained preparations. The teacher should provide this information or direct pupils to written accounts of the complete system.

Teaching procedure

Associated materials
S(M) 2.1, 2.3

The gut has been chosen because it is easily seen and dissected. Some members of the class might well be directed to prepare other organs for microscopy.

Pieces of gut wall immersed in alcohol or ethylene glycol mono ethyl ether for a few hours or overnight usually have the appearance shown in figure 13 of *Laboratory guide (M)*.

The preparation of leaf midrib tissue should take only a minute or two and could be delegated to one member of the class.

Questions and answers

What function do you think the rings or loops in the tracheae perform?

a The rings may prevent the tubes from being squashed flat, and so blocked by pressure of the tissues round them.

If there are ringed vessels in the midrib of a leaf, too, does this suggest they do a job similar to that of an insect's tracheae? Do the vessels in the plant appear to contain air?

b Yes, but plant vessels are not silver and presumably contain water or sap, not air. Perhaps these are subject to pressure from the surrounding cells and might become blocked for this reason. (The rings prevent collapse due to low pressure in the vessels.)

How do tracheae end in the gut wall? Is there any evidence that they, like blood capillaries, eventually join larger tracheae to enable circulation of air in one direction?

c The smallest branches appear to end blindly. There is no visible evidence that they join together like a capillary bed.

If you find a trachea which appears to be discontinuous as in figure 13, does this give you any help in interpreting the 'blind' endings of the smallest tracheae?

d Tracheae appear discontinuous, after immersion in liquid, like those in figure 13 of *Laboratory guide (M)*. The 'blind' endings may be filled with liquid, thus preventing a clear view of the real endings.

Now that you have looked at the breathing movements of a living locust and the arrangement of tracheae inside a dead one, how do you think these animals bring about the exchange of gas between their internal organs and the surrounding air? Consider the size of the tracheae.

e Breathing movements, by disturbing the tracheae and air sacs, presumably shift air to and fro to some extent along the tubes. Some movement of gases must be due to diffusion but this would be expected to be slow, considering the diameter of the smallest tracheae (the thinner the tubes the greater is the resistance to the flow of fluids). The system seems to require additional 'pumps' of some kind to bring about gas exchange between internal organs and the outside air.

2.4 The breathing apparatus of mammals

Principles

The dissection of a mammal differs considerably from that of a locust; a secondary aim of this dissection is to extend the experience of students so that they become aware of general, gross differences in organization between insects and mammals.

The main conclusion to be drawn from it is the fact that air goes to the lungs, not directly to every part of the body, and that another medium (blood) carries the dissolved gases to the body tissues. Students will probably be aware of this principle already.

Teaching procedure

Associated materials
S(M) 2.1, 2.9
S(C) 2.6

Mice are suggested for dissection because they are cheap and readily available. Rats, guinea pigs, or rabbits are preferable because of their size. Mice are too small to be used for the U-tube manometer investigation but if one or two rats are obtained for the whole class, this should be sufficient to enable everyone to appreciate Procedure stages (12)–(15).

A collection of hearts should be kept, in alcohol, for the work of L(M) 3.4.

Students should note the positions of the main abdominal organs for future reference.

Practical problems

Dexterity is required to make a good joint between a cut trachea and a cannula or glass jet, but it is a task well within the capability of most students.

The dissection of mice requires good illumination and the frequent use of a binocular microscope. After the thorax has been fully opened it may be helpful to cover the dissected mouse with water; this will help to separate the organs and remove blood.

Questions and answers

Living muscle can contract and become taut. At other times it can be relaxed, and hardly tense at all. Do the muscles of the dead mouse appear to be contracted or relaxed?

a Muscles of a freshly killed mouse are usually relaxed.

The diaphragm is muscle. Was it tight or loose when you first examined it? Is the state of the diaphragm likely to be due to muscle contraction?

b Tight: this could be rigor mortis or tension induced by something other than active contraction.

Describe the tension of the diaphragm when the thorax has been opened. If the tension has changed how do you account for this?

c Diaphragm is slack, at least on the side nearest the puncture.

How can you distinguish between the oesophagus and the trachea; is the difference between them related to their functions?

d The trachea is ventral, in the same relative position as our own windpipe. It has rings or, more precisely, half-hoops (of cartilage).

Is there any similarity between the trachea of a mouse and a trachea in a locust?

e Yes; the many transverse hoops.

If gases pass from the outside air to the lungs, how do they pass on to all the other tissues of the body? Try to put your answer in the form of a simple hypothesis based on your mammalian dissection rather than on previous knowledge.

f The only vessels connected with the lungs, other than the trachea and bronchi, are blood vessels. Presumably blood carries gases to and from the lungs.

A rise in the level of the fluid in the open side of the U-tube indicates a rise in pressure. When you moved the diaphragm, did you cause any changes in pressure in the trachea? What does your answer to this question suggest to you about the organs we use to breathe and the way they work?

g Yes; pulling the diaphragm back causes a fall in pressure. This would correspond to the domed diaphragm becoming tighter, in life, and causing air to enter the lungs.

Was there a change in pressure after the thorax had been opened? What does your answer imply or suggest?

h The diaphragm has little or no effect on air pressure in the trachea once the thorax has been perforated. The lungs are not perforated; the action of the diaphragm must be indirect. (This is a point at which the teacher could introduce or revise the part played by the pleural membranes and cavity.)

What volume of air did you use to inflate the lungs of the rat to their full capacity? How does this compare with an estimate of the volume of the thorax in which they are normally contained?

i The volume used was much more than the volume of the thorax.

Give a word that describes one physical quality of lungs that you saw when you suddenly removed the syringe.

j Elastic. The lungs tend to return to their original size when the syringe is removed.

2.5 The fine structure of the lungs

Principles

Although this is the third investigation in the chapter when students use a microscope it draws more attention to interpretation than before. The preparations of leaf epidermis and gut wall are thin but, in a sense, complete structures. The leaf section is transverse, fairly easy to relate to a whole leaf, and probably familiar to many students from diagrams in elementary textbooks. A lung section has no visible orientation in relation to the whole organ and cuts many structures at various angles. Accurate interpretation is a difficult task. A section never looks like a diagram of a lung; students should not expect this.

Teaching procedure

Associated materials
S(M) 2.1, 2.6, 2.7
S(C) 2.6

It is essential to obtain good preparations and know the stains used. The teacher can vary the detail and depth of this part of the chapter to suit the needs of each particular class. This is an opportunity to introduce some of the terminology of histology, if desired.

Students cannot be expected to form a clear picture of the air sacs and alveoli from prepared lung sections; they must look in textbooks. They can and should derive some idea of the extreme thinness of the walls which separate air from blood.

Questions and answers

How many different kinds of tubes are present in the prepared slide of a lung section?

a Two main kinds; one containing blood corpuscles, the other, empty space.

What are the distinctive features of the tube linings?

b The empty ones have a folded lining of distinct cells. Blood-filled spaces have a smooth lining lacking the appearance of cells.

Are there any signs of rings or hoops, as there were in locust tracheae? (Remember you have been examining a section, not complete tissue.)

c There may be horseshoe- or C-shaped structures in the wall of some tubes. This is probably cartilage but students will not recognize it as such unless slides of cartilage or a textbook are provided.

Your lungs produce mucus which is sometimes brought up the trachea. Can you see cells in the bronchial epithelia which might be responsible for secreting mucus and for moving it? You can only guess here, as there is no way of examining living tissue.

d Goblet cells are usually fairly obvious; their function can be learned from histology texts, not deduced. Ciliated epithelium should be clearly visible; here, students might make an intelligent guess concerning its ability to move mucus. They will again need to consult a text.

Comment on the distribution of elastic fibres, bearing in mind how a whole lung behaves after it has been inflated.

e Elastic fibres are distributed generally through the lung tissues. It may appear that their elasticity could be due to an elastic coat round the lungs, but the slide shows that this is not so.

From your measurements and estimates work out how far a gas molecule would have to travel from the centre of an average tissue space to the side, and from the side of a space through the wall into a blood vessel.
Draw an air sac to scale.

f The point of importance here is that the gas space is large compared with the thickness of the wall surrounding it. This corresponds with the notion of diffusion in gas being some ten thousand times faster than diffusion in water.

Review the breathing systems of locusts (insect) and mice (mammal). Air, as such, goes only as far as the lungs of a mammal. Blood carries oxygen and carbon dioxide throughout the body, as many of you will know. Remember when you compare this system with the tracheal one of insects that locusts are large insects, but even the largest insect is minute compared with the largest mammals.

g The obvious differences in the insect and mammal systems should be brought out here; direct supply of air in one case, localized organs (lungs) in the other. Insects are thus severely limited by the rate of diffusion of air. No insect is more than about an inch thick but mammals are not thus restricted. Blood carries many things as well as dissolved gases; tracheae carry only gases.

Why do you think that breathing systems exist at all? If the outer surface of the body were permeable to oxygen and carbon dioxide there would be no need for tracheal systems or lungs.

h This question recalls the opening remarks about the waterproof and gasproof nature of skins and cuticles. Leaves, insects, and mice would become desiccated and damaged if they were not covered by impermeable, protective skins.

2.6 The capacity of the human lungs

Principles

The act of breathing maintains air of constant composition in the alveoli. This idea of dynamic equilibrium is by no means self-evident. It is commonly believed, by students, that oxygen entering the nose passes directly into the blood. A spirometer can be used to find the vital capacity of lungs and the various subdivisions of this volume. This information, together with a knowledge of dead spaces, can lead to better understanding of the breathing process.

Teaching procedure

Associated materials
S(M) 2.1, 2.4, 2.5, 2.6, 2.7
S(C) 2.6

Spirometry of one subject provides enough results for the whole class. There is no need to take valuable lesson time repeating a procedure which is by now familiar.

The end of the investigation provides a good opportunity to review the essential features of an ideal organ of gas exchange, namely, thin membranes permeable to gases, large surface area, and some form of ventilating mechanism.

Questions and answers

What are the following volumes for the subject: tidal volume, expiratory reserve volume, inspiratory reserve volume? (See figure 20.)

a –

What is the vital capacity, i.e. the sum of the three volumes discovered in (a)*?*

b –

You can estimate the total lung capacity by multiplying the expiratory reserve volume by six. This has been found to provide a reasonably accurate figure. Work out the total lung capacity of the subject.

c –

Calculate from (b) *and* (c) *the residual volume.*

d –

Calculate the volume of air left in the lungs at the end of a normal expiration. Look at figure 20.

e ~~Res~~Ex piratory reserve plus residual volume.

Calculate the dead space of your experimental subject.

f –

Deduct this volume from the tidal volume and express the result as a percentage of the volume of air already present in the lungs (expiratory reserve plus residual volume).

g

$$\frac{\text{(tidal volume} - \text{dead space)}}{\text{(expiratory reserve} + \text{residual volume)}} \times 100$$

Comment on the statement, 'breathing brings fresh air into close proximity with blood capillaries in the lungs', in the light of your calculations. Summarize the physical phenomena and bodily activities responsible for gas exchange.

h This question is intended to bring out the idea of dynamic equilibrium and partial renewal of air in the lungs at each breath. Gas exchange depends ultimately on diffusion but is greatly affected by complex organs which cause mass movements of air – ventilation.

Additional bibliography

General reading

Leaves and leaf surfaces. All botany textbooks give information on the topic; an example is:
James, W. O. (1963) *An introduction to plant physiology*. 6th edition. Oxford University Press.

References

For an account of the method of forcing air out of leaves:
Nuffield O-level Biology (1966) Text Year III *The maintenance of life*. Longmans/Penguin.

For further explanation of making replicas of surfaces:
Sampson, J. (1961) 'A method of replicating dry or moist surfaces for examination by light microscopy.' *Nature*. **191**, 932–3.

General information on insect tracheal system:
Barrass, R. (1964) *The locust*. Butterworth.
Wigglesworth, V. (1956) *Insect physiology*. Methuen.

For help in interpretation of lung and other histological preparations:
Freeman, W. H. and Bracegirdle, B. (1966) *An atlas of histology*. Heinemann.

For general information, including information on dissection, about the structure and function of mammals including human beings:
Comroe, J. H. (1966) 'The lung.' *Scientific American*. February **214**:2, 57.
Winton, F. R. and Bayliss, L. E. (1962) *Human physiology*. 5th edition. Churchill.

For greater detail about the physiology of human lungs:
Cotes, J. E. (1965) *Lung function*. Blackwell Scientific Publications.

Extension work I

Gas exchange systems: the gill system of the dogfish

Review

The study of respiratory organs in locusts and mammals, carried out in Chapter 2, introduces the facts of gaseous exchange in animals that breathe air; however, it gives no indication of the way in which aquatic organisms obtain their oxygen. The purpose of the following investigations is to deal with this important topic by studying the gill system of a dogfish.

Though this animal is quite easy to obtain and is a convenient size for dissection, it is seldom possible for students to see living specimens in the laboratory. Freshwater fish which can be kept living for study are teleosts with smaller, more compact gills, but the inexperienced would find it difficult to dissect these. The work on dogfish gills can lead naturally to a fuller dissection of part of the circulatory system (Extension Work II) and for this reason the chapter gives precise instructions for preliminary dissection. Throughout such work, it is hoped that the teacher will never make students follow instructions blindly but will always help them to see each step as part of an enquiry into how organs work in the living animal.

The histology of gills is studied as a concomitant of dissection, providing a rigorous test of interpretation. In this, as in other exercises, questions play an important part in guiding the students' thought and actions. This is especially true when they are trying, from the structure of gills, to deduce how these are ventilated.

Illustrated answers can be given to some questions but drawing dissections and slides is not a primary aim and may actually detract from the main objective, which is to understand the structure of gill systems in terms of their function.

The sequence of topics is:

1 External features and preliminary dissection.
2 The anatomy of a branchial bar.
3 Histology of the gill lamellae.
4 The mechanism of ventilation.

Assumptions

- The dissection of the dogfish should follow the study of gas exchange in an insect and a mammal (L(M) 2.2–2.5), and students should therefore well understand features associated with respiratory surfaces. They also need:
- To realize that the diffusion of oxygen in water is about 6000 times slower than in air and that water is roughly 40 times more viscous than air. This will help them when assessing the structural differences between the gills of a fish and the lungs of a mammal.
- Sufficient knowledge of histology to enable them to distinguish between such tissues as cartilage and muscles.
- Knowledge of the terminology used in most textbooks for the dogfish system. (Students new to the subject should be sure of the meaning of terms such as anterior, posterior, dorsal, ventral, transverse, and longitudinal, before starting their practical work.)
- To understand the difference between drawings and diagrams, when making records of work done. A drawing of an organism, dissection, or organ is a complete picture accurate in every detail. A diagram expresses an idea, relationship, or function but may be incomplete or inaccurate in some respects. The illustrations of this investigation in *Laboratory guide (M)* are diagrams though part of figure 25 is complete enough to be called a drawing.

Definitions of terms

Branchiae (gills) – Thin-walled plate-like or filamentous respiratory surfaces richly supplied with blood vessels and kept moist by the medium in which the organism lives.

Branchial (gill) lamellae – Plate-like branchiae (gills).

Branchial clefts (gill slits) – Openings from the pharynx to the external environment which allow the passage of the respiratory medium; internal clefts open from the pharynx into pouches, and external clefts open from the pouches to the outside environment.

Branchial (gill) pouches – Chambers between the internal and external clefts; the walls of pouches are lined with lamellae.

Branchial (gill) bar – All the tissue between successive branchial pouches and composed of skeletal tissue, blood vessels, muscles, lamellae, a cranial nerve, and an interbranchial septum which is joined to the body wall dorsally and ventrally.

Visceral arch – The term visceral arch is sometimes used for a gill bar, but this leads to confusion since the term is more properly used for the components of the visceral skeleton, including the jaws and hyoid arch.

Branchial arch – The skeletal component of a branchial bar that supports the pharynx.

Interbranchial septum – A layer of connective tissue extending from the skeletal arch into the septum. The interbranchial septum contains blood vessels, nerves, muscles, and branchial rays. It also supports the lamellae in elasmobranchs but in teleosts the septum is reduced or absent.

E1.1 External features and preliminary dissection

Principles

Fish, like mammals and insects, require oxygen, but unlike them, they obtain it from water, not air. The object of this section is to examine the gills of a dogfish as specialized respiratory surfaces, noting any features of the gill structure which may be adaptations for their function.

Teaching procedure

Associated materials
S(M) 2.1, 2.8, 3.4

If possible, students should observe living dogfish or sharks in an aquarium. Failing this they should see the breathing movements on film. It is important that they regard a dissection as an aid to understanding *living* animals. Any method of dissection which realizes this aim is a good one; following a set of instructions, as an end in itself, should be discouraged.

Practical problems

If the work of this investigation is to be followed later by Extension Work II ('Transport inside organisms; circulation in the dogfish'), each student will require a whole fish and can use it for the practical work of both series of investigations. For Extension Work I alone, one fish will supply portions of branchial bars sufficient for several students.

Questions and answers

From your examination (stage 1), which structural features do you think could act as valves controlling the direction of water as shown by the carmine particles?

a The valves of the mouth are not conspicuous in the dogfish; they are small, passively operated flaps. Valves are more conspicuous in bony fish. (The term valve may seem a little extravagant for the septal flaps but during the expansion phase the pressure of the surrounding water forces the septa against the body wall and effectively closes the external clefts.) Only the spiracular valves are operated by muscles; these lie on the posterior surface of the aperture.

Describe the distribution of lamellae in each of the pouches of one side.

b Students should note that there are lamellae on each side of the pouches and also that they are absent from the posterior surface of the fifth pouch.

Make a simple diagram of the pharynx showing the direction of flow of water through it.

c Students should remember that a diagram should show anatomical relationships as clearly as possible but not necessarily be a visual facsimile.

How do you think the fish propels the water along the paths indicated by your diagram? Relate your hypothesis to observations made so far in this dissection.

d The intrinsic muscles are cut transversely. When these contract they will force water out of the pharynx. Other muscles will presumably restore the pharynx to its former shape when water enters. The valve flaps prevent backflow of water. (Students should begin to see that a full answer to this question may be complex. See figure 2.)

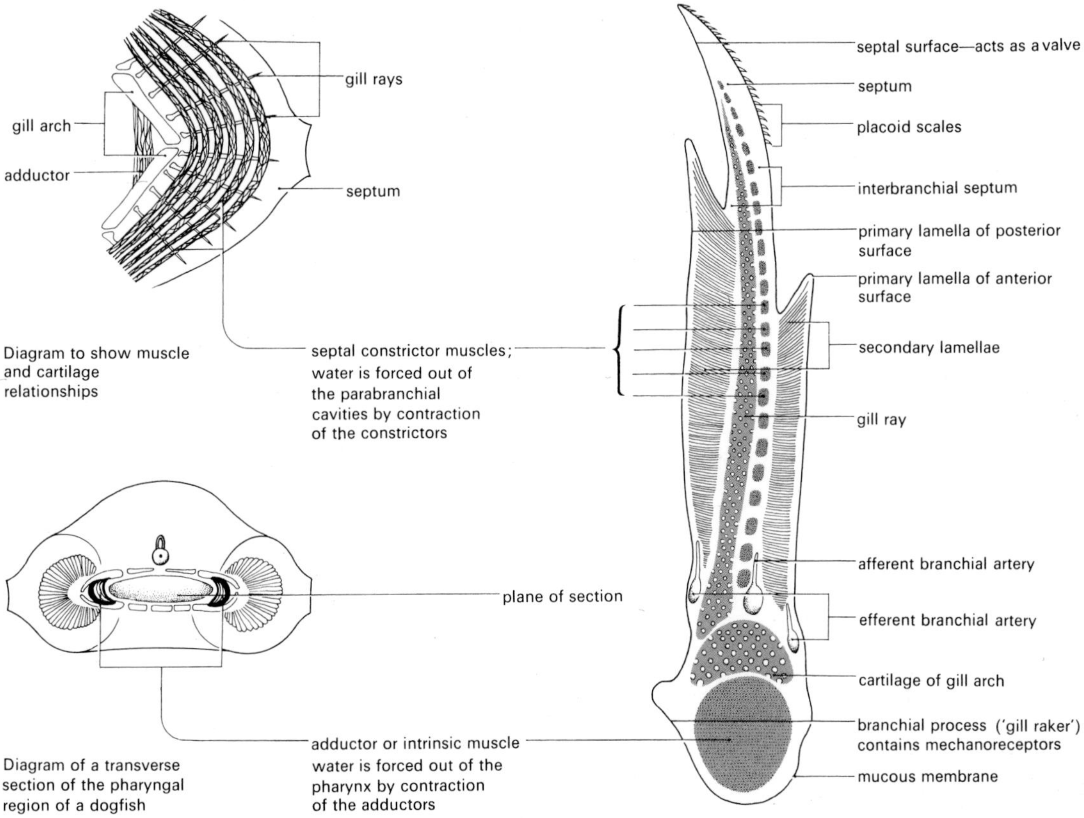

Figure 2
Diagram of a tranverse section of a branchial bar.

E1.2 The anatomy of a branchial bar

Principles

This is a continuation of the investigation which requires much more precise dissection on a fairly small piece of tissue. The gill lamellae should appear as obvious features of interest demanding further study.

Teaching procedure

Associated materials
S(M) 2.1, 2.8, 3.4

If time allows, the teacher can profitably extend this investigation by providing a bony fish such as a herring. This will enable students to compare the gill systems of a teleost and an elasmobranch.

Questions and answers

Describe the distribution of primary lamellae on both surfaces of the cut portion of branchial bar.
How are the secondary lamellae arranged with respect to the primaries?

a and *b* These questions are partly answered by figure 25 in *Laboratory guide (M)*, but they are necessary to draw attention to the lamellae, details of which can easily be overlooked.

Describe the skeletal components in a branchial bar. Do any of them extend into the septum? (You would find it helpful to inspect a preserved and mounted dogfish skeleton.)

c Transversely cut epibranchial or ceratobranchial cartilages are present with longitudinally cut branchial rays.

What muscle tissue can you find in the portion of branchial bar? What do you think happens in the living fish when this muscle contracts?

d Intrinsic muscle cut transversely; see question (*d*) in E1.1. The function of the muscles lying alongside the branchial ray is to cause contraction of the parabranchial cavity.

By what possible pathways can oxygen, absorbed from the surrounding water, pass from the branchial bar to other parts of the body?

e There is only one reasonable hypothesis. Dissection reveals blood vessels, so presumably dissolved oxygen is carried by the blood. Other channels or systems could be present but unrevealed by dissection.

E1.3 Histology of the gill lamellae

Principles

To complete the anatomical investigation of the gill system from a functional point of view students need to refer to the histology of gills. Unfortunately, most school laboratories are not equipped for preparing dissected material for microscopic investigation so it will be necessary to use slides prepared elsewhere.

Teaching procedure

Associated materials
S(M) 2.1, 2.8, 3.4

Students should be made aware of the staining techniques used and the meaning of colours they see in prepared slides. They should also be acquainted with the appearance of cartilage, muscle, and other tissues *before* examining gill slides.

The class could make a model in paper, card, or Plasticine, as a communal enterprise, with each member contributing ideas for the model.

Practical problems

Interpreting a two-dimensional section as part of a three-dimensional structure is a most difficult task even for experienced observers.

The success of this exercise depends on prepared slides of high quality. If these are unobtainable students can make use of photomicrographs. These are economical in cost and time, but the students, who study only a selected and restricted part of a gill section, gain less experience from them.

Questions and answers

In what respects do the lamellae, as seen in section, meet the specification for an 'ideal absorptive organ'?

a
1 A thin, permeable surface – the lamella has an epithelium only one cell thick.
2 The surface area of the lamellae is large.
3 Exposure to an oxygen-bearing medium – the lamellae are in contact with water.
4 The oxygen-bearing medium is continually replenished as its oxygen is depleted – water is moved past the lamellae.
5 The oxygen, once absorbed, is removed from the surface – the lamellae and gill bars contain blood vessels.

If oxygen is absorbed by the lamellae from the environment, how does it pass from them to the branchial bar? Give your reasons, based on observations of gill sections under the microscope.

b Sections reveal that the lamellae contain numerous blood vessels.

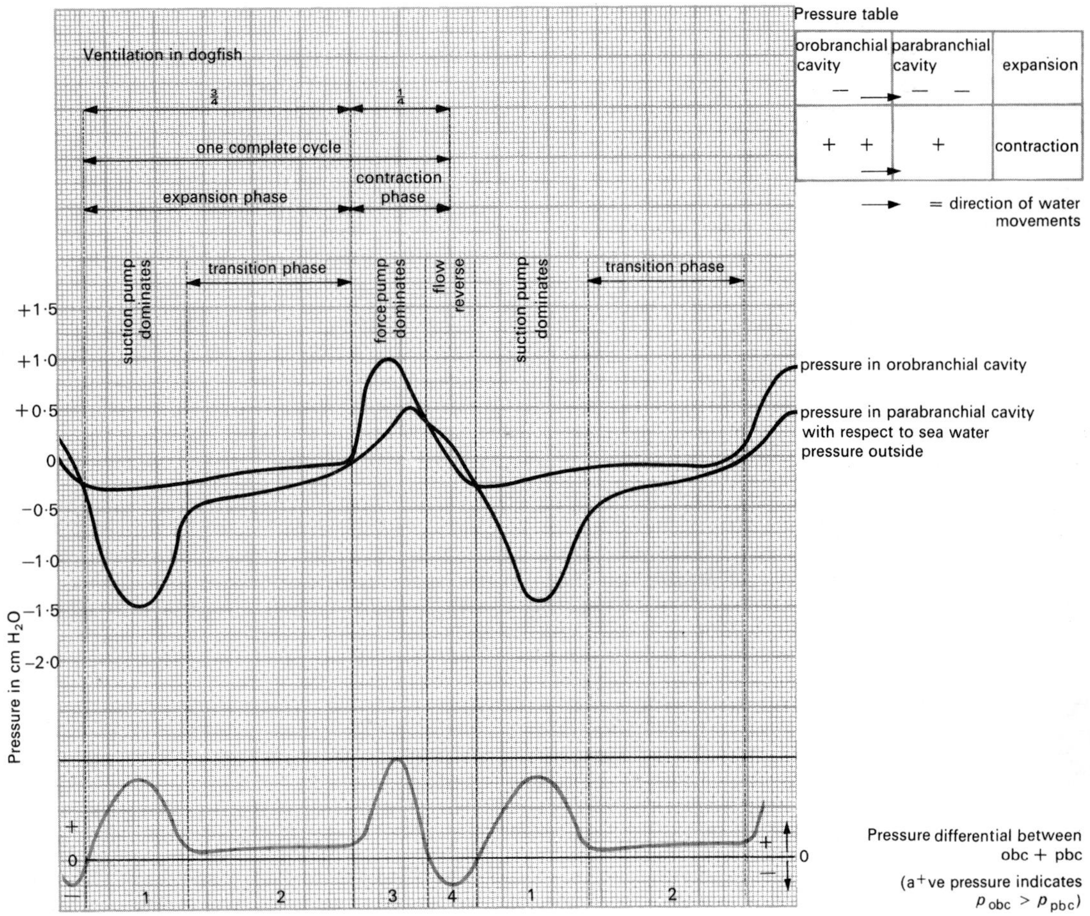

Figure 3
Pressure in orobranchial and parabranchial cavities.

What mechanism can you suggest for the ventilation of the secondary lamellae?

c The mechanism for ventilating the secondary lamellae is not well understood. One possibility is that, during the expansion phase, water flowing from the orobranchial cavity into the parabranchial cavity will not be able to escape through the external gill slits because they are closed throughout this phase. There would therefore be a tendency for this water to be forced between the secondary lamellae. During the contraction phase the rapid rise in orobranchial pressure (see figure 3) could also serve to force water along this route, particularly if the lamellae in the live animal meet across the external branchial cleft, as they do in bony fish. Under these conditions the easiest pathway for the water would be through the spaces between the secondary lamellae and out along the septum. The situation in teleosts is more readily understood and could be referred to with advantage.

What features in common have the gill lamellae of a fish and the air sacs of a mammal's lung? Comment on the significance of these common features.

d The common features include a large (total) surface area and an extremely thin superficial layer (epithelium) over the capillaries. The features are adaptations to the function of uptake or exchange of materials by diffusion.

E1.4 The mechanism of ventilation

Principles

Associated materials
S(M) 2.8

This is an exercise in deduction, using some observations from the practical work of previous investigations, some new information, and a series of questions, to present a sequence of ideas. When they have followed this sequence students should be able to write a more reasoned and better account of gill ventilation than they would unaided by preliminary questions.

Questions and answers

Ventilation of the gills involves a cycle of events. As water enters and leaves, the pharynx appears to get larger and smaller. During the expansion phase, when water is entering the pharynx, what happens to the orobranchial volume and pressure? (Refer to figure 76 for the meaning of the terminology.)

a During this phase the walls of the orobranchial cavity will be moving outwards; volume will increase and pressure decrease. Pressure relative to the assumed constant (zero) value for sea water can be represented in a diagram by a single negative symbol; the pressure outside now exceeds orobranchial pressure and water tends to flow into the fish. This water flow closes the septal valves. (See figure 3.)

Now consider the cartilaginous branchial rays that exert an outward force. What will happen to the volume and pressure in the parabranchial cavity due to this force?

b Any outward movement of the branchial rays will expand the parabranchial cavities and reduce their pressure.

Are the two cavities in free communication or is there a barrier that would delay pressures being equalized should they differ? What anatomical structures could form a barrier between the orobranchial cavities?

c Although the two cavities are in communication in a live fish, the lamellae meet and so constitute a barrier which would oppose the immediate equalization of pressures.

What would happen to the water in the pharynx if there were a difference in pressure between the two cavities?

d Water would flow from the high pressure region to that of lower pressure.

Measurements made on anaesthetized dogfish show that parabranchial pressure falls below that of the orobranchial cavity during the expansion phase.
1 *What effect will this have on the flow of water?*
2 *Can this water escape from the fish?*
3 *If not where will it be driven?*
4 *Does this in any way serve to ventilate the respiratory surface?*

e
1 Water will be caused to flow from the orobranchial cavity into the parabranchial cavity.
2 No, the septal valves are still closed.
3 Between the secondary lamellae.
4 Yes, by forcing the oxygen-bearing medium over the lamellae.

1 *When the contraction phase begins will pressures be equal?*
2 *If not which cavity will have the greater pressure?*

f
1 No; contraction of the pharynx will raise orobranchial pressure but owing to the barrier of the lamellae this increase will not be immediately communicated to the parabranchial cavity. Orobranchial pressure can be represented by two pluses and parabranchial by one plus sign (see figure 3).
2 The orobranchial cavity.

Due to this difference in pressure, what will happen to the flow of water?

g Water will flow from the orobranchial cavity into the parabranchial cavity and out through the gill slits.

1 *How many pumps operate to ventilate the respiratory surface?*
2 *What kind of pumps are they – pressure or suction pumps?*
3 *Do they act independently or are they synchronized?*
4 *Is the flow of water over the gill lamellae continuous or intermittent?*
5 *Is the ejection of water from the external clefts continuous or intermittent?*

h
1 Two.
2 The muscles and cartilages of the pharynx form a pressure pump; the branchial rays and septa form a suction pump.
3 They act independently, or alternately.
4 Continuous, or nearly so (see figure 3).
5 Intermittent.

Summarize your answers (a) *to* (h) *by writing a short account describing how the gill lamellae of the dogfish are ventilated.*

i –

Additional bibliography

General reading

Marshall, G. and Hughes, G. M. (1965) *The physiology of mammals and other vertebrates.* Cambridge University Press.
Krogh, A. (1941) *The comparative physiology of respiratory mechanisms.* University of Pennsylvania Press.

References

Darbyshire, A. D. (1907) 'On the direction of the aqueous current in the spiracle of the dogfish.' *J. Linn. Soc. (Zool).* **30**, 36–94.
Hughes, G. M. (1960) 'The mechanism of gill ventilation in the dogfish and skate.' *J. exp. Biol.* **37**, 28–45.
Satchell, G. H. (1959) 'Respiratory reflexes in the dogfish.' *J. exp. Biol.* **36**, 63–71.

Chapter 3

Transport inside organisms

Chapter review

Having studied the mechanisms and systems by which certain organisms exchange materials with their environment, students should see how these materials are moved between the exchange mechanisms and body tissues. The aim of this chapter is to consider the limitations of simple diffusion and look for mass flow in animals and plants.

Some useful creatures will be found in the model communities set up for Chapter 1. This serves to draw attention again to the aquatic habitat and to the way in which pond organisms obtain their oxygen.

Preparing a frog heart for experiments requires skill in dissection which has a different aim from that practised in the previous chapter. Microscopy follows the same pattern as before, and is used to promote critical enquiry into the relation between the structure of organs and their function.

The movement of metabolites inside plants is a difficult subject for practical work in schools; secondhand evidence must be used to focus attention on this problematical field of plant physiology.

The sequence of topics is:

1 Movement inside plant cells.
– Movement inside animals.
2 Circulation in animals.
3 The heart in action.
4 The structure of hearts.
5 Blood vessels.
6 Transport inside plants.

Assumptions

Little previous knowledge is essential but some basic ideas will be helpful:

- The concept of diffusion in liquids, from which much of the argument stems.
- Notions of the simple physics of liquid flow, e.g. of friction between moving liquids and their containers, and of the consequent resistance to flow offered by vessels of small bore.
- Knowledge of the general distribution of tissues in a plant stem including cortex, phloem, and xylem. (Little detail of these is given within this chapter.) However, preconceived ideas about the blood system are not necessary and may prove to be a disadvantage.

3.1 Movement inside plant cells (preliminary)

Principles

A leaf of *Elodea* is chosen because it is thin. This is highly significant. Leaves of water plants are usually thin and/or highly branched. It is to be hoped that students will ask why this particular leaf is used rather than an aerial one. The much slower rate of diffusion in water than in air is believed to be connected with the anatomical features referred to above.

Leaf cells of *Elodea* may show cyclosis; that is, protoplasmic streaming within cells. This provides a useful starting point for discussion of the 'activity' of plants compared with that of animals, and the need for the movement of materials inside plants.

Teaching procedure

Associated materials
S(C) 1.4, 1.5, 2.1, 2.2

Leaves from a green, healthy *Elodea* plant should be mounted in a drop of water from the same tank or pond.

Practical problems

Cyclosis is often much slower than many textbooks suggest and it is necessary to observe the specimen carefully for several minutes. Even so, cyclosis is capricious in the sense that it may not appear at all. This does not mean that the practical period has been wasted. It is hoped that students will understand why there may be no visible activity in a leaf by contrast with part of an animal. There is no need for mass-flow devices in a thin organ; diffusion alone will account for sufficient movement of materials.

Questions and answers

Can you observe any moving particles? If so, is the movement from cell to cell or confined within cells?

a Yes or no! If there are moving particles, their circulation is confined to individual cells.

What functions do you think these movements could be performing?

b The circulation of materials, such as food substances.

Movement inside animals

The work of Chapter 2 should have drawn attention to the different means by which tissues of locusts and mice obtain their oxygen. All students will probably be well aware that oxygen is carried by blood. At this stage they may need to do brief revision before proceeding to the next investigation.

3.2 Circulation in animals

Principles

Though the fact of circulation in animals is common knowledge it is not easy to observe. True circulation, blood going round and round, is hard to see; often mere movement of red cells in a capillary bed is presented as circulation, but strictly speaking it is not. By examining the transparent limbs of small Crustacea we can see blood entering and leaving them. This does take us a little nearer true circulation.

Examination of the gills of *Asellus* reveals movement of blood inside opposite in direction to the flow of water outside. This introduces the idea of counter–flow, an important principle in the efficient operation of any exchange mechanism.

Teaching procedure

Associated materials
S(M) 3.1, 3.4
Film loop 'Capillary circulation of blood' NBP–45

This investigation is divided into two parts. The first is extremely easy and good observations should be reported within a short time of capturing and mounting the small crustaceans. The second part, involving the displacement of gill plates, is a little more difficult but is well within the capabilities of most students. Thus, the investigation as a whole can be adjusted to suit a class of any range of ability. The theoretical aspects of circulation can also be demonstrated according to the intellectual requirements of the class, for example, by restricting ideas to simple movement of fluid in crustacean appendages or using the gills as examples of a counter current device for efficient exchange.

Practical problems

Almost any *Asellus*, however pigmented, has antennae transparent enough to reveal moving blood. Students may find it difficult to displace one of the gill plates without crushing the animal. If no gill appears, the best plan is to try another *Asellus* rather than continue with the first. If moving blood is seen to stop this is a sure sign that too much pressure has been applied and the animal is unlikely to recover, even though appendages may continue to twitch for some time. This raises an interesting point concerning a definition of death.

Questions and answers A

Can you see any moving objects inside any of the limbs? Record your observations accurately with the aid of simple sketches.

a Distinct particles, or corpuscles, can be seen moving together in streams in most appendages.

Do the particles or corpuscles within a limb all move in the same direction?

b No. There are usually at least two streams moving in opposite directions. Sometimes there are two flowing into a limb and one back to the main body, or vice versa. (See figure 4.)

Can you see blood vessels in any of the limbs or antennae?

c No; in places the appendages seem full of moving fluid (blood) and there must be partitions of some kind allowing a two-way flow. The partitions themselves are invisible.

Is the rate of flow of corpuscles regular?

d No, it is irregular or pulsatile.

Questions and answers B

Suggest one reason why the structure appears colourless in contrast to other parts of the body.

e The walls of the 'structure' might be much thinner than the rest of the body covering.

Can you see particles moving inside this structure and, if so, describe the motion and its direction in relation to the whole body?

f Particles are visible, moving in the colourless plate. The direction of movement is from behind, forward as shown in figure 4.

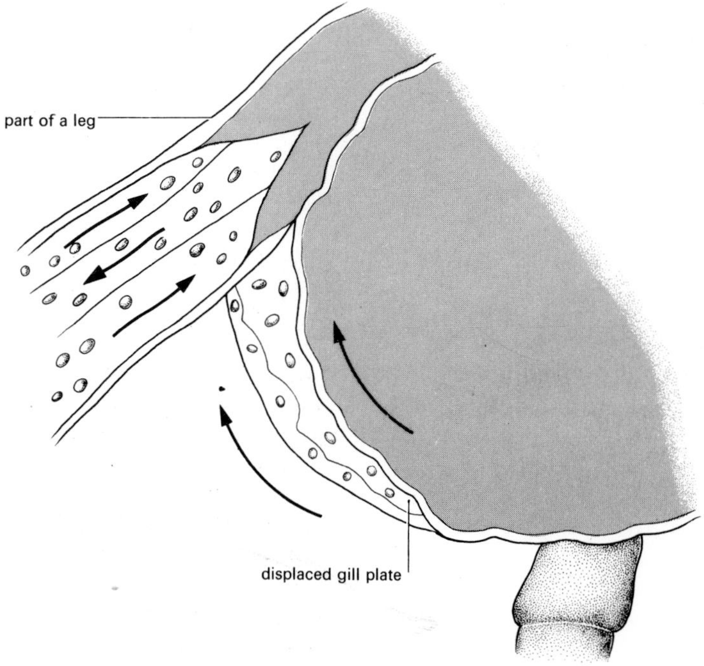

Figure 4
Blood flow in portions of *Asellus*.

How does this direction compare with that of water outside the body when you observe it in the specimen tube?

g As far as we can see, water is being moved backwards (from front to rear) over the posterior parts of the body.

Structures of this kind are termed 'gills' by the writers of textbooks. What evidence have you obtained to support the idea that they do, in fact, function as gills?

h The 'gills' are plate-like and probably have thin walls. Blood moves in one direction while water is continually propelled past the 'gills' in the opposite direction. This appears to be an ideal exchange device incorporating the counter flow principle. It is most important that this kind of argument should not be taken as proof that these structures are responsible for the entire uptake of oxygen by the animal. In large Crustacea, e.g. the lobster, ninety-seven per cent of oxygen is taken up by gills, but in small forms similar to *Asellus* the gills may be responsible for only sixty or seventy per cent of total oxygen uptake. The thickness of the body wall is a poor indication of its permeability to oxygen. The anatomy of the gill plates is given in standard texts together with further ideas on observing blood flow.

3.3 The heart in action

Principles

Ideally, students should see a heart within a living organism, pumping blood round the body. They can do this to a limited extent with crustaceans and other small semi-transparent creatures. Some authors claim that *Asellus* is a satisfactory subject but usually pigment obscures the central organs.

There is little doubt that experiments on a living frog heart have considerable impact on students. Having acquired some technique in the dissection of dead animals, they can now apply this in a more testing situation. The general aim of this investigation is to let students see for themselves that a heart is a remarkable organ which continues to function in an otherwise 'dead' animal. A variety of experiments can be performed; the selection presented in *Laboratory guide (M)* is intended to suggest rather than compel.

Teaching procedure

Associated materials
S(M) 3.2, 3.3

Experiments on the frog heart could, if carried out in a callous fashion, make a bad impression and be a disservice to biology. Pithing (destruction of the brain and spinal cord) is an operation to be carried out by the teacher or trained technician (NEVER BY STUDENTS) where it cannot be seen by members of the class. The exact legal position is not clear and there is every reason for exercising caution and common sense. It is common practice to stun the frogs before pithing. Though this is frowned upon by some physiologists, perfectly good heart activity usually results. Though it may be helpful to teachers and technicians to see a film loop demonstrating this operation it is probably not wise to show it to students because, as Bryant points out,

'. . . The showing of a film of an animal under experiment should be regarded as equivalent to demonstrating the actual experiment depicted . . .'. It is important that students should check that the pithed frogs give no response to stimulus. They should jab feet, legs and arms lightly with a pin and if any response occurs then or during dissection immediately put the frogs in a closed container full of chloroform vapour. Such frogs should be killed and used for other dissections.

Use of pithed frogs is likely to bring up the whole question of what is meant by 'death' and the question of suffering on the part of animals. It should be pointed out that an animal without a central nervous system is unlikely to feel pain. For those who require absolute assurance this may not be enough.

The more extensive the preparation and rehearsal of this practical exercise, the more likely it is to work well. It is one which requires organization in advance.

Practical problems

The first steps of pithing a frog present little problem. Many people prefer to stun the animal by holding it by the legs, ventral side up, and bringing the head down sharply against the edge of a bench. Hold the stunned frog firmly in a duster, dorsal side up, and bend the head downwards. Slide the point of a blunt seeker back along the mid-line of the head until it slips into the depression of the foramen magnum. Press the point of the seeker firmly into this depression and forwards into the brain. Pull it back with upwards pressure to destroy the brain but do not remove the seeker completely. Turn the seeker round through 180 degrees and find the neural canal; this can be difficult. Press the seeker back as far as it will go. The frog usually goes into spasm with this action. This is an automatic response which does not indicate pain or suffering. Remove the seeker with an upward pressure. Test the frog for reflexes by pinching each foot. If this fails to evoke a response pithing has been successful. There is almost no bleeding and the appearance of a pithed frog is perfectly acceptable to students. Techniques involving the beheading of frogs, though simple and swift, are not desirable, as the student is presented with a most unpleasant, mutilated animal with which to experiment.

Inserting the hook into the ventricle sometimes presents difficulties but not if it is held firmly by forceps; artery forceps are ideal for this purpose.

If smoked paper is being used for the kymograph remove the drum and fix a sheet of glazed paper to it. Rotate this over a smoky flame made by burning coal gas which has passed through a container of cottonwool soaked in benzene. The soot layer should be thin and even since a thick layer could present too much friction for the recording arm of the heart lever. Smoking should be done in a fume cupboard or near an open window. A scraper (usually made of a triangular piece of celluloid or a modified pin) should be used, attached to the end of the lever. The heart lever should be arranged so that the scraper point or pen is in contact with the drum and is working evenly.

When recordings have been made, the smoked paper should be removed with the utmost care and dipped through a trough of liquid varnish. Alternatively, hang it up and spray with artist's fixative from an aerosol. Allow to dry.

If an electrical stimulator specially made for such physiology experiments is not available, an induction coil working from a 1·5–3·0 volt battery will serve. Some difficulty may be experienced in finding the small cardiac branch of the vagus nerve and applying wire electrodes to it. Care, dexterity, and practice are needed for this part of the exercise.

Questions and answers

Examine the tracings made by normal heart beat before heat and chemical or electrical treatment. Are the peaks simple, that is, V-shapes? If not, what kind of heart activity would account for the shapes obtained?
Which part of a frog's heart contract and in what sequence?

a and *b* When a frog heart beats, contraction of the sinus venosus is followed by contraction of the atria, then that of the ventricle, and finally that of the base of the aorta. Because several parts of the heart contract in sequence the trace recorded on the kymograph drum is not a single inverted V but a more complex shape. (See figure 5.) By watching the heart as a record is being made, each part of the resulting trace can be related to the contracting components concerned.

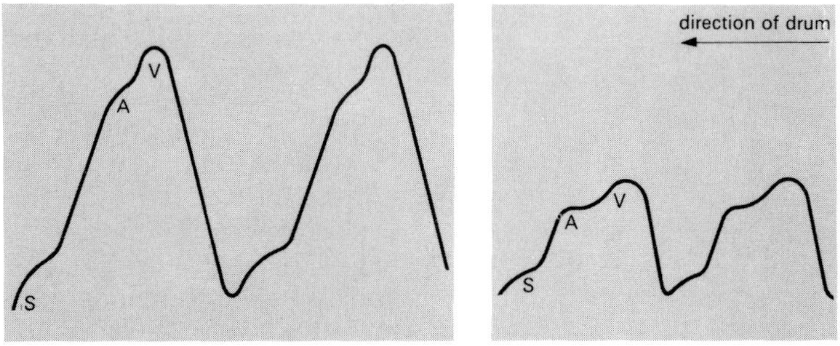

Much depends on the method of attachment of the heart to the lever. Here, contraction causes an *upward* movement of the heart lever. Also, the speed of the kymograph drum obviously affects the shape of the trace.

S = portion related to the contraction of sinus venosus
A = portion related to the contraction of atria
V = portion related to the contraction of ventricle

Figure 5
Examples of recordings of a frog's heart.

What is the effect of temperature on heart rate?

c The higher the temperature, the faster is the frequency of heart beat. Some examples from actual experiments are as follows:

Temperature	*Number of beats in the same period of time*
10° C	5
18° C	18
24° C	31
30° C	43

Note: A variant of this experiment can form a basis for discussion. Place a glass rod in Ringer's solution of known temperature, then apply the rod to the sinus venosus. Compare the traces thus obtained with those when Ringer's solution was poured over the whole heart.

What effect does acetyl-choline have on the heart?

d Acetyl-choline usually reduces the frequency of heart beat.

What effect does adrenaline have on the heart?

e Adrenaline usually accelerates heart beat – its effect is not always as marked as expected, when administered in the way suggested.

What happens to the heart beat frequency when the vagus nerve is stimulated electrically?

f The heart is inhibited by stimulation of the cardiac branch of the vagus nerve.

Would you expect the cutting of the vagus nerve to have any effect on the heart? Give the reasons for your answer.

g No. The vagus nerve is presumably connected to the brain which has been destroyed by pithing. Cutting of the vagus merely confirms this fact.

Two concepts emerge from this work which may be new to students. One is that the heart will continue to beat even when isolated from the nervous system. The other is that when a nerve is stimulated this may *stop* an action, contrary to the idea that 'messages' along nerves cause actions to take place. If then the vagus functions as a 'brake', does the frog heart have an 'accelerator' and if so, what is it?

3.4 The structure of hearts

Principles

From elementary biology lessons, first aid classes, or general reading all the members of the class will probably think they know how a heart is constructed. A real mammal heart, as opposed to a textbook diagram of one, is a most complicated, three dimensional structure. The aim of this section is to widen the definition of 'heart' in the minds of students and encourage them to approach heart anatomy with critical minds. From the brief examination of the frogs used in the previous investigation and the mice dissected in

Chapter 2, it is not likely that the concept of double circulation will have revealed itself. For this and other details of blood systems, students must consult textbooks.

Teaching procedure

Associated materials
S(M) 3.2

After the rigorous discipline necessary for the successful operations in the last investigation, this one can be left to the students' inclinations and enterprise. They should be able to select appropriate planes in which to cut hearts so as to reveal as much internal structure as possible.

Questions and answers

Describe the heart of a locust as far as possible from the preserved tissue at your disposal.

a The 'heart' is a long tube with slight bulges corresponding with the segments of the body.

What external features do the hearts of rats and sheep have in common which distinguish them from a frog's heart?

b Hearts of mammals are clearly divided into two atria and less clearly into two ventricles. There is no sinus venosus. Frog hearts have two atria, a single ventricle, and a sinus venosus.

Which hearts exhibit signs of possessing their own circulatory system?

c Hearts of mammals have a network of vessels visible over the outside surfaces. These are the coronary vessels and are conspicuous in large hearts. Frog hearts do not appear to have them.

How does the total volume of the atria compare with the total volume of the ventricular space in any one heart?

d The total volume of the atria should equal that of the ventricles. In the living heart this could hardly be otherwise, blood being an incompressible fluid.

Is there any anatomical evidence that ventricles cause higher blood pressure than atria?

e Difference in the thickness of ventricular and atrial walls. If heart wall is largely muscle, a thick piece can presumably exert more force when it contracts than a thin one. If this is so, then more force will be exerted by the ventricles than the atria, causing a higher blood pressure. By the same reasoning we should be able to deduce that higher pressure is caused in the left ventricle than the right.

How are valves prevented from 'blowing back' into atria when ventricles contract?

f Valves between atria and ventricles are tied by strings – the *chordae tendinae* – to papillary muscles on the inner surfaces of the ventricles. The way in which valves work can be shown by means of a film loop or a simple model.

Does your examination of heart sections suggest that the pressure produced by the two ventricles is equal or unequal? Give your reasons.

g See (*e*) above. Pressure in the pulmonary circulation of mammals is much less than in the systemic circulation.

What is the function of each of the chambers of the mammalian and the frog's heart? Base your answers on your own observations and information from textbooks. What is meant by 'double' circulation?

h The function of heart ventricles is not in doubt; they serve as the main 'pumps' for blood circulation. Though most textbooks go into elaborate detail about the structure of the atria and other parts of the heart, they are extraordinarily reticent about their function. Because muscle cannot expand actively, merely contract, it is said that some opposing force must operate to return a muscle to its original length, after contraction. What opens or dilates a ventricle after it has contracted? Some authorities claim that the atria serve as priming pumps, pushing blood into ventricles, so opening them after contraction (systole). Most texts are less specific and merely state that atrial systole causes the rapid filling of ventricles. Some dilation of the ventricles may result from the elasticity of the ventricle walls in their relaxed state (i.e. during diastole). All this has a bearing on the frog heart, as here, there are two priming pumps in series: sinus venosus and right atrium leading to the ventricle. Does the sinus venosus force blood into the atrium to dilate it fully? The dangers of arguing function from structure without adequate recourse to experiments are well displayed by the old ideas concerning passage of blood through the frog's heart. Unfortunately, textbooks which expound an elaborate story of oxygenated blood from the left atrium being forced out of the ventricle into the carotid arteries are still to be found in schools. A concise amount of modern work and reasoning is given by Foxon, who also provides a detailed account of the experimental methods used. (See Additional Bibliography.) These form a possible starting point for discussion of double circulation in terrestrial vertebrates.

3.5 Blood vessels

Principles

Blood circulating round the body travels at different velocities and under a gradient of pressure. The vessels through which it passes are adapted to these changing circumstances and the aim of this section is to encourage students to relate the structure of vessels to their functions. The study is limited to prepared sections of aorta, artery, and vein, and so it is not comprehensive. There is no reference, for example, to valves in veins. A much longer and more detailed series of exercises must be devised if justice is to be done to this complex and absorbing subject.

Teaching procedure

Associated materials
S(M) 3.1, 3.3, 3.6

Each student should be given (in turn) a single slide with three sections of aorta, artery, and vein mounted on it. If these happen to be mounted on separate labelled slides it might be advantageous to cover the labels in some way, in order to encourage deduction and identification.

Questions and answers

Which of the three vessels do you think contained blood at high pressure (that is, are arteries)? Give your reasons.

a Two sections, aorta and artery, have much thicker walls than the other (vein). Common sense suggests that the latter is the low pressure vessel.

Which of these sections was taken from an artery nearest to the heart (the aorta)? State your reasons.

b By the same reasoning the vessel with the thickest wall should withstand the greatest pressure and therefore be situated nearest the heart in a hydrodynamic system; pressure falls with distance.

What possible function can elastic tissue have in the wall of a blood vessel? What type of blood vessel does it occur in?

c The elasticity of the aorta and great arteries 'smoothes' the pulsatile flow from the heart. This is not always an easy concept to convey and a simple model can be useful. See figure 6.

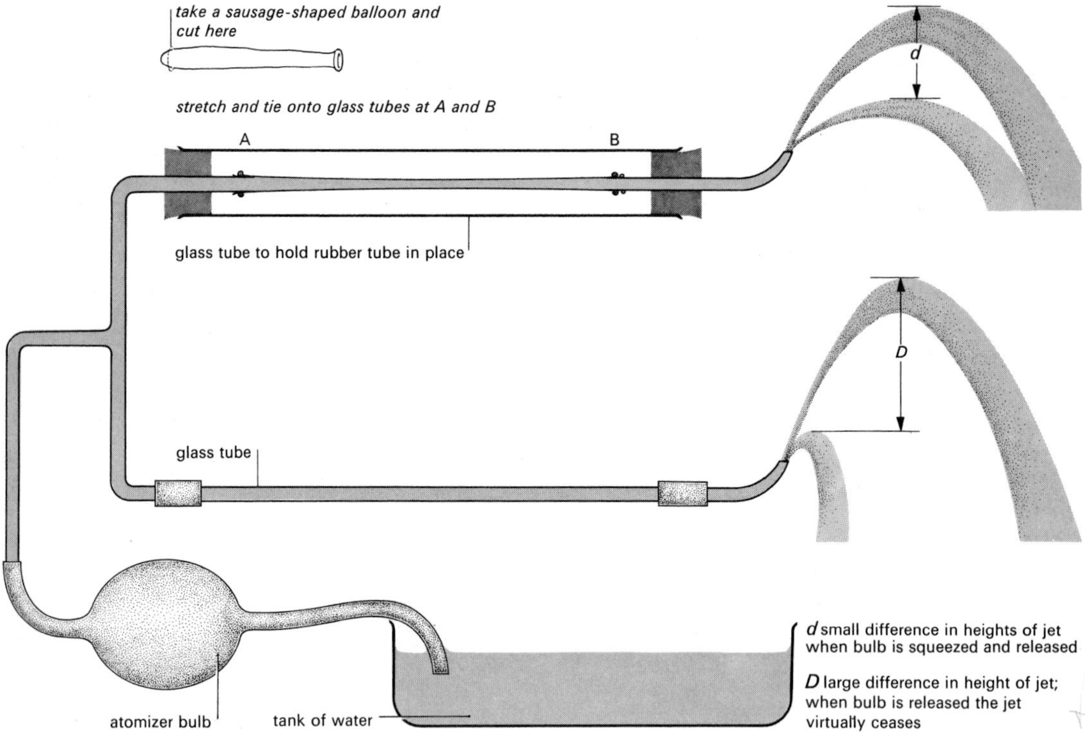

Figure 6
Model to show the different effects of elastic and rigid tubes.

3.6 Transport inside plants

Principles

If students have the illusion that all the elementary questions about plants and animals have been answered, a glance at translocation should shatter it. Though a great deal is known about the types of chemicals transported through plants and their speed of passage, hardly anything is understood about the method involved. We focus attention on this aspect of plant physiology by referring to secondhand evidence – an autoradiograph of plants containing labelled sucrose. This simple experiment could be performed in schools but it is costly. An opportunity of using other labelled material and making autoradiographs is provided later, in L(M) 7.2.

Teaching procedure

Associated materials
S(C) 1.3, 1.4, 1.5, 2.1, 2.2, 2.3, 2.5
Film loop 'Handling radioisotopes I: Carbon-14'

The exercise essentially requires no equipment but students should be given an opportunity of looking at a prepared longitudinal section of a stem, under a microscope.

Questions and answers

Describe the distribution of radioactive carbon in the control shoot after twenty-four hours, as shown in the autoradiograph. How does the distribution of ^{14}C differ in the two shoots?

a In the control shoot (A) radioactive carbon is present in the fed leaf, the entire stem, and a few leaves near the apex. There is a marked difference in the two shoots. In the experimental shoot (B) there is abundant ^{14}C as far as the ringed portion of the stem. Beyond this there is only a faint trace in the stem and none at the apex.

Examine the micrograph of a privet section (figure 37). What can you deduce about the probable pathway of the radioactive carbon?

b The path taken by ^{14}C would seem to lie in the outer part of the stem (cortex and phloem), not the xylem.

The total length of the shoot used was about 25 cm. What statements can you make about the speed of conduction of radioactive carbon in the living shoots?

c The ^{14}C must have travelled from the fed leaf to the apex (A), a distance of about 18 cm, in 24 hours at a rate of over 7 mm per hour. It may have travelled much faster than this.

Additional bibliography

General reading

Plant physiology:
Galston, A. W. (1961) *The life of the green plant*. Prentice-Hall.
James, W. O. (1963) *An introduction to plant physiology*. Oxford University Press.
Thomas, M. (1935) *Plant physiology*. Churchill.

Crustacea:
Borrodaile, L. A., Eastham, L. E. S., Potts, F. A., and Saunders, J. T. (1932) *The Invertebrata*. Cambridge University Press.
Parker, T. S. and Haswell, W. A. (1898) *A textbook of zoology*. Macmillan.

References

Human and other circulations:
Bell, G. H., Davidson, J. N., and Scarborough, H. (1961) *Textbook of physiology and biochemistry*. Livingstone.
Clegg, A. G. and Clegg, P. C. (1962) *Biology of the mammal*. Heinemann.
Foxon, G. E. H. (1952) 'The mode of action of the heart in the frog.' *New Biology*, **12**, 113–127, Penguin.

Other references:
Bryant, J. J. (1967) *Biology teaching in schools involving experiment with animals or pupils*. Association for Science Education.
Foxon, G. E. H. (1951) 'A radiographic study of the passage of the blood through the heart of the frog and the toad.' *Proc. Zoo. Soc. Lond.* **121**, 529.
Rowett, G. H. Q. (1963) *A guide to dissection*. John Murray.
Silen, L. (1954) 'The circulation of isopods.' *Acta Zool. (Stockholm)*, **35**, 11.
Thaine, R. (1964) 'The protoplasmic streaming theory of phloem transport.' *J. exp. Bot.* **15**, 470.
Thomas, A. J. (1954) 'The oxygen uptake of the lobster.' *J. exp. Biol.* **31**, 228.

Chapter 4

Transport media

Chapter review

This chapter terminates one phase of enquiry and begins another. A study of the exchange of gases between organisms and their environment leads, because of the mechanisms involved, to a consideration of transport media in general and blood in particular. The study of blood has so many aspects that a whole course of biology might well be devoted to it; only the function of transport is considered in this chapter.

This does not attempt to give any comprehensive treatment of oxygen or carbon dioxide. *Study guide (M)* gives some details of oxyhaemoglobin dissociation. For topics such as the Bohr effect and chloride shift, standard texts should be consulted.

The second phase of enquiry considers first the transport in blood of materials other than oxygen. Estimations of glucose concentration in blood provide an introduction to Chapter 5 on nutrition.

Though blood is the major topic of the chapter, it also considers plants and, to a limited extent, sap.

The sequence of topics is:

1 Examination of human blood.
2 The carriage of oxygen.
3 Haemoglobin reactions.
4 Transport of materials other than gases in plants and animals.

Assumptions

The main subject of this chapter can be taken to a fairly advanced level or presented in a simple form to suit the needs and scientific background of students.

– To appreciate the full significance of the work on erythrocytes and haemoglobin, students should understand the following concepts and terms:

Permeability of cell membranes.
Osmosis; hypotonic, hypertonic, and isotonic solutions.
Solubility of gases, Henry's Law, absorption coefficients, partial pressure.

In *Laboratory guide (M)* technical terms are strictly limited so that students are unlikely to be discouraged from reading and investigating because they do not know them. It may be that interest in work with blood will stimulate enquiry into such aspects of physical chemistry as are outlined above.

4.1 Examination of human blood (preliminary)

Principles

The investigation employs two techniques for the microscopic examination of blood. Both place emphasis on the erythrocytes and ignore the white cells and platelets. In conjunction with previous work, this investigation highlights the role of blood as a medium of transport. The study of white cells would be irrelevant in this context and can be considered later. For similar reasons, clotting and functions of blood other than transport are likewise not mentioned in this chapter.

Teaching procedure

Associated materials
S(M) 4.1, 4.6
S(C) 2.4

Because blood changes rapidly once it is released from the body it is essential to use fresh samples whenever possible. Students should be able to obtain drops of reasonable size from thumb or forefinger but this should never be demanded of them if they are really opposed to the idea. The teacher should always be willing to provide some, in such cases. It is most important that all students should follow a strict procedure in obtaining blood samples and never deviate from it. It is essential to use sterile lancets. Also, the reasons for care and discipline should be pointed out to students as part of their biological training.

The use of saponin or household detergent has a bearing on a subsequent technique, considered in L(M) 4.2; it should be included if possible. By comparing a dry blood smear with a drop of fresh blood students may gain some idea of the effect of histological treatment on tissues. These preparations also provide a good opportunity to consider optifacts even though the diameter of an erythrocyte is many times greater than the resolution of a light microscope. How well students understand this subject will depend to some extent on their individual scientific backgrounds.

Questions and answers

How many different kinds of corpuscle can be seen in untreated blood?

a Erythrocytes can be seen easily; other (white) cells may be seen with difficulty. Students who know already about several types of white cell may claim to see more.

What is the size (diameter and thickness in microns) of the erythrocytes or red blood corpuscles?

b Average diameter 7·2 μm. Average thickness near the periphery 2·2 μm.

How are the erythrocytes grouped together? Illustrate your answer with a simple, accurate drawing.

c Rouleaux formation is obvious in shed blood but is not necessarily a common condition in blood vessels.

In what ways are the corpuscles affected by the various liquids used in stage (6)? Can you account for your observations? Seek information from textbooks if necessary (see Bibliography).

d Distilled water and very weak solutions cause water to enter erythrocytes by osmosis, making them swell and burst–haemolysis. Sodium chloride solution (8·9 g/dm³) is isotonic and should not have any visible effect on erythrocytes.

Detergents affect the membranes of erythrocytes causing haemolysis. Strong solutions draw water out of corpuscles by osmosis, causing them to shrink, often into fantastic shapes. The commonest is a crenated form looking like the fruit of a horse chestnut.

How does the blood of the dry smear differ in appearance from a drop of fresh blood?

e No rouleaux can be seen. The red corpuscles are often irregular rather than disc-shaped. They are far more distinct.

4.2 The carriage of oxygen

Principles

Students will have been told from an early age that blood carries oxygen round the body. The aim of this section is to stimulate thought about the extraordinary properties of blood which make it so well adapted for this function. The section also describes some procedures by which students may attempt to release oxygen from blood and see for themselves the oxygen 'capacity' of haemoglobin. These procedures should be regarded as qualitative rather than strictly quantitative.

No reference to the carriage of carbon dioxide in blood is made in this chapter.

Teaching procedure

Associated materials
S(M) 4.2, 4.3, 4.4, 4.5

The practical work of this section is essentially confirmatory rather than experimental. It may be argued that too much time is taken covering knowledge which will be familiar, namely that blood has a large 'capacity' for oxygen. Though this is true enough, these exercises provide opportunities for students to devise their own apparatus for a specific task. The methods outlined for large and small quantities of blood are only suggestions and both require some ingenuity in order to complete the devices so that they work properly. The idea that laboratory investigations are always fully covered by a complete set of instructions should be discouraged.

Practical problems

It is often difficult to obtain an adequate supply of blood in quantities of more than 10 cm^3. It may be impossible to acquire blood from an abattoir and, if so, the class should adopt the method using a single drop of human blood. To use 2 or 3 cm^3 of blood in a respirometer it is necessary to have a vessel which contains potassium ferricyanide solution inside one of the large test-tubes. Arrangements must be made so that this can be tipped over during the experiment to allow the solution to mix with the blood. Barcroft made a miniature version of the apparatus suitable for a single drop of human blood but this is probably too difficult to construct in a school laboratory. The single-drop device described in *Laboratory guide (M)* employs a different approach but the same basic principle. The glass bending and dexterity required should be well within the capability of students.

Questions and answers

From results obtained through procedures A or B, what was the percentage of gas displaced from the blood sample by potassium ferricyanide?

a Blood within the body will hold up to about 20 cm^3 oxygen per 100 cm^3. The yield from the experimental procedures is likely to be considerably less. In theory, excess potassium ferricyanide should oxidize all iron(II) atoms of oxyhaemoglobin to iron(III) and cause all oxygen to be liberated. The results actually obtained should be considered adequate if they indicate that substantially more oxygen is carried by a quantity of blood than by the same quantity of water.

If we assume that the gas is oxygen, do your results confirm the hypothesis that blood can contain more oxygen per unit of volume than water?

b They should do so.

How would you set about testing the composition of the gas displaced from a sample of blood?

c By applying methods similar to those used in Chapter 1 for the analysis of air.

Which groups of animals have 'free' haemoglobin and which have red corpuscles?

d Haemoglobin is found 'free' in solution in many invertebrate animals. In vertebrates it is found in cells which have nuclei and in smaller non-nucleated corpuscles such as those in mammals.

Is an advantage gained by animals which have their haemoglobin in corpuscles, and, if so, what is it?

e The commonest suggestion is that when haemoglobin is enclosed in corpuscles blood can contain far more haemoglobin that it could in 'free' solution because its effective osmotic pressure is reduced. As soon as haemolysis occurs and haemoglobin is released into the plasma, the osmotic pressure of the blood rises greatly. Such a condition causes water to be drawn into the capillaries, out of tissues. Other authorities point out that free haemoglobin (like other proteins) has a high viscosity. If all haemoglobin at present in a man's corpuscles were released his blood would flow like syrup, putting an impossible load on the heart.

Are the erythrocytes of all animals shaped like human red cells? Is a biconcave disc a shape well adapted to the carriage of oxygen?

f No; mammals have biconcave erythrocytes; other animals such as amphibia and fish have red cells which contain a nucleus. These are larger than the mammalian type and more or less spherical in shape. A biconcave disc has a larger surface area than a sphere of the same volume. Materials may be able to diffuse in and out of a mammalian erythrocyte more rapidly than a spherical body of the same volume. The biconcave shape allows erythrocytes to bend into a cup shape when being forced through capillaries narrower than about 5–7 microns. This may be more significant than the surface area/volume argument.

4.3 Haemoglobin reactions

Principles

Haemoglobin reacts not only with oxygen but also with carbon dioxide and carbon monoxide. If supplies of citrated blood are available this can be demonstrated quickly and easily.

Teaching procedure

Associated materials
S(M) 4.2, 4.3, 4.4, 4.5, 4.6

The procedure for exposing blood to gases is so simple that students can be allowed a free hand in setting up the apparatus and devising their own criteria of comparison.

If some form of colorimeter is available the procedure should be modified so that it may be used; ideally both machine *and* eye should be used to compare blood samples.

Practical problems

The major difficulty, as before, is obtaining enough blood. It is unreasonable to expect convincing results from a miniature version of the apparatus using single drops of human blood. A second difficulty is acquiring gases such as oxygen and nitrogen. If cylinders are not available it is unwise to attempt the exercise; the time and trouble required for gas production are not justified by the unreliable results which are likely. Finally, the exercise depends on subjective judgments of colour. Students should be encouraged to standardize the light used to compare blood samples and to devise means of overcoming differences of colour vision in different individuals. Gas should not be bubbled through blood as this often causes excessive frothing.

Questions and answers

How many different colours of blood have you observed? Be careful to distinguish between different colours and varying shades or intensities of the same colour.

a and *b* The answers, of course, depend on the number of gases used. Nitrogen and other gases which do not form specific compounds with haemoglobin 'sweep' oxygen out of blood, thus producing the colour of haemoglobin. Carbon

If we assume that each colour indicates a different compound of haemoglobin, how many such compounds have been formed?

dioxide combines with haemoglobin to form carbohaemoglobin (or carbaminohaemoglobin) which has a different absorption spectrum from haemoglobin. However, it may be impossible to distinguish this difference by merely looking at blood in a tube. The situation is further complicated by the fact that the colour of haemoglobin changes to some extent with pH.

Oxygen causes a clear change in colour (cherry red), distinct from blood exposed to air. These colours are reversible in the sense that they can be changed back and forth by changing the type of gas used.

Coal gas, containing carbon monoxide, produces another variety of red coloration. It is often stated that the compound formed, carboxyhaemoglobin, is stable and that the colour is not changed by subsequent exposure of the blood to oxygen. This is not always borne out by the experimental procedure such as is used here, which makes use of pure oxygen rather than air. Carboxyhaemoglobin does dissociate in the presence of high oxygen concentrations; this principle is important in the treatment of carbon monoxide poisoning. Combination of haemoglobin with nitric oxide is analogous with its reaction to carbon monoxide.

To summarize, students should obtain different red coloration using oxygen, carbon monoxide (coal gas), and air. Nitrogen and other 'inert' gases give a dark red colour of pure haemoglobin from which it is difficult to distinguish carbohaemoglobin produced with carbon dioxide.

Coal gas consists mainly of hydrogen and methane (about 80 per cent) and some carbon monoxide, ethylene, and nitrogen (20 per cent). Which of these gases do you think combines with haemoglobin? Account for your answer; you may need to refer to a textbook (see Bibliography).

c It is reasonable to suppose that hydrogen or methane produces the red colour of carbohaemoglobin. This can be tested by the use of hydrogen gas, if available. (A supply of methane is less likely to be at hand.)

The poisonous effect of carbon monoxide is so well known that this is the most likely answer to be given.

4.4 Transport of materials other than gases in plants and animals

Principles

This section represents a turning point in the train of thought begun in the first chapter. Blood carries more than just oxygen and carbon dioxide. By turning our attention to one of these other materials, glucose, we prepare a way to the next topic, food and digestion. The wording of many elementary biology texts suggests that the function of transport in blood is like the function of a conveyor belt or goods train, with freight being loaded on at one point and unloaded at another. One effect of this is the misleading idea that urea, when produced by the liver, is carried direct to the kidneys for excretion; this should be discouraged. The difficult task of trying to find differences in glucose concentration in different parts of the blood stream should also discourage such thinking. It is preferable to conceive of blood as a medium of fairly constant composition, flowing to all parts of the body, maintaining a constant internal environment for cells. The section is limited to a study of glucose because this is one component of blood which can be easily estimated and is also of great importance in the life of organisms. Another substance which could be estimated in a similar way is urea.

Teaching procedure

Associated materials
S(M) 4.7, 4.8
S(C) 1.3, 1.4, 1.5, 2.4

It is suggested that students try out the procedure using Dextrostix on a drop of their own blood, then using a drop of plant sap, and then awaiting an opportunity for testing animal blood. This will occur in the work of the next chapter and the delay in completing the procedure should therefore not be long. Information about the whole circulatory system of a mammal is required when planning blood sampling. This can be obtained from any standard zoology text, and it can serve as revision and consolidation of some of the work in previous chapters and as preparation for Chapter 5.

For estimation of urea, use Azostix.

Practical problems

The term 'sap' is used in its most general sense as the fluid which exudes from a cut surface of a plant. It may come from xylem vessels, phloem sieve tubes, or other cells which have been cut. The teacher should point this out to students, who may believe that sap comes only from the phloem. Sap appears on the cut surface of the lower part of a stem when there is a plentiful supply of water to the roots.

With Dextrostix, only a drop of blood is required for glucose estimation, but even this amount may be hard to find in a single blood vessel of a small mammal. Rats, and more especially mice, have remarkably little blood. With care, it is possible to collect a drop of blood from the hepatic portal vein and another from the dorsal aorta.

Questions and answers

What is the concentration of glucose in blood from your thumb?

a –

Is glucose present in plant sap; if so in what concentration?

b Dextrostix commonly gives a positive indication of the presence of glucose. Much will depend on the state of the plant. It is easiest to collect from the lower cut surface, and this suggests that glucose may have been travelling up the plant from the roots. There are several differing hypotheses to account for the presence of the glucose and it should be noted that, in general, carbohydrate is translocated more as sucrose than glucose. It is unfortunate that a simple specific test is not at present available for this compound.

Does sap contain material visible under the microscope? If so, describe it and try to interpret what you see.

c Yes; 'sap' from young stems of *Impatiens* invariably contains a few chloroplasts and, often, needle-like crystals. Transverse and longitudinal sections reveal the presence of these materials in cortex cells and it may be assumed that they have been released from cut cells and are not necessarily present in the phloem or xylem vessels.

From which vessels of the mammal did you sample blood? Was there a difference in glucose concentration? What can you infer from this result?

d It is suggested that blood samples should be taken from vessels supplying the gut and from the hepatic portal vein. If the animal was fed shortly before being killed for dissection there is a reasonable chance that the content of glucose will be higher in vessels draining the ileum than in those supplying it. It is normal practice to provide laboratory animals with a continuous supply of food and in such circumstances differences of concentration of glucose in the two types of blood vessel are far less marked. The ability to control the feeding of an animal during the day before dissection is a great advantage but no animal should be subjected to conditions liable to cause pain, stress, or interference with or departure from the animal's normal condition of well being.

Additional bibliography

General reading

Nuffield O-level Biology (1966) Text Year IV *Living things in action*. Longmans/Penguin.
Tullis, J. L. (1953) *Blood cells and plasma proteins*. Academic Press.

References

Ames Company. *A handbook of routine diagnostic tests*.
Barcroft, J. (1908) 'Improvements in the technique of blood gas analysis.' *J. Physiol.* **39**, 411.
Bryant, J. J. (1967) *Biology teaching in schools involving experiment or demonstration with animals or with pupils*. Association for Science Education.
Evans Electroselenium, Ltd. *Colorimetric methods*.
Mitchell, P. H. (1938) *A textbook of general physiology*. McGraw-Hill.

Extension work II

Transport inside organisms: circulation in the dogfish

Review

The dissection of the branchial arteries of the dogfish is a traditional part of school biology. Here we are not so much concerned with a training in techniques of dissection as encouraging students to enquire into the anatomy of a dogfish from a functional point of view. The investigations here could be undertaken as a continuation of Extension Work I or as separate studies.

The investigations trace the path of blood circulating from the heart, through the gills, and into the dorsal aorta. They require more careful and elaborate techniques of dissection than in other investigations in *Laboratory guide (M)*.

The microanatomy or histology of the gills presents a formidable problem of interpretation to students. The work throughout demands mental reconstruction of the dissected and sectioned fish to make a coherent picture of the gills and blood system as they function in the living animal. It provides a good example of the way the function of organs can be deduced from this structure. This is particularly so with the study of the heart.

The sequence of topics is:

1 Exposure of the heart.
2 Blood vessels joining the heart and gill system.
3 The drainage of blood from the gills.
4 Further study of the heart.
5 Passage of blood through the gills.

Assumptions

- This work should not be attempted until simpler dissections such as those in Chapters 2 and 3 have been completed.
- Students should be aware, through this experience, of the general aims of dissection and how they are achieved. Some useful practical hints are summarized in E2.1.

E2.1 Exposure of the heart

Principles

The fact emerges from the study of respiratory surfaces of mammals (Chapter 2) and fish (Extension Work I) that they are intimately associated with the blood system. This investigation is concerned with tracing the exact path taken by blood from the point of entry into the heart, through the gills to the dorsal aorta. To complete the circulatory path from the dorsal aorta back to the sinus venosus would require a difficult and time-consuming dissection and it is not mentioned in the following procedures. It may, of course, be attempted if teachers and students so wish.

Teaching procedure

Associated materials
S(M) 2.8, 3.1, 3.4, 3.5, 3.6, 3.7

Though the following dissection is a continuation of E1.1 it may be done on its own with a quick identification and examination of the gills in place of the thorough investigation carried out in E1.1–E1.4. Students should bear in mind that they are investigating part of a circulatory system transporting oxygen (amongst other things) to all parts of the body. Such a system requires a pump, vessels, and valves and students should discover these by dissection. The dorsal approach to the heart has been used so that the efferent and afferent branchial arteries can be related to each other and the gill lamellae.

If preserved dogfish skeleton, 'museum' specimen dissections, and thick transverse sections of whole fish (steaks) are available, students should examine them when trying to answer the questions.

Practical problems

No student should be restricted to the use of a single dogfish. The knowledge that one serious mistake will ruin his only major dissection is likely to have an inhibiting effect on a student, leading to slow, timid, and ineffectual work. A second chance should be available to all and it should be possible to learn from errors. As this is a rigorous dissection the following hints may help to guide students:

1 Keep dissecting instruments in good condition.
2 Study the instructions given and attempt them one at a time.
3 To separate organs use blunt instruments such as forceps or fingers whenever possible.
4 Stretch structures to separate them and pin them apart.
5 Never cut anything unless it is necessary to do so.
6 Never cut blindly; always clear the structure to be cut so that the position and effect of the cut can be foreseen.
7 When dissecting blood vessels place the blunt edge of a scalpel alongside the vessel and cut upwards, never across.
8 Use a bench lamp to illuminate the region being dissected.
9 Use a lens, preferably mounted on a stand, to see small structures.

10 Remove or deflect obscuring structures that are not part of the system being investigated.
11 Determine the course of blood vessels by gently pulling them and observing deflections of the structures to which they are attached.
12 Trace blood vessels to their fullest extent.
13 Pin out a finished dissection to give the best possible display of the system investigated.

Questions and answers

Will blood pressure be high or low in the sinus venosus?

a Low.

What causes blood to flow into the atrium from the sinus venosus?

b The pressure in the sinus venosus must exceed that of the atrium; the pressure difference is produced by contraction of the sinus venosus.

What is the function of the atrium?

c To fill the ventricle with blood, and possibly act as a priming pump.

How is a uni-directional flow of blood ensured?

d By means of valves.

Which chamber forces blood out from the heart and drives it through the vascular system?

e The ventricle.

How is the chamber you selected in (e) *adapted for its function?*

f It has thick muscular walls.

Will the pressure of blood leaving the heart be high or low?

g High.

What purpose is served by the conus arteriosus?

h It assists the ventricle in forcing blood into the ventral aorta (this cannot be deduced from mere inspection).

How are its walls adapted for this function?

i They are thick and muscular.

What prevents the wall of the pericardial cavity from moving?

j The pericardium walls are attached to rigid skeletal structures, i.e., pectoral girdle and basibranchial cartilage.

E2.2 Blood vessels joining the heart and gill system

Principles

This is a continuation of the previous investigation with the same overall aims and methods.

Teaching procedure

Associated materials
S(M) 2.8, 3.1, 3.4, 3.5, 3.6, 3.7

The discovery of a blood vessel often leads to premature attempts to rush on with the dissection and find all the other vessels as quickly as possible. The first essential is to remove all connective tissue from the limited part of the arterial system that has been exposed; in the long run faster progress is achieved by patiently cleaning up each small area than by more adventurous methods.

Difficulty is commonly encountered over the removal of the coracobranchial muscles, chiefly because students fail to free these muscles from connective tissue before excising them; the natural reaction of the class will be that it is rather fussy to take such pains over a structure that they consider has nothing to do with the dissection. But the reason for this procedure is that these muscles *are* very much a part of the dissection – they are landmarks which lead to the arteries; this is an excellent example of the way in which procedures make use of relationships. It could be explained to the class that the difficulty presented by the fifth afferent branchial artery is entirely due to its relationships; it is tightly surrounded by the fourth and fifth coracobranchial muscles, leaving little room for the insertion of instruments, and its origin is embedded in tough connective tissue at the base of the aorta. Knowing this they could then verify all that has been said for themselves, but they should not spend too much time on this vessel.

Questions about the functions of the muscles and skeletal components of the pharynx really relate to the ventilation of the gill lamellae but the answers could not have been given from the work done in Extension Work I.

The tracing of the afferent branchial arteries appears to be easier when performed from the inner surface of the arch.

Questions and answers

What do you consider to be the function of the pillar muscles?

a By their contraction they decrease the volume of the pharynx and so serve to pump water through the branchial pouches.

What purpose is served by the various cartilages of the branchial skeleton?

b They support the pharynx and provide points of attachment for muscles such as pillar muscles.

How are the pillar muscles related to the branchial skeleton and the pectoral girdle?

c They are attached to them: the posterior end of each pillar muscle is attached to the coracoid region of the pectoral girdle; the anterior ends are attached to the junction of the hypobranchials with the elastobranchials, except the fifth, which is attached to the basibranchial.

What correlation is there between thickness of wall and likely blood pressure?

d Vessels in which pressure is likely to be high have thicker walls than vessels in which pressure is low.

What sort of blood, oxygenated or deoxygenated, do you think flows in the vessels you have dissected?

e Deoxygenated.

For what purpose is blood being pumped to the branchial bars?

f To collect oxygen.

Make an illustrated record of the parts of your dissection which show the probable course of blood from the sinus venosus to any one branchial bar.

g –

E2.3 The drainage of blood from the gills

Principles

If the path of blood circulation is followed strictly students should investigate blood vessels in the gill lamellae. This sequence may be followed (see E2.5) but it is probably better for practical reasons to place the four parts of the dissection together as suggested here.

Teaching procedure

Associated materials
S(M) 2.8, 3.1, 3.4, 3.5, 3.6, 3.7

The students can follow the investigation through the Procedure and Questions. However it is at about this stage in the dissection that questions about veins might well arise. This provides an opportunity for discussion and reference to textbooks on the system of blood sinuses typical of fish; and it may be related to the low blood pressure of a single circulation compared with that in the double circulation of mammals. Alternatively, this subject could be dealt with after the dissection of the heart.

The epibranchial arteries are relatively simple to find and the chief difficulty is to expose an efferent loop satisfactorily. Provided the cartilages are removed without damaging the mucous membrane there is reasonable hope that the procedure suggested will succeed. This depends upon knowing exactly where to look for the loops and here a model of the branchial arch will be invaluable.

Questions and answers

Which have the thicker walls, the epibranchial arteries or the afferent branchials? (To find the answer you will have to remove and examine pieces of each vessel.)

a Afferent branchial arteries.

How do you account for any difference in thickness?

b Higher blood pressure in afferent branchial arteries.

What sort of blood, oxygenated or deoxygenated, do you think the epibranchial arteries contain?

c Oxygenated.

By what route is this blood distributed to the rest of the body?

d Dorsal aorta and its tributaries.

How do you think the blood pressure in the dorsal aorta compares with that in the ventral aorta? Account for the differences you suggest.

e Lower in dorsal aorta; a drop in pressure occurs across the capillary beds of the gill lamellae.

How does blood from the heart reach either *the right pectoral fin* or *the muscles of the tail? Make a diagram of your dissection with arrows to indicate the direction of blood flow.*

f Ventral aorta – afferent branchial arteries – capillary bed of the gill lamellae – efferent branchial arteries – epibranchial arteries – dorsal aorta – right subclavian artery.

E2.4 Further study of the heart

Principles

This item of investigation is placed here purely for convenience. It is unwise to disturb the heart until the vessels from it have been properly seen. It could be left until the gill histology has been dealt with but the storage of a partly dissected animal never improves its condition. The object of examining the heart is to deduce the way in which it works so far as this is possible without access to a living animal. The work of L(M) 3.3 and L(M) 3.4 is relevant here.

Teaching procedure

Associated materials
S(M) 3.2, 3.3, 3.5, 3.6, 3.7

The dissection of the heart is simple and straightforward. It should not take much time to complete, so that there is ample opportunity for a thorough inspection while answering the questions.

Questions and answers

1 *Is the sino-atrial valve symmetrically placed?*
2 *What prevents the sino-atrial valve from opening when the atrium contracts?*
3 *How many flaps are there in the sino-atrial valve?*
4 *How are the flaps arranged?*

a
1 Yes.
2 There are no retaining tendons so, presumably, inelastic connective tissue in the valve flaps prevents them from being forced into the sinus venosus; this can be tested by manipulating the flaps.
3 Two.
4 There are a left and a right flap with a vertical aperture between.

1 *Is the atrio-ventricular valve symmetrically arranged?*
2 *What prevents the atrio-ventricular valve from opening when the ventricle contracts?*
3 *How many flaps are there in the atrio-ventricular valve?*
4 *How are the flaps arranged?*

b
1 No, it is slightly to the left of the mid-line.
2 Fibrous strands – the chordae tendinae.
3 Two.
4 There are an anterior and a posterior flap with a horizontal aperture between.

1 *How many rows of valves are there in the conus arteriosus?*
2 *How many valves are there in each row?*
3 *Are the valves all the same?*
4 *What prevents these valves from opening when blood pressure in the ventral aorta exceeds ventricular pressure?*

c
1 Two.
2 Three.
3 No. The three valves of the anterior row are typical pocket valves, but the three valves of the posterior row are shallow and scarcely amount to pockets – they are attached to the anterior valves by tendons.
4 Such a pressure difference would force blood back towards the heart but this would fill the pockets and so close the valves.

What is your theory of the action of the heart? Illustrate your answer with sketches or diagrams of the dissected heart. Does your theory of the action of the heart fit in with the direction of flow you indicated in the diagram of the arterial system?

d –

E2.5 Passage of blood through the gills

Principles

Students now complete their study of the path of blood from the heart to the dorsal aorta by inspecting the gill lamellae under the microscope. This investigation also provides an exercise in the interpretation of two-dimensional sections as part of a three-dimensional structure, an important aspect of many anatomical studies.

Teaching procedure

Associated materials
S(M) 2.8, 3.1, 3.4, 3.7

The practical work of this investigation can only be done with good histological material in which capillaries can readily be distinguished. The sections are cut through various planes and this should be explained to the class. A useful aid to teaching is a crude paper model of a primary lamella with some secondaries fastened to it with adhesive tape. Such a model can be bent into the sort of distorted form the lamellae have in fixed material. A ruler, represent-

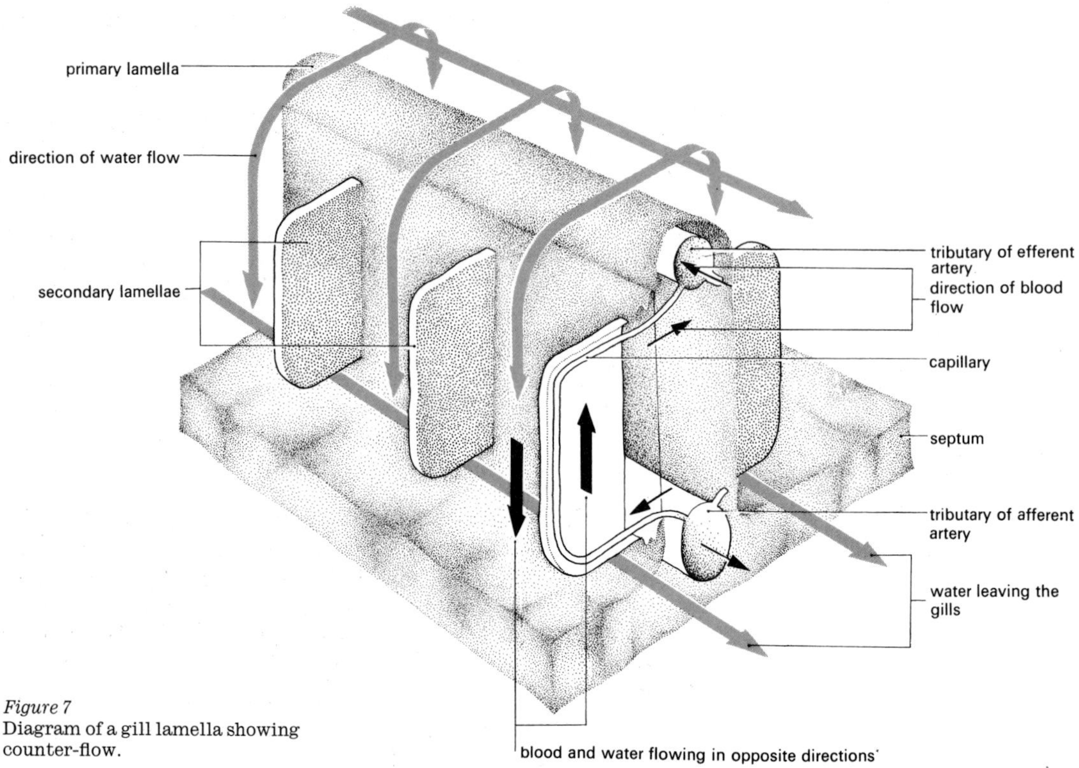

Figure 7
Diagram of a gill lamella showing counter-flow.

ing the razor edge, held against the paper model, will immediately illustrate the idea that sections cut from distorted material present problems of interpretation. (See figure 7.)

In an undistorted section the plane of a transverse section will either pass through the whole length of a primary lamella or it will miss this altogether and pass through all the secondary lamellae it supports. In the sections provided for the class there will be some regions where only secondaries are visible, others where the secondaries can be seen to be attached to the primary, and several regions showing more than one series of secondaries of indeterminate origin. A brief discussion of this problem should make it clearer.

It is essential that the class revise branchial arch structure before looking at the slides, and a model should be demonstrated, but the model must not be a complete one, showing the distribution of the capillaries. This would make the exercise superfluous.

The first necessity is for the student to orientate the various parts of the section; he should identify the primary and secondary lamellae and distinguish the cartilage of branchial skeleton components from muscle.

The student should also make a crude sketch of the course of the afferent and efferent arteries along a branchial arch and construct a diagram from the slide of their positions in a section. This diagram will define the problem, which is to find the link between the vessels.

Demonstration by the teacher will help students to locate the branches of the afferent tributaries more quickly. It may only be necessary to confirm the students' identification and so give them confidence in their ability to do this work.

The afferent tributary can only be traced to the bases of secondary lamellae in exceptional sections. Therefore connecting it to the bulbous swellings at the base of the secondaries is a deductive exercise.

From the swellings it is quite easy to locate the capillaries. They are cut many times in each lamella, as one would expect from a knowledge of the network of a capillary bed, and the brighter students may be able to reconstruct this network arrangement from their own observations.

The efferent tributaries are usually easier to find than the proximal afferent tributaries. They are situated along the distal edge of the secondaries.

When the students have completed the exercise they could, with benefit, make three-dimensional models with Plasticine – nothing elaborate, just a summing up of their findings. Paper models take longer to construct but are of a more permanent nature.

Questions and answers

How wide are the capillaries of the lamellae compared with the size of the red blood corpuscles?

a Barely wide enough to allow the passage of an erythrocyte.

Using the diameter of a red blood corpuscle as a unit, compare the following: the thickness of a capillary wall, that of the outer layer (epidermis) of a secondary lamella, and that of tissue which lies between them.

b Capillary walls and outer epidermis are extremely thin and of the same order of size as an erythrocyte (one diameter). Thickness of connective tissue varies. The close proximity of sea water and blood should be well understood. (The collagen fibres of the connective tissue appears red with Van Gieson stain, blue with Azan, and green with Masson.)

If the gill lamellae are responsible for the exchange of substances between sea water and the blood, what are these substances and how are the lamellae suited for such exchange?

c Oxygen and carbon dioxide. Extremely thin tissue and large surface area of the lamellae suit them for their function of exchange.

In which direction do you think the blood might flow in the capillaries of a secondary lamella compared with the water outside? Do you think that the exchange of substances between the sea water outside and the blood in the capillaries would be facilitated by flow in opposite directions or by flow in the same direction? Or do you think it would be the same in either case? Give the reasons for your answer.

d Water probably flows past the lamellae in the opposite direction to the blood (counter-flow). In any exchange system counter-flow increases the efficiency (see figure 7).

Can you suggest any reasons to account for the fact that dogfish die when out of the sea, in spite of the much higher concentration of oxygen in air compared with that in sea water?

e The lamellae are large enough in area and thin enough to allow adequate absorption of oxygen but their shape is quite unsuited to air. During dissection students will probably have seen that the secondary lamellae lie squashed together. Though their surface area in water is large, their effective surface area in air is reduced enormously. The ventilation mechanism of the pharynx is unsuited to a gaseous medium. The converse question, 'Why do mammals (with lungs) drown?' may also be raised at this point.

Summarize the chief differences between the circulation of blood through the gills and body of a dogfish, and through the lungs and body of a mammal. Can the differences be related to the differing sources of oxygen, sea water, and air?

f The summary should mention single and double circulation and the much higher blood pressures achieved by mammals than by fish. A point worth making is that fish do not seem to benefit from a single circulation and a low pressure blood supply but they survive well enough in water. Such a system seems to be quite unsuited to the active life of an animal living on land. The question requires a broad appreciation of the differences between aquatic and terrestial life, going beyond the topic of respiratory surfaces alone.

Additional bibliography

General reading

Francis, E. T. B. (1955) 'The vertebrate heart I.' *Sch. Sci. Rev.* **37**, 73–85.
Francis, E. T. B. (1956) 'The vertebrate heart II.' *Sch. Sci. Rev.* **37**, 226–223.
Rowett, H. G. Q. (1950) Dissection Guides II *The dogfish.* John Murray.
Whitehouse, R. H. and Grove, A. J. (1949) *The dissection of the dogfish.* 2nd edition. University Tutorial Press.
Yapp, W. B. (1960) *An introduction to animal physiology.* 2nd edition. Oxford University Press.

References

Hazelhoff, E. H. and Evenhius, H. (1952) 'Importance of the counter current principle for oxygen uptake in fishes.' *Nature*, **169**, 77.
Satchell, G. H. (1960) 'The reflex coordination of the heart beat with respiration in the dogfish.' *J. exp. Biol.* **37**, 719–31.
Wendell Burger, J. and Bradley, S. E. (1951) 'The general form of circulation in the dogfish, *Squalus acanthias*.' *J. All. comp. phys.* **37**, 389–402.

Chapter 5

Digestion and absorption

Chapter review

The ways in which materials enter living organisms is a continuing theme of this series of chapters. Now that students have investigated the uptake of oxygen, this chapter directs attention to the fate of food. There is no detailed reference here to the nature of food itself, diets, or methods of ingestion, nor is there any mention of teeth. For such information students must look elsewhere.

The practical work emphasizes digestion as a phenomenon common to a wide range of organisms, including plants, and not merely as a function of alimentary canals. The one food material mentioned by name is starch. This is used because it is experimentally convenient and also a familiar substance. The next chapter, which is concerned with enzymology, considers the chemistry of the digestion of starch. The present aim is to understand how digestion is necessary as a preliminary to absorption and to see both these functions in relation to the structure of alimentary organs.

The sequence of topics is:

1 Digestion by micro-organisms and tissues.
2 Digestive organs; a model gut.
3 The double function of the alimentary canal.
4 Fine structure of the intestinal wall.

Assumptions

– Some knowledge of digestion; whereas in previous chapters little knowledge has been assumed, it would be unrealistic to suppose that students already know nothing of digestion. Even without formal teaching in biology, children become aware that we require a mixed and balanced diet which we digest in our stomachs and intestines. Many probably realize that the 'goodness' of food passes into the bloodstream. This kind of information is almost unavoidable and is derived from science books for children, radio and television programmes, and advertisements for patent medicines and foods.

- Some additional factual information is necessary if the student is to gain a comprehensive grasp of digestion. This may be sought in standard references and texts.

  Note: An elementary knowledge of carbohydrate chemistry may be an advantage for the work of this chapter; it is essential for the next. Similarly, students should have access to elementary information about proteins and amino acids.

5.1 Digestion by micro-organisms and tissues (preliminary)

Principles

The use of starch/agar plates is standard practice for showing that germinating cereal grains produce a starch-digesting enzyme. The appearance of a clear zone round each grain, against a blue background (starch-iodine complex), has considerable visual impact and appeal. The scope of this technique can be extended to include all manner of tissues and colonies of micro-organisms. Plates are superior to vessels of starch solution because the relative volumes of starch/agar and organisms are not critical, whereas they are when starch solution is used. Also, colours of intermediate breakdown complexes cannot be seen as well in solution as they can in agar.

At first, students may see no parallel with the work of earlier chapters in which they investigated interchange between organism and environment, but the starch/agar plates should demonstrate clearly that organisms do affect a relatively large volume or zone around them. A difficulty may arise if the clear zone round an organism is thought to represent food which has been eaten; the questions at the end of the section should help to allay such misunderstanding.

A second aim of this section is to relate digestive action of micro-organisms, germinating grain, and animal gut, thus stressing a similarity between saprophytic and holozoic nutrition. At the same time the relationship between the outside environment and the portion of it enclosed by the alimentary canal can be pointed out.

Teaching procedure

Associated materials
S(M) 5.3, 5.6, 5.7, 6.2, 6.5

The technique is so simple to understand and carry out that students should be able to manage it almost entirely for themselves. The practical work should precede discussion about digestion and not follow it, since the results can stimulate productive questioning. The list of suitable items mentioned in *Laboratory guide (M)* is by no means exhaustive and additional ideas, however unlikely, should be encouraged. The technique can be modified and extended in all sorts of ways. Measuring the diameter of a zone can give a semi-quantitative estimate of the potency of enzymes.

Practical problems

Once it has been seen that some micro-organisms are capable of digesting starch, it may be argued that items such as organs or tissues which appear to do this are really carriers of micro-organisms. This is one reason for practising sterile techniques and using sterile materials as far as possible. For example, barley grains should be surface sterilized before being placed on agar. Clear and useful results can be obtained without recourse to strict, sterile practice, and the method suggested in *Laboratory guide (M)* saves time and energy.

The fact that some portions of locust gut may have more effect on starch than others is not a problem but gives a significant lead into subsequent investigations of the chapter.

Questions and answers

Unchanged starch forms a deep blue colour with iodine solution. Which organisms or other items are associated with colourless zones?

a From the list, all the items should show a clear zone except water. The need for a control should be obvious.

Are such zones immediately touching the items themselves or do they extend beyond them?

b No, they extend beyond the items in all directions. This is important as evidence of a diffusible agent at work. We know this as an enzyme or mixture of enzymes. Chapter 6 discusses these further.

What can you say about the chemical composition of the non-blue zones of agar? What further tests could you perform on these plates?

c All that can be said of the clear zones is that they contain no starch. It is important to discover if the zones are nothing but agar and water or whether they contain a starch derivative or breakdown product. Agar can be removed from the clear zones by means of a cork borer and tested with Benedict's reagent for the presence of reducing sugar. Portions of unaffected starch/agar should also be tested in the same way.

What other colours have you observed besides blue? How do you account for them?

d Some items, particularly germinating cereal grains, produce clear zones with a distinct purple fringe or periphery. This should arouse some comment. The colour suggests that starch may be digested in at least two ways and that perhaps the purple represents an intermediate breakdown product of starch. This is, in fact, due to α-amylodextrin.

In the light of your answers to (a), (b), *and* (c), *relate this investigation to the process of digestion. If animal and plant tissue and micro-organisms can affect starch in the same way, is there any significance in this similarity?*

e Some micro-organisms and tissues produce a substance which changes the chemical constitution of starch. This may be accidental or highly significant; it all depends on the product of the chemical change. Benedict's test reveals that starch is replaced by reducing sugar. Sugars have smaller molecules, diffuse more rapidly, and permeate certain membranes more easily than starch. Digestion in the gut precedes absorption and this may be so with micro-organisms. Young plants use the food stored in seeds; presumably, this has to be absorbed and transported round the plant in a diffusable form.

5.2 Digestive organs; a model gut

Principles

Having noted that pieces of locust gut decompose starch, it is important to see this as a significant process, of use to the living organism. The need for digestion as a preliminary step towards absorption may be well known to students already but they should find this investigation useful, if only confirmatory. The use of real gut wall is technically difficult and an artificial cellulose membrane is the next best thing. Incidentally, this also serves to emphasize once again the value of using models to simulate real situations.

Teaching procedure

Associated materials
S(M) 5.1, 5.2, 5.4, 5.5, 5.6, 6.2, 6.5

It is worth pointing out that Visking tubing is made for dialysis and that it probably works as a molecular sieve, incapable of active transport. Living membranes are far more complex. Cellulose should be looked upon only as a convenient material for a model of the gut and not be confused with plant cell walls, as this might cause misunderstanding.

Practical problems

Pieces of gut produce small amounts of enzyme so the volume of substrate used should not exceed that stated in the instructions. Important, too, is the volume of water outside the cellulose bags. This should be as small as possible so that the concentration of reducing sugar is large enough, at the end of the period of dialysis, to produce a positive result with Benedict's reagent.

Questions and answers

Iodine forms a blue compound with starch; Benedict's solution forms an orange precipitate when heated with reducing sugars. In which samples did you find starch and in which did you find reducing sugar?

a Expected observations:

	Macerated gut + starch suspension		Starch suspension alone	
	inside bag	outside bag	inside bag	outside bag
Iodine test	blue	yellow	blue	yellow
Benedict's test	orange precipitate	orange precipitate	no change	no change

From your observations alone, is there any evidence that gut tissue changes starch to reducing sugar? If so, explain it clearly.

b Reducing sugar may have been present in the gut tissue all the time. From the previous exercise it is known that starch is altered not only by locust gut but by other tissues too. Some of these are likely to be free of maltose and can be tested.

Can you add to this evidence by inspecting the starch/agar plates in 5.1*?*

c Yes; plates can be taken from cold store and portions of the clear zones tested with Benedict's solution for the presence of reducing sugar.

Consider the answers to question (a)*. What do these observations and the properties of cellulose tubing suggest to you about the problem of digestion for a living locust feeding on starch-filled leaves?*

d If the properties of the cellulose bag in any way resemble those of animal gut, then we have a simple model of digestion/absorption. Starch cannot permeate the membrane but, if it is converted to reducing sugar, the latter can then do so. The cellulose bag thus simulates the gut of a locust that has eaten starch; the water outside the bag represents the cells of the locust's body.

5.3 The double function of the alimentary canal

Principles

There is more in this investigation than dissecting an animal to identify the parts of the gut. As well as finding out something of the structure of the alimentary canal, it is intended that students should also discover two things which the mammal gut does when alive. After work with a pithed frog (L(M) 3.3) there should be no surprise at finding that intestines can continue to move after the animal is dead provided, as before, that certain conditions are maintained. Peristalsis may well be familiar to students, as a name. Gut movements, when actually observed, prove to be more complex than simple motion in one direction.

An attempt is also made to see if digestion has taken place in the animal before death. Though not easy, it is certainly possible to show that a greater variety of amino acids exists in the intestine than in the stomach. This is done by introducing a form of chromatography, a technique of great importance in biological research.

Teaching procedure

Associated materials
S(M) 5.1, 5.2, 5.4, 5.5, 5.6, 6.2

In order to get the best results and for reasons of economy, it is probably desirable that students should dissect mice either singly or working in pairs. In addition, one or two freshly killed rats should also be used. Though intestinal movement is best seen in mice, these animals are so small that it is difficult to extract the gut contents and also to examine the internal surface of their minute intestines. It is best if the teacher sets up chromatograms in the first instance, thus providing an example to be copied later by students. (Chapter 7 discusses chromatography again.)

The same rats should be used as for the blood tests outlined in L(M) 4.4.

Dissection in order to observe the parts of the alimentary canal and intestinal movement, the testing of blood, and analysing the contents of the gut call for cooperation among the whole class rather than individual work.

Practical problems

Intestinal activity decreases rapidly with time even though fresh, warm Ringer's solution is continually applied to the dissection. If all the members of a class begin dissecting at the same moment, it is likely that by the time they examine gut linings under the microscope, there will be little if any visible movement of the villi. One way of overcoming this difficulty is to kill a few of the mice later in the practical session and get a few students who have watched the dissection to proceed directly and quickly to this stage of the exercise.

Use of ready-made thin layer strips makes the whole operation possible within the time limits of a laboratory period. To obtain the best results place successive drops of extract on the strip, allowing each one to dry before adding the next. In this way a small but concentrated spot of extract is built up and there is a good chance that a number of amino acid spots will be just visible after standing in solvent for one to two hours.

Questions and answers

Which parts of the alimentary canal appeared to move; how do you account for the movement?

a In life, the whole gut is capable of moving, but under experimental conditions the small intestine is most likely to be seen to move. Movement is worm-like, due presumably to the muscle in the gut wall itself which is arranged in a manner similar to that in earthworms.

It is commonly known that food passes along the alimentary tract from mouth to anus. Do the gut movements appear to move food in this direction? If not, what did the movements appear to do to the food inside the gut?

b Three types of movement may be seen:
1 Pendular movement due to contraction and relaxation of longitudinal muscle.
2 Segmentation caused by contraction and relaxation of circular muscle.
Both these types of movement help to mix the gut contents.
3 Peristalsis caused by rhythmic contractions of circular and longitudinal muscle fibres which move the food along the gut.

Does the inside surface of the alimentary canal appear to be adapted to a digestive or absorptive function, or both? Apply the question to each part of the gut you examined, and state the reasons for your conclusions.

c The digestive function cannot be related to the internal gut surface as seen by the naked eye or with a hand lens; microscopic examination is necessary. Absorption depends on the surface area and this can be related to visible features. Unlike the stomach and caecum, the ileum has a large surface area compared with the volume of digested food contained. The internal surface of the ileum and duodenum is like a 'fur' with the many small projections (villi) which increase the surface area and make the intestine more likely to have a greater efficiency as an absorber. This feature is not found in the oesophagus, stomach, caecum, or rectum, though their inner surfaces are found to be ridged or folded.

The solvent rising up thin layer plates separates the various products of digestion of proteins; ninhydrin forms coloured compounds with amino acids. From your observations is there any evidence that protein has been digested?

d A larger number of spots may be seen on chromatograms of the contents of the ileum than on those of the stomach. This implies that there is a greater variety of amino acids in the ileum than in the stomach. Digestion breaks down protein molecules into their constituent amino acids, so an increase in the number of free amino acids suggests that digestion has taken place.

Which part of the gut is chiefly responsible for absorbing digested food? (Confirm your answer by reference to a textbook.) It would be reasonable to assume that absorption occurs in the last part through which food passes on its journey along the alimentary canal. How do you account for the fact that this is not so?

e The ileum is the portion of alimentary canal considered responsible for the absorption of digestive products into the blood stream. The question is asked in order to stimulate interest in the position and function of the caecum, colon, and rectum. Does any digestion take place posterior to the to the ileum? It is said that the caecum contains bacteria which break down cellulose. Clearly, this is a much larger organ in animals like rabbits which eat much cellulose, than in rats or mice. If digestion does occur in the caecum, where are the products absorbed? An attempt to answer this question can lead to an understanding of the significance of coprophagy in rabbits and certain other mammals. The process occurs to a lesser extent in rats and mice.

5.4 Fine structure of the intestinal wall

Principles

As with lung tissue – L(M) 2.5 – a natural sequel to dissection and macroscopic examination is to make a microscopic study of the ileum. Ideally, students should be able to prepare their own sections of gut but this is a time-consuming process. A transverse section of ileum is much easier to orientate in relation to the whole organ than a lung section but it still presents difficulties in the way of interpretation. Students should try to build up a three-dimensional picture of the gut wall in their minds. This model should be related as far as possible to the real size of the gut and the incredibly large surface involved. Another point of importance is the part played by stains in histology. For example, the P.A.S. staining technique provides evidence of the secretion of mucus by goblet cells in the mucous membrane.

Reference could be made here to the lung as the other absorptive organ studied. The marked differences in the structure of ileum and lung might well stimulate profitable discussion.

Teaching procedure

Associated materials
S(M) 5.4

The questions are intended to encourage an approach to histology that enquires into the functions of tissues and a search for signs of adaptation of structure to function in the living animal. *Laboratory guide (M)* gives little special terminology, so that teachers can introduce it from standard texts if they wish, or ignore it if they feel it is inappropriate to the needs of their students. The procedure is concerned only with sections of the ileum. The investigations suggested do not necessarily preclude similar studies of stomach, duodenum, and other parts of the alimentary tract, if the necessary materials are available and if time permits.

Questions and answers

Describe the general form of the internal surface of the section. Does your description agree with that of the piece of ileum cut from the dissected animal?

a The internal surface of the ileum consists of large numbers of finger-like projections (villi). This cannot be deduced solely from a transverse section, which rather resembles a series of ridges. 'Islands' of tissue in a prepared section indicate the presence of cylindrical, finger-like structures and this is borne out by the previous examination (L(M) 5.3 Procedure stage 10).

Where are blood vessels situated in the wall of the intestine? Refer to figure 59 which is a photomicrograph of an injected specimen. By what route can digestive products pass into the blood stream of a living animal?

b Figure 59 in *Laboratory guide (M)* shows capillaries to be centrally situated within each villus, not immediately next to its surface. Products of digestion must therefore pass through an outer region before entering the blood system. It is possible to estimate the shortest distance travelled through the epithelium of a villus and hence to conclude that it is much greater than the thickness of epithelia in the alveoli of the lungs.

Note: Laboratory guide (M) makes no reference to lacteals or the lymphatic system, because these are difficult to discern in prepared sections. Students should not conclude that all products of digestion necessarily pass only into the blood system.

Do you consider the ileum to be an organ well adapted for the absorption of digested food? Give your reasons.

c The ileum may be said to be adapted for absorption because of its enormous surface area relative to its volume. It can be regarded as a thin tube, the inner surface of which is covered with many minute projections.

If your section is stained with P.A.S. (periodic acid, Schiff method), mucus and the cells producing it will show up clearly, stained deep pink. These are called goblet cells on account of their shape. Comment on their frequency and distribution; what part do you think mucus plays in the action of the alimentary canal? Can you identify other secretory cells? If so, record their position with the aid of a simple, outline sketch.

d Goblet cells appear as single, conspicuous entities in a P.A.S. preparation. They are distributed fairly evenly over the inner surface of the ileum. Few students will seriously consider mucus as an agent of digestion, knowing that enzymes are responsible for this. Mucus, being slimy, is most likely to act as a lubricant which facilitates the movement of digested food and protects the villi from physical damage due to friction.

Other secretory cells in the crypts of Lieberkühn are not so easy to identify and a good, illustrated textbook is probably an essential aid in their investigation.

On the same or another sketch record the position of muscle tissue. If this contracts in the living animal, what movement of the intestine is brought about?

e Students should, by now, be familiar with the appearance of plain muscle but should take care, when comparing slides with illustrations in books, to distinguish between longitudinal and transverse sections. Confusion can arise over the relative positions of circular and longitudinal muscle layers. Contraction of circular muscle causes the diameter of the gut to decrease and its length to increase in consequence; contraction of longitudinal muscle causes the length to decrease and diameter to increase in consequence.

Look at figure 60, an electron micrograph of a minute portion of the inner surface of ileum. There are about 200 000 000 finger-like projections per square millimetre of surface. Comment on the possible significance of these structures with reference to question (c).

f The electron micrograph shows that villi seem to be covered by yet smaller villi. (It is important to emphasize the difference in scale of figures 59 and 60 in *Laboratory guide (M)*.) Presumably this is a third structural feature giving increase in surface area. This question can lead to the idea of absorption by pinocytosis.

This is a good stage at which to draw together the ideas in the previous chapter with those in the present one so that, for example, the presence of glucose in the blood can be seen in relation to the processes of digestion and absorption.

Additional bibliography

General reading

Grove, A. J. and Newell, G. E. (1961) *Animal biology*. University Tutorial Press.
Hogg, M. (1966) *A biology of man* Vol II. Heinemann.
Holter, H. (1961) 'How things get into cells.' *Scientific American* **205**, 3, 167–180.
Marshal, G. and Hughes, G. M. (1965) *The physiology of mammals and other vertebrates*. Cambridge University Press.
Nuffield O-level Biology (1966) Text and Teachers' Guide Year III *The maintenance of life*. Longmans/Penguin.

References

Ham, A. W. and Leeson, T. S. (1965) *Histology*. 5th edition. Lippincott.
Nuffield O-level Biology (1966) Text Year IV *Living things in action*. Longmans/Penguin.
Rowett, H. G. Q. (1960) *The rat as a small mammal*. 2nd edition. Murray.
Thomas, J. G. (1963) *Dissection of the locust*. Witherby.
Winton, F. R. and Bayliss, L. E. (1962) *Human physiology*. Churchill.

Chapter 6

Enzymes and organisms

Chapter review

The work of this chapter is largely concerned with starch because students will have become familiar with it through the work of the last chapter and can follow its hydrolysis and synthesis simply and quantitatively.

Amylase enzymes are first extracted from germinating grain and then used to demonstrate the course of a typical enzyme-controlled reaction. This knowledge of some of the properties of one enzyme can be used to test yeast fermentation to see if this is also an enzymic process.

The chapter ends by considering the synthesis of starch by an enzyme extracted from potatoes. This emphasizes the importance of enzymes in synthesis and is relevant to the work in Chapter 7.

The sequence of topics is:

1 Enzyme extraction.
2 The course of an enzyme-controlled reaction.
3 Enzyme activity in whole organisms.
4 An enzyme-controlled synthesis.

Assumptions

– Students require little background knowledge. They should be familiar with the name 'enzyme' and with a list of enzyme properties. The practical work is so outlined that it will be easy to rearrange investigations to suit the previous experience of students. These investigations are not intended to provide a full picture of enzyme characteristics; they must be supplemented by other sources of information.

– The use of structural formulae here requires little background knowledge beyond the simplest concept of chemical valency, C:4, O:2, and H:1. (There are no double bonds in the examples given.)

6.1 Enzyme extraction (preliminary)

Principles

There are a number of purified enzymes which may be obtained easily from suppliers. However the danger of using these is that they may appear to students as chemicals dissociated from living organisms. Salivary amylase is much easier to obtain than amylase from germinating grain but extraction of the latter provides an example of a method which, though simple, is widely used to obtain enzyme. However students should appreciate that not all enzyme extraction is as easy as that of amylase.

Teaching procedure

Associated materials
S(M) 5.3, 6.1, 6.2

It is desirable that students should carry out the extraction process themselves. However it may be most economical if one or two members of the class prepare enzymes for the rest. The exercise can be usefully increased in scope by using barley grains at different stages of germination, e.g. dry grain, grain soaked for 24 hours, and grains germinated for the period suggested in *Laboratory guide (M)* or for a longer period. The potency of each enzyme extracted can be compared experimentally and related to the requirements of the normal development of the plant.

Practical problems

Occasionally germinating grain produces unpleasant fungal growths. This is best prevented by surface sterilization with 1 per cent hypochlorite solution. In fact, this is more important in theory than in practice. If students follow the line of argument in the last chapter, they may claim that enzyme activity is due, wholly or in part, to micro-organisms rather than to the grain itself. Thus the former have to be eliminated.

Mercury(II) chloride can be used. It is mentioned in L(M) 6.1 as an enzyme poison. Care has to be taken because it is exceedingly poisonous.

Questions and answers

Which parts of the germinating barley do you think have been discarded in the extraction process?

a Husks or pericarps with insoluble endosperm.

What tests could be profitably performed on the discarded material?

b Iodine solution could be used to test for the presence of starch, Benedict's test for the presence of reducing sugar.

Of what use would results of these tests be?

c As we are looking for a starch-digesting enzyme (revealed by work in 5.1) the presence of starch in grain is most significant.

6.2 The course of an enzyme-controlled reaction

Principles

The idea that amylase digests starch is known from 5.1 and probably as background knowledge. The aim here is to quantify the process, using the iodine test, and to follow the course of the reaction. Once this has been done and the characteristics of the normal reaction have been established, it is possible to discover one or two of the properties of the enzyme by modifying the experimental conditions.

It is important that students realize that they cannot generalize about all enzymes from one example and, conversely, that some of the general properties already learned may not apply to amylase.

For the sake of simplicity, the single word amylase is used but there are normally two forms of this enzyme present in germinating barley. Dry barley grains contain mainly maltogenic β-amylase which hydrolyses only straight-chain amylase. Four-day-old, germinating barley contains this together with dextrogenic α-amylase capable of breaking down the amylose and amylopectin moieties of starch.

That the amylopectin is digested after the amylose is revealed by the purple/violet intermediate colour found in the starch/agar plates of 5.1. Maltogenic amylase is more sensitive to heat treatment than dextrogenic amylase and its activity is greatly diminished if it is subjected to a temperature of 70° C for fifteen minutes. This could be the basis for a further investigation.

Teaching procedure

Associated materials
S(M) 6.1, 6.2, 6.3, 6.4, 6.5, 6.8

Several students could share a single colorimeter. This is preferable to using less sensitive visual methods of comparing colours. Once a satisfactory technique has been established and measurements obtained which lie along a smooth line of a graph, the way is clear for further investigations. These should be devised, as far as possible, by students themselves. For newcomers to the subject the irreversible effect of high temperature is one of the most important characteristics of enzymes. This property can be used to show that fermentation – see L(M) 6.3 – is concerned with enzymes. Those already familiar with this property might turn their attention to the poisoning effect of salts of heavy metals.

Practical problems

Reliable colorimeters are essential for this work though they need not be elaborate or expensive. Whether the students use manufactured or home-made ones the teacher must allow them time to find out by preliminary trial how to obtain consistent readings. For example, the making of a conversion graph – see L(M) 6.2 Procedure stage 11 – is a good preliminary exercise. The readings obtained should lie on a smooth curve.

Students may suggest that instead of taking samples from a reacting mixture they simply add iodine to it in the sample tube and take readings at intervals. This works well in that it produces a characteristic curve but it is difficult to understand what is happening chemically. If, when the mixture has gone completely colourless, more iodine is added, a dense blue colour is formed, showing that much undigested starch remains. Because the chemistry of the starch/iodine compound is obscure it may be safer to adhere to the customary practice of taking samples.

Questions and answers

Draw a graph of starch concentration (from the conversion described below) against time and compare it with figure 65. In what ways are the two graphs similar? How do they differ?

a Ideally the graphs of starch and casein digestion will be similar. Amylase extracts vary; low enzyme yield gives a slow reaction, high temperature a rapid one. The shape of the curve indicates rapid reaction to begin with, progressively declining in *rate* until no starch remains. Students should be encouraged to propose reasons for the curves obtained. See figure 8.

Figure 8
Graph showing the progress of starch hydrolysis by barley extract.

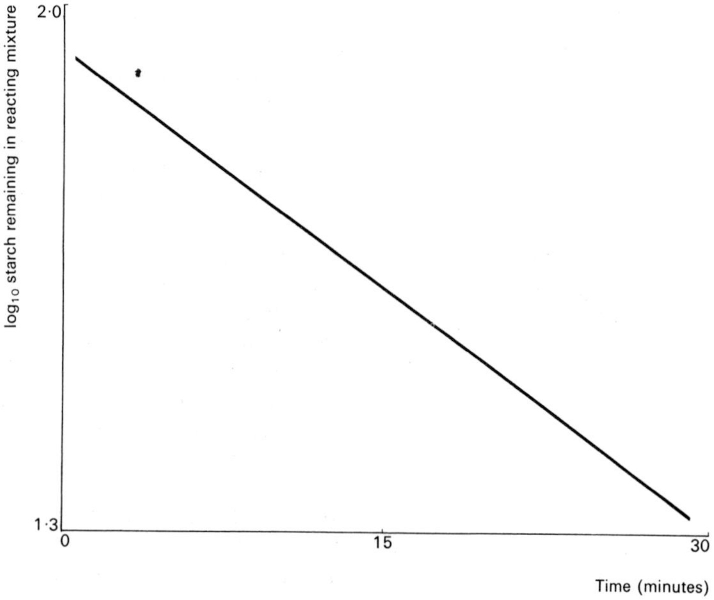

Look up the logarithm (base 10) of each value of starch concentration and then plot log concentrations against time. What information does the graph provide that the previous one did not reveal?

b The points should be on or near a straight line showing that the original concentrations bear an exponential (logarithmic) relationship with time. This cannot be assumed or deduced merely by looking at the previous graph of starch concentration against time.

Name one phenomenon, not necessarily biological, which shows a similar relationship with time. Is there a similar underlying principle related to starch digestion and the phenomenon you have named?

c One example is the cooling curve (the temperature/time curve of a cooling body). Another, to be considered in the next chapter, is radioactive decay. With digestion and radioactive decay, the rate of decrease is related to the amount of material remaining. It is like water running out of a burette, being fast at first, getting slower as the head of water decreases. This model is also analogous to the cooling curve, heat loss being related to temperature difference.

How would you modify the above procedure to investigate either the effect of temperature (0 to 100°) or the effect of acidity and alkalinity on starch digestion? Give sufficient experimental details to serve as adequate instructions.

d Example: note the time (t) required for the enzyme/substrate mixture at 15° C to give about one-third of a full scale deflection of the colorimeter. Set up identical reacting mixtures at different temperatures such as 30° C, 45° C, 60° C, 70° C, and 90° C. After exactly t minutes, add a sample to the iodine solution and record the intensity of colour. Repeat for each temperature. Convert the reading into starch concentrations and plot a graph of these quantities against temperature. To investigate the effect of pH set up a similar experiment, keep the temperature constant, but add acid and alkali to make a range of pH values.

Taking into consideration the results from the tests using iodine solution and Benedict's solution, state exactly what reaction has taken place in the mixture of starch and enzyme extract.

e From using iodine alone all that can be concluded is that starch disappears. Benedict's test shows the presence of reducing sugar and if there were none in the extract at the outset then it must have been formed during the reaction. That maltose is formed cannot be deduced from these tests.

6.3 Enzyme activity in whole organisms

Principles

The purpose of this investigation is to allow students to relate the activities of organisms to the enzymes they possess. It is important that they should not regard enzymes merely as aids to digestion. Frequently, students do hold this unfortunate idea.

Many eminent scientists of the nineteenth century were confused by the ability of mere chemicals to carry out fermentation, a process considered to be the function of complete organisms. Similar views are sometimes held by students today. Fermentation is the function of chemicals and conditions within an organism. The same applies to the processes of nutrition and respiration. Thus, to identify something, such as yeast, as living or non-living, students must construct a composite picture, including other characteristics such as growth and reproduction.

Students should see that yeast fermentation is affected by temperature and other factors in much the same way as any enzyme process. (Some students have been known to refer to the 'death' of an enzyme at high temperature; this is a danger to guard against.)

From the investigation it may well appear that fermentation is controlled by a single enzyme, as, indeed, it was thought to be at one time (the enzyme zymase). It is difficult to provide an opportunity for students to discover that a multi-stage process and a multi-enzyme system are involved. It may be best to provide information on this from books and accept the limitations of time and technique. One possible suggestion is given as answer *(d)* below.

Teaching procedure

Associated materials
S(M) 6.2, 6.3, 6.5, 6.6, 6.7, 6.8, 7.8

Alternative forms of apparatus are suggested. It should be possible to provide at least one respirometer per pair of students. The experiments carried out will depend on the numbers available and the previous knowledge and experience of students. One of the most important elementary investigations is the comparison between the activity of normal yeast and that of boiled yeast.

Practical problems

There are many forms of respirometer suitable for this investigation. The type illustrated in figure 72 in *Laboratory guide (M)* is easy to operate and suitable for a number of different experiments. Students should be able to distinguish between the underlying principles of different models. Essentially the version suggested for use is a differential respirometer. The manometer registers a difference between the vessel containing organisms and a compensating vessel. If the syringe piston is left in one position throughout an experiment (i.e. not used) and the change in manometer fluid is recorded then the respirometer is being used as a Barcroft differential respirometer. If the syringe is used to restore the manometric fluid to its original position, from time to time, then the respirometer is being used as a form of Dixon-Barcroft constant pressure manometer.

There are two main problems likely to be encountered in the investigation. One concerns erratic respirometer readings due to temperature fluctuation. This can be remedied by using efficient thermostat-controlled water baths and allowing sufficient time for equilibration of temperature between the outside water and the centre of the vessels containing yeast suspension.

The second difficulty concerns the yeast, different samples of which may vary in their ability to ferment sugar. Dried yeast, as supplied by bakers, health stores, and school suppliers, though often less active per unit weight than fresh bakers' yeast, is possibly more reliable in the long term. It is advisable to mix the substrate (sucrose) and dry yeast an hour or two in advance or, alternatively, to allow the mixture to stand overnight and add more substrate just before it is needed. The recommended concentration of yeast is so great that carbon dioxide should be produced in considerable volume. This will make the investigation quick and the respirometer readings more reliable.

Questions and answers

Describe the experiment devised at stage (13) and state the results obtained. Do these provide evidence supporting the hypothesis that the action of yeast on sucrose is enzyme-controlled?

a The simplest experiment is to compare gas production by normal yeast and by an equivalent quantity heated to 90–100° C for several minutes and then allowed to cool. This can be done as two separate experiments or by placing boiled yeast in the compensating vessel. (If it produces any gas at all it will make restoration of the manometric fluid difficult.)

How would you determine the composition of the gas evolved?

b That carbon dioxide is produced by fermentation can be regarded as almost common knowledge. The gas can be identified using a solution of calcium hydroxide.

How would you identify the other products of fermentation? What are they?

c The other product, ethanol, is not easy to identify in small quantities of fermenting mixture unless the class has access to a vapour phase chromatograph. (A 'school' version as used by the chemistry department would be quite adequate to detect ethanol.)

Alternatively, brew a large volume of yeast and sucrose (1 dm^3) and distil off the ethanol. Later identify it by its boiling point.

Using chemicals and apparatus mentioned previously in this chapter, how would you discover if there was a change in the amount of sucrose during the course of fermentation?

d Take a sample of the mixture soon after the yeast has been added to the sucrose solution. Spin down the yeast in a centrifuge and test the clear liquid by first hydrolysing it with dilute acid and then testing with Benedict's solution. Having obtained a red precipitate, repeat the procedure with a fermenting mixture which has almost ceased to give off gas. A much reduced or absent precipitate indicates that sucrose has been used up. (This method is better adapted for use with glucose or maltose. There is then no need for hydrolysis with acid.)

Design an experiment, not necessarily using a respirometer, to show whether one or a number of enzymes are concerned in fermentation. You will require a wider knowledge of enzyme properties than that derived from the work of this chapter alone.

e This question requires careful examination of the literature and an answer based on experiments performed by the students may be impossible. Students who have read accounts of the work of Harden and Young, Robison and Neuberg may wish to repeat one of the simpler experiments. The simplest of these involves the addition of sodium sulphite to fermenting yeast. The bisulphite compound of acetaldehyde is formed instead of ethanol. This suggests that acetaldehyde is a normal precursor of ethanol and that fermentation is a multi-stage process. From this one may conjecture that it is also a multi-enzyme system.

6.4 An enzyme-controlled synthesis

Principles

Students should obtain for themselves a clear indication that enzymes are responsible for metabolic synthesis as well as breakdown reactions. It is fortunate that one of the few syntheses which can be observed in a normal school practical session is that for starch which can be studied quantitatively.

A point to be emphasized is that simple carbohydrates such as glucose, maltose, and sucrose cannot be synthesized into starch, only a phosphorylated sugar, glucose:1:phosphate. The significance of this is considerable and students should well understand it at least by the end of Chapter 7. Starch synthesis requires energy and this is presumably derived from cell respiration. It is significant that glucose:1:phosphate is an intermediate of respiration produced by reaction with ATP and not by simple reaction between glucose and phosphoric acid.

Teaching procedure

Associated materials
S(M) 6.2, 6.3, 6.4, 6.5, 6.6, 6.7, 6.8

This investigation follows the lines of L(M) 6.1 and 6.2 involving extraction and the use of a colorimeter.

Practical problems

The quantities of materials given in *Laboratory guide (M)* should be modified to suit individual requirements.

Potatoes of medium size and age are most satisfactory. Large potatoes sometimes produce a poor yield of phosphorylase enzyme. Small, 'new' potatoes have such small grains of starch that these are difficult or impossible to spin down.

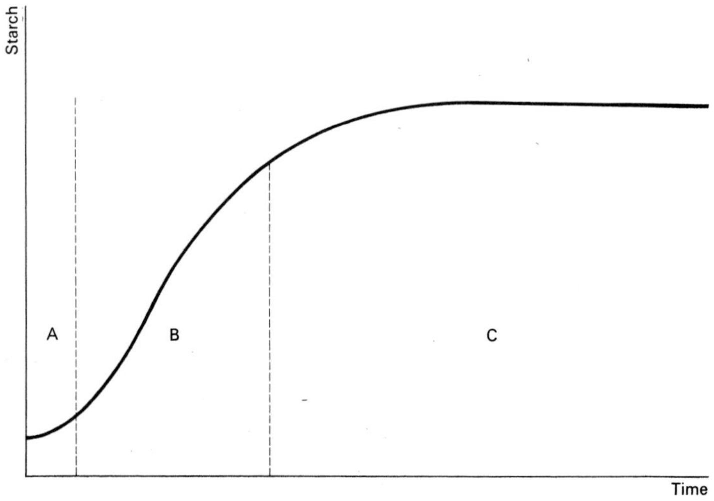

Figure 9
The progress of starch synthesis.
A = lag phase
B = synthesis
C = substrate used up

Questions and answers

Describe the appearance of the mixtures at the end of the investigation. Which of the substrates produced starch after the addition of potato enzyme extract?

a Glucose:1:phosphate. All the mixtures may appear a little darker at the end of the experiment. This has nothing to do with starch formation but is due to the action of polyphenol oxidase and is the same process as that causing apples to go brown when cut. The enzyme mixed with glucose phosphate becomes turbid and if a drop is examined under a microscope, granules (4–10 microns in diameter) may be seen.

Compare the graphs obtained in this investigation with that of starch digestion (6.2). Describe any similarities and differences between them.

b See figure 9.

State the difference which you consider most significant and suggest a hypothesis to account for it. How would you test the hypothesis?

c The graph follows an expected path; a rise in starch concentration to a maximum when all the glucose phosphate has been used up. One curious feature which may be seen is an initial lag phase. Hanes (see Additional bibliography) showed that synthesis was autocatalytic because the lag phase was decreased by adding small amounts of soluble starch to the reacting mixture of enzyme and glucose phosphate. Proposing such a hypothesis of autocatalysis is possibly beyond the capabilities of most students at this stage but it is worth describing it as an example of the way graphs may be used to develop hypotheses.

It has been assumed throughout that the reaction investigated is controlled by an enzyme in potatoes. How would you test the hypothesis that an enzyme or enzymes are responsible for starch synthesis?

d Heat the enzyme extract. Add enzyme poisons, acid, or alkali. Any or all of these, if they reduce the rate of synthesis, lend support to the idea that an enzyme is involved. The presence of protein could be tested; all known enzymes are proteinaceous.

Make a list of likely substrates for the potato enzyme which might be tested in addition to glucose, maltose, and sucrose.

e There would seem to be little point in trying other non-phosphorylated carbohydrates. Other possibilities include: phosphoric acid with glucose; or glucose with a phosphate; glucose:6:phosphate; glucose with ATP.

Additional bibliography

General reading

Baldwin, E. (1949) *Dynamic aspects of biochemistry*. Cambridge University Press.
Baron, W. M. M. (1963) *Organisation in plant*. Edward Arnold.
James, W. O. (1953) *Plant respiration*. Oxford University Press.
Jevons, F. R. (1965) *The biochemical approach to life*. Allen & Unwin.
Nuffield O-level Biology (1966) Text and Teachers' Guide Year III. *The maintenance of life*. Longmans/Penguin.
Eggleston, J. F. (1970) Nuffield Advanced Biological Science Topic Review *Thinking quantitively I: Descriptions and models*. Penguin. (Considers the use of graphs for constructing hypotheses.)

References

Hanes, C. S. (1940) *Proc. Roy. Soc.* (London) 'The breakdown and synthesis of starch by an enzyme system from pea seeds', **128B**, 421 and 'The reversible formation of starch from glucose-1-phosphate catalysed by potato phosphorylase', **129B**, 174.

Chapter 7

Photosynthesis

Chapter review

For such a large and complex topic as photosynthesis, we do not attempt an integrated sequence of investigations but, instead, propose five distinct practical approaches. Each employs a different technique to obtain different information.

The traditionally accepted identification of photosynthesis with starch production is put in doubt partly by considering the implications of the work on starch synthesis performed in the last chapter, and partly by experiments with leaf discs floating on glucose solution.

Use of radioactive carbon enables the student to relate the fixation of carbon dioxide to light and the presence of chlorophyll in living leaves. Students can discover a more precise relationship between light intensity and photosynthesis by measuring the oxygen produced by pond weed.

Like previous chapters, this one emphasizes the relationship between the structure of an organ and its function. It examines leaves as photosynthetic organs. An indication of the essential presence of chlorophyll in all true plants can be gained by chromatographic studies of a number of plants containing different pigments.

The sequence of topics is:

1 The production of starch by leaves.
2 The uptake of carbon dioxide.
3 The evolution of oxygen.
4 Leaf structure.
5 Leaf pigments.

Assumptions

– A knowledge of the basic facts of photosynthesis. With or without previous training in biology, most students will probably know that organic materials are synthesized from carbon dioxide and water in the presence of light and chlorophyll. The work of this chapter reaffirms some (not all) of these facts by practical investigations.

- Familiarity with the *in vitro* synthesis of starch, the solubility of oxygen in water, and the technique of chromatography. These topics are all used here and are also mentioned in previous chapters. The Inverse Square Law (7.3) should present no problems.
- Some understanding of radioactivity, a new topic. Students should understand that radioactivity is a phenomenon of atomic nuclei and therefore invulnerable to chemical change. This makes it impossible to alter the rate or type of radioactive decay by change of temperature or chemical reaction. For the same reason a radioactive isotope of an element behaves chemically in a plant exactly as does its non-radioactive counterparts. The teacher should emphasize the importance of radio isotopes generally in research.
- It is desirable for students to be fully aware of the different forms of radiation though they are concerned, here, with only one (beta radiation). They should understand, in principle, the form and function of a simple Geiger-Müller tube, ratemeter, and scaler, and the method of detecting radiation by photographic film – autoradiography.

7.1 The production of starch by leaves

Principles

Experiments on plants carried out in middle-school biology have long depended on starch tests as evidence of photosynthesis. These lead to a definition of photosynthesis in terms of an equation:

$$\text{carbon dioxide} + \text{water} + \text{light} \xrightarrow{\text{chlorophyll}} \text{oxygen} + \text{starch}.$$

The aim of this investigation is to let students find that leaves are capable of producing starch in the dark, but only from a suitable precursor and in the presence of oxygen. From this, the idea should emerge that starch production may serve as a perfectly good indicator of photosynthesis but, by itself, is not light-dependent or an essential part of the process. Photosynthesis has to be defined without reference to starch.

Teaching procedure

Associated materials
S(M) 1.4, 1.5, 7.1, 7.2, 7.3, 7.4

There are at least two ways of presenting the ideas of this investigation besides that of strictly adhering to the Procedure in *Laboratory guide (M)*. The first of these is to have stages (1) to (6) already completed and present the apparatus to students with the request to carry out stage (7). This saves the class's time but reduces the scope of the investigation to a single operation: a starch test. The second way is to abandon a practical approach and present the students with the results of such an experiment.

Practical problems

Starch production by leaf discs on glucose solution differs markedly from one species to another. *Impatiens* has been known to give adequate results, *Nicotiana* is probably more reliable. How glucose enters the leaf discs is of interest. It has been reported that if the discs are floated upside down on the solution, no starch is formed. This implies that entry occurs through the stomata but if this is so, how does oxygen enter? This is perhaps a topic for further enquiry.

Questions and answers

In which conditions did leaf discs produce starch?

a In illuminated leaf discs and in the darkened discs exposed to air. Not in those in dark, anaerobic conditions.

What are leaf discs deprived of when they are made to sink (see stage 5)?

b Air; that is, nitrogen, oxygen, carbon dioxide, and the rare gases.

Propose a hypothesis to account for the results. How could you test it?

c To produce starch, leaves in the dark require oxygen. (From previous work, e.g. 6.4, students can infer that the synthesis of starch from glucose requires the transfer of energy and this is more likely to require oxygen than nitrogen or carbon dioxide.) Set up discs floating on glucose solution as before but in an atmosphere of nitrogen. If no starch is formed, the hypothesis is supported.

Do the results of the investigation affect the validity of the starch test as an indicator of photosynthetic activity? If so, give details.

d Yes; the elementary notion of photosynthesis

$$\text{carbon dioxide} + \text{water} + \text{light} \xrightarrow{\text{chlorophyll}} \text{starch} + \text{oxygen}$$

must be modified, as, for example,

$$\text{carbon dioxide} + \text{water} + \text{light} \xrightarrow{\text{chlorophyll}} x + \text{oxygen} \rightarrow \text{starch}.$$

If the substance x is always converted to starch by leaves, then the starch test is a valid one for photosynthesis. In other words (except in those plants which never produce starch), photosynthesis always results in starch but starch is not always the direct result of photosynthesis.

7.2 The uptake of carbon dioxide

Principles

After casting doubt on an established means of detecting photosynthesis, it is most important to follow with something more positive. The use of radioactive tracers into research photosynthesis has been crucial. Without it we should have little, if any, firm ideas about the fate of carbon dioxide in living leaves. The aim of this investigation is to enable students to establish a link between light and the uptake or fixation of carbon dioxide. By using variegated plants, the necessity of chlorophyll can also be demonstrated. It is important to understand that there is no substitute for this technique. The mere disappearance of carbon dioxide from air surrounding a plant does not provide the same kind of evidence as that from the use of tracers.

Teaching procedure

Associated materials
S(M) 1.4, 1.5, 7.2, 7.5, 7.9
Film loop 'Handling radioisotopes I: Carbon-14'

A second aim is to familiarize students with the ways of handling radioactive substances and the interpretation of autoradiographs. Illustrations of these in textbooks have less impact than autoradiographs made in the school laboratory. It may be more difficult to interpret these but students will learn more lessons.

The procedure, though written as instructions for individual students, is best conducted as a single experiment for the whole class. (Students under the age of sixteen years are not permitted to handle open sources of radioactivity such as tablets of $Na_2{}^{14}CO_3$.)

One or two leafy shoots provide many leaves which may be shared amongst the class for making autoradiographs. Even if apparatus and fume cupboards allow more than one experiment to be performed at a time, it is wiser to examine the results of one before starting another.

It may be necessary to increase the intensity or duration of illumination or modify the technique in other ways in the light of experience.

If a scaler is available, students should take counts from unit areas of darkened, illuminated, and variegated leaves. Evidence thus gained is a useful addition to that from autoradiography.

Practical problems

Open sources of some radioisotopes, including ^{14}C, are available to schools in quantities more than enough for a number of experiments of the type included. The amounts involved are so small that damage to the health of students is virtually impossible. This fact should not encourage them to be careless. Tablets of sodium carbonate ($Na_2{}^{14}CO_3$) are strongly recommended as a convenient, easily handled form of radiocarbon. Such tablets (each containing 50μ Ci of ^{14}C) may be purchased by schools which have applied for and received permission from the Department of Education and Science. Teachers making application must satisfy the Department that they have undergone appropriate training. Details of this training requirement, the amounts of isotope which may be purchased, and the rules of laboratory are laid down in publications available, free of charge, from the Department of Education and Science, Curzon Street, London W.1.

Use sodium carbonate in preference to barium carbonate because, if dust is inhaled, it may remain localized in the respiratory tract for a considerable time because of its insolubility. Indoor plants such as *Zebrina* spp. assimilate carbon dioxide rapidly in the conditions indicated by *Laboratory guide (M)* and are recommended for this work. Enclosing the mounted leaves in a polythene bag reduces the amount of radiation reaching the film. Sealing the leaves in a bag avoids accidental loss of leaf fragments in the darkroom and elsewhere. This safety precaution is recommended even though it slightly reduces sensitization of the photographic film.

Questions and answers

What conclusions can you draw from your observations?

a Compare the autoradiographs, with reference to the leaves from which they were made. Black areas of film should correspond with leaf areas illuminated during the experiment. Transparent *masks* may diminish the light falling on the leaves so that a lighter portion of black film may be produced. If variegated leaves were used, areas of different intensities of colour should correspond with the patterns formed on the processed film.

Do all the blackened areas associated with leaf images correspond with your expectations?

b Though in general an affirmative answer is likely, closer inspection may reveal a black line corresponding with the mid-rib or veins of the leaf and there may be other interesting anomalies.

Examine the centre or mid-rib portion of the leaf images on the film and report your findings.

c It is important for students to realize that film can be blackened by chemicals and uneven pressure as well as by radiation. Patches of grey or black in places well away from carbon-14 are not uncommon in first attempts at an unfamiliar technique.

Are there any blackened portions of the film outside the leaf positions? If so, how do you account for them?

d The answer cannot be deduced and will either be known from previous reading or guessed. Radioactive carbon is assimilated into all carbon-containing components of the plant rapidly, as was shown by Calvin and others (see Additional Bibliography). It is important that students are not misled into thinking that the radioactive carbon dioxide is merely trapped, in this form, in the leaf cells.

In what compound or compounds do you think the radioactive carbon was combined at the time of cutting leaves from the shoot?

e Expose a leafy shoot to air containing $^{14}CO_2$ as before and then make an extract and run a paper chromatogram. When this is completed, place the chromatogram against a piece of X-ray film to make an autoradiograph. The *hot* spots on the paper will cause blackening of the film. Such a technique can be carried out successfully in a school laboratory but because of the small amounts of radioactive isotope in each spot of separated component a much longer period must be allowed for autoradiography; of the order of 1–2 weeks. Extracts can be made by grinding the plant tissue and letting it stand in a minimal amount of ethanol for several hours.

7.3 The evolution of oxygen

Principles

It is important to remind students that photosynthesis is not confined to plants living in the atmosphere and indeed that the process began at a time when all life was aquatic. We suggest *Elodea* for this investigation because it is easy to obtain, culture, and handle, and produces gas bubbles. Because carbon is taken in as dissolved bicarbonate ions and oxygen is given off as a gas there is no need for analyses of either liquid or gas phase. Methods of measuring oxygen evolution from an aerial leaf involve fairly sophisticated equipment such as a Warburg apparatus; we avoid this by using *Elodea*.

It is possible to adapt the technique using pond weed to investigate the principle of limiting factors. The rate of oxygen production is limited by the availability of bicarbonate ions. If the experiment is begun in pure water or low bicarbonate concentration, gas production should reach a maximum and then rise again as more bicarbonate is added.

Teaching procedure

The type of apparatus described in *Laboratory guide (M)* is simple enough for students to have access to it individually. As an alternative technique, the bubbles emerging from a shoot of *Elodea* may be counted in known periods of time. Counting should be regarded as a last resort if the quantity of gas emerging is too small to collect. Bubbles are usually too erratic for reliable quantitative work.

Practical problems

Associated materials
S(M) 1.3, 1.4, 1.5, 1.6, 7.1, 7.6, 7.7

Elodea has a reputation for unreliable performance and there are quite a number of suggested recipes and remedies. Part of the oxygen given off by an aquatic plant will dissolve in the water until it is saturated. If gas production is rapid and the *Elodea* shoot is near the surface, this effect is minimized. The precaution of saturating the water with oxygen before starting the experiment may be taken. This will enrich bubbles of any gas given off with oxygen and must be taken into account when analysing samples (see the answer to question *c* below). A less artificial method is to use water from the aquarium tank in which the *Elodea* was already bubbling. This water is also saturated with oxygen but as a result of photosynthetic activity, not human intervention. We do not recommend adding bicarbonate ions to the water simply to aid the production of oxygen or as an additional experiment; potassium bicarbonate is said to be less toxic than sodium bicarbonate. It is more difficult to control change in the ionic concentration than light intensity and students should not undertake the former until they have successfully completed the simpler technique described in *Laboratory guide (M)*. Small, bright sources of light are better than large ones. Projector bulbs have produced better results than larger bulbs of equivalent power.

Questions and answers

State any relationship between gas production and light intensity which has been demonstrated by your results.

a The amount of gas collected per unit of time is inversely proportional to the square of the distance from the light source. The graph, ideally, should be linear, but some scatter of points is likely.

How would you confirm, experimentally, that the light intensity decreases with the square of the distance?

b By means of a light meter. There are serious theoretical drawbacks; for example, the calibration of the light meter should be considered. Meters may respond variously to different wavelengths of light. A meter used alongside a plant immersed in water may give misleading results. If students understand this point, the information contained in figure 10 may be of further interest.

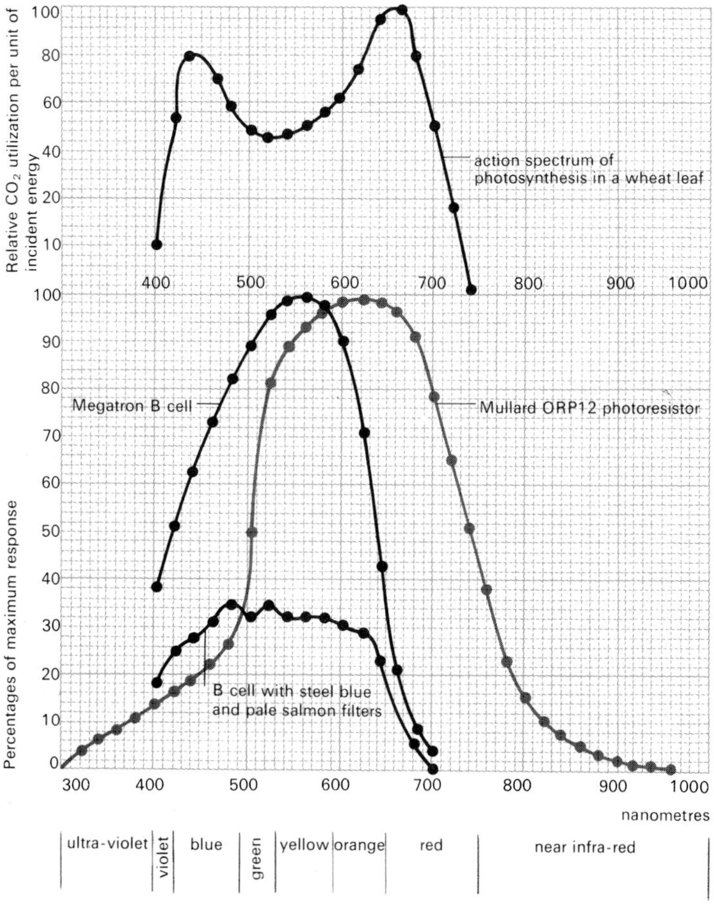

Figure 10
Spectral sensitivities and an action spectrum.

What is the composition of the gas analysed? How do you account for it?

c The gas collected is unlikely to be pure oxygen and such a result raises obvious questions concerning the nature of the other gases present and how their presence can be explained.

As a bubble of oxygen rises through the water, some tends to dissolve, and nitrogen already present in the water comes out of solution into the bubble. The composition of collected gas therefore depends partly on the metabolism of the plant and partly on the contents of the water. If a sample of gas is collected over water which has part of its surface exposed to air, as in the traditional *Elodea* demonstration, the composition of the sample becomes in time, more and more like that of the atmosphere. (According to Dalton's extension of Henry's Law, 'The amount of any one gas dissolved from a mixture of gases is proportional to its partial pressure when the gas has come into equilibrium with the liquid.' The solubility coefficients, volume of gas dissolved by one volume of water, of oxygen and nitrogen at 20° C, are 0·031 and 0·016 respectively.) This is probably why gas collected over pond weed during several days cannot rekindle a glowing splint. This discussion should not mislead students into thinking that the oxygen produced by photosynthesis is derived from *dissolved* oxygen in the water.

7.4 Leaf structure

Principles

This investigation is intended to draw the attention of students to leaves as organs adapted to the process of photosynthesis. The similarities of leaf form should be stressed rather than the diversity of outline shapes. To function efficiently, cells containing chloroplasts must be exposed to sunlight, carbon dioxide (or bicarbonate ions), and water. The typical laminate leaf form is therefore ideal. Students should revise the work of 2.1 and relate it to photosynthesis. They should examine as much fresh leaf material as time permits, supplementing it by prepared sections where necessary.

Teaching procedure

Associated materials
S(M) 2.2, 7.4
S(P) 1.6, 7.1

Having already made epidermal strips (investigation 2.1), students should be encouraged to use any means at their disposal to investigate leaf structure for themselves. They can gain much by examining fragments of leaves under a microscope and should not waste time trying to obtain perfect transverse sections cut by hand. There is a place for prepared, microtome sections. These should not predominate but can aid students in formulating a three-dimensional mental model of living leaves. Lactic acid can be used to clear leaves.

Practical problems

The usual method of using pith to support leaves when cutting them by hand produces a large amount of unwanted material which has then to be separated from the leaf sections. Rolling the leaves may provide a better alternative with some specimens. *Zebrina* spp., though excellent for many purposes, have leaves with a curious anatomy which should not be regarded as typical.

Questions and answers

How many different kinds of cell, judged by their shape, can you see in a leaf of Elodea*? Describe the size and contents of the cells.*

a Only two or three. Most cells appear remarkably similar; brick-like in shape. The majority are packed with green *corpuscles* or chloroplasts but they are colourless at the edges and near the mid-line of the leaf. Some cells at the edge may project as small spikes. Diameters of cells and chloroplasts should be measured.

How many different kinds of cell (judged by size and shape) can you see in a section of broad leaf of a dicotyledonous plant? Give a brief, illustrated account of each type.

b At least six kinds; epidermis, palisade mesophyll, spongy mesophyll, guard cells, various cells of vascular tissue.

By two simple plan drawings, compare the organization of cells in a broad leaf (dicotyledon) with that in a narrow leaf (monocotyledon).

c Figure 11 illustrates this.

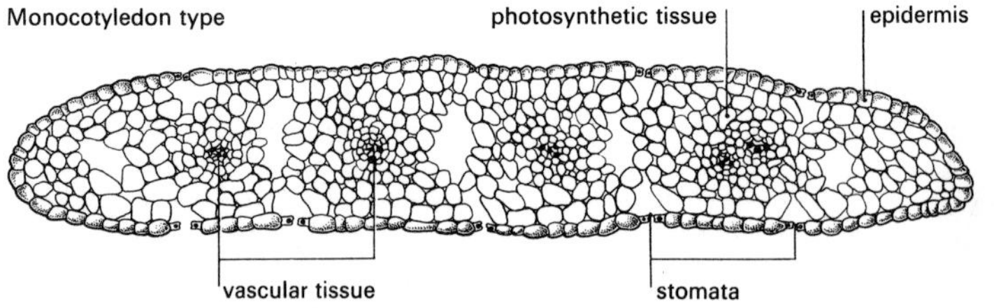

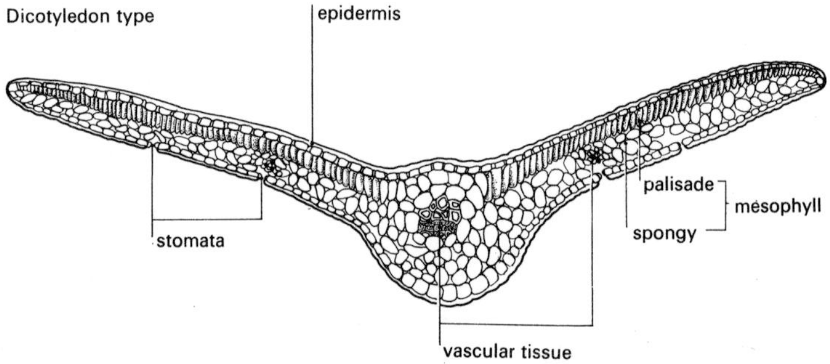

Figure 11
Plan drawing of two kinds of leaf in transverse section.

Describe the contents of the cells of a freshly cut leaf. Compare them, with respect to colour, size, and shape, to the contents of Elodea *leaf cells.*

d Mesophyll cells contain green chloroplasts. These are similar to the chloroplasts of *Elodea*. The chloroplasts are denser in the palisade cells, less dense in spongy mesophyll cells, and absent from epidermal cells.

Describe any items of debris which occur commonly and which you think are important in the whole leaf. Do those in iodine solution differ from those in water?

e Large numbers of chloroplasts escape from cut cells together with starch grains (coloured blue by iodine solution). Shapes and colours may be seen clearly in isolation.

What structural features of the leaves examined so far can be regarded as adaptations to a photosynthetic function?

f

1 Cells containing large numbers of chloroplasts are clustered in a thin layer on the *upper*, more illuminated side. (Leaves of monocotyledon plants do not follow this plan. Their leaves are equally illuminated on both sides, being supported more or less vertically.)

2 Guard cells provide a means of entry and exit for gases.

3 Spaces in the spongy mesophyll allow diffusion of gases.

4 Vascular tissue provides water and support.

5 The large surface area/volume ratio and the small distance between the surfaces favour the rapid exchange of gases by diffusion between photosynthesizing tissue and the environment.

Note: (*1*) to (*4*) apply to aerial leaves; only (*5*) applies to *Elodea*.

7.5 Leaf pigments

Principles

Chromatography of leaf pigments is rapid and easy. It can be used to compare the pigments of leaves of many plants of different colours. The aim is to show that two pigments (chlorophyll *a* and chlorophyll *b*), are always present, that some are common, and that some appear to be peculiar to the plant from which they are extracted. This study should prompt questions concerning the role of the chlorophylls in photosynthesis, the parts played by other common pigments, and the possible significance of the rarer pigments. The fact that variegated leaves are commoner in gardens and hot houses than in nature should not pass unnoticed.

Teaching procedure

Associated materials
S(M) 7.4

Because two or three *runs* can be carried out in one practical session, students can be left to perfect their own techniques by trial, error, and discussion. Each student or group might well make an extract from a different coloured plant.

Practical problems

Chromatographic separation of pigments has been criticized because, once they have been extracted from the leaf, light affects them adversely. The dried paper reveals, not pigment spots, but the breakdown products of leaf pigments. Students may compare extractions and runs in light and dark experimentally, but without this refinement, there is still some value in discovering that leaves contain more than one type of pigment.

Questions and answers

Do all the pigment extracts contain the same variety of components? If not, give details.
Are some component pigments common to all the extracts?

a and *b* Ordinary leaves usually contain five pigments which appear (reading from top to bottom of the paper) as follows: carotene (yellow), phaeophytin (grey), xanthophyll (yellow), chlorophyll *a* (blue-green), and chlorophyll *b* (green).

What conclusions can you draw from answers (a) *and* (b) *concerning the role of pigments in photosynthesis? Try to find, from textbooks, the function performed by plant pigments.*

c Chlorophylls seem to be essential (this cannot be assumed from the practical work alone). Other pigments may also have a function in photosynthesis. There is a tendency to regard chlorophyll as the only pigment of importance. A question could emerge from the practical work: 'Do some plants contain chlorophylls along with no additional pigments?' Pigments peculiar to one or a small number of species can hardly be regarded as essential to photosynthesis.

Additional bibliography

General reading

Bassham, J. A. and Calvin, M. (1957) *The path of carbon in photosynthesis.* Prentice-Hall.
Faires, R. A. and Parks, B. H. (1960) *Radioisotope laboratory techniques.* 2nd edition. Newnes.
Lehninger, A. L. (1965) *Bioenergetics.* Benjamin.
Simon, E. W., Dormer, K. J. and Hartshorne, J. N. (1966) *Lowson's botany.* 4th edition. University Tutorial Press.

References

Audus, L. J. (1953) 'A simplified version of an apparatus for the measurement of oxygen evolution in the photosynthesis of *Elodea*.' *Sch. Sci. Rev.*, **35**, 120–121.
Fogg, G. E. (1963) *The growth of plants.* Penguin. (Contains much useful material on photosynthesis including photographic evidence from a leaf disc experiment, plate 10; pp. 144–145.)
Jones, H. (1951) 'A simple bubbler for investigating the effect of varying external conditions on the rate of photosynthesis.' *Sch. Sci. Rev.*, **32**, 391–392. (Deals with the use of *Ranunculus aquatilis*, water crowfoot, instead of *Elodea*.)
Lorch, J. W. (1962) 'The leaf of *Ricinus*–an ideal object for teaching leaf structure. *Sch. Sci. Rev.*, **43**, 434–437. (Outlines a clearing technique using lactic acid.)
Moore, E. J. (1931) 'Formation of starch from sugar in darkness.' *Science Master's Book*, Series I, Part II. Murray.
Nuffield O-level Biology (1966) Teachers' Guide Year III *The maintenance of life.* Longmans/Penguin. (Details on starch production from leaf discs in the dark, 141; *Elodea* bubbling, 126–130.)
Overman, R. T. and Clark, H. M. (1960) *Radioisotope techniques.* McGraw-Hill.
The Radiochemical Centre, Amersham; *Catalogue of radioactive products.* (Provides a full list of the available compounds containing ^{14}C and other isotopes.)

Extension work III

Metabolic systems

Review

Students investigate metabolism to a limited extent in Chapters 1, 6, and 7. Here, some of the ideas considered there are pursued a little further.

It is possible to compare metabolic activity in different conditions or different organisms through a study of oxygen uptake. A simple, yet reliable method of doing this is introduced and then used, to determine respiratory quotients. This ratio is not presented as a totally dependable means of identifying respiratory substrates but, on the contrary, as an example of something in science which can be both useful and misleading.

The materials extracted from plants and animals for the work of Chapters 5 and 6 are chemically robust and thus ideal for teaching purposes. However, they are not typical of the more delicate systems of enzymes so characteristic of metabolism. We outline two more difficult investigations to exemplify the complex techniques required to extract and experiment with respiratory and photosynthetic systems.

The sequence of topics is:

1 The uptake of oxygen as a measure of metabolism.
2 Respiratory quotient.
3 Investigation of an intermediate respiratory reaction.
4 Chloroplast activity in photosynthesis.

Assumptions

- Familiarity with the use of a simple respirometer and with methods of enzyme extraction. Chapter 6 prepares students for this work.
- Some knowledge of three chemical concepts. This may require some attention.

The most important concept is *oxidation-reduction*. For this work it is not sufficient to define it as addition or removal of oxygen. Oxidation is considered in relation to succinic acid and is presented as the removal of hydrogen atoms because this may be a little more familiar to students than the notion of electron transfer.

Osmosis is the second concept. To explain the use of sucrose in extraction media, it is necessary to refer to osmosis in mitochondria and chloroplasts. Though this subject has not been formally introduced before, it is assumed that most students are aware of this phenomenon in one form or another.

The third term which may cause difficulty is *buffer solution*. This can be introduced by stating that these solutions are so composed that they maintain constant pH despite the addition of acid or alkali. A full explanation is essential to understand the biological implications of mitochondrion and chloroplast activity.

E3.1 The uptake of oxygen as a measure of metabolism

Principles

Gas changes, particularly the uptake of oxygen, act as indicators of the biochemical activity of organisms and their tissues. The importance of manometric methods in measuring tissue metabolism should be emphasized. A variety of manometers have been designed. In research, the Warburg apparatus is most commonly used but the respirometer described in *Laboratory guide (M)* is simpler to construct and use.

Teaching procedure

Associated materials
S(M) 1.1, 1.4, 1.6, 1.8, 2.4, 2.5, 6.2, 6.3, 8.3

It should be pointed out again (see Chapter 6) that the respirometer can be used either as a Barcroft differential respirometer or as a Dixon-Barcroft constant pressure manometer.

Practical problems

Almost all anomalous results obtained with respirometers are due to fluctuations of temperature either at the initial phase of equilibration or during the running of the experiment.

Questions and answers

When the graph of manometer readings against time is a straight line, what can be said about the uptake of oxygen by organisms in the respirometer?

a The rate of oxygen uptake is constant.

How much oxygen was absorbed by the organisms? State the amount as cubic millimetres (mm³) per hour per milligramme (mg) of living material.

b There is no 'right' answer to this question. Rates of oxygen absorption depend not only on temperature but on the state of development of the organisms and other imponderables.

How does a rise in temperature affect the rate of oxygen uptake? How can the effect be best expressed?

c The higher the temperature the greater the oxygen uptake (to a maximum when enzyme damage begins).
Calculated by using Q_{10}, that is:

$$\frac{\text{Rate of oxygen uptake at temperature } (t+10)^\circ\text{ C}}{\text{Rate of oxygen uptake at } t^\circ\text{ C}}$$

What rates of oxygen uptake would you expect if you raised the temperature to 40° C or 50° C? Give your reasons.

d This is a difficult question because Q_{10} of seedlings decreases with a rise in temperature. If oxygen uptake almost doubled between 20–30° C, it might seem reasonable to suppose that it would double again for the next 10° C. Figures range from Q_{10} 1·6–1·8 at 20–30° C to Q_{10} 0·6–1·0 at 40–50°C.

E3.2 Respiratory quotient

Principles

This investigation uses the same techniques with slight modification. The respiratory quotient provides further information about respiration. However, its use is limited.

Teaching procedure

Associated materials
S(M) 1.1, 1.4, 1.6, 2.4, 2.5, 6.2, 6.3, 8.3

Students should be guided neither to accept R.Q. as a certain indicator of respiratory substrate nor to dismiss it as a useless ratio.

Practical problems

It is best to use oil-bearing seeds for this investigation. If seeds containing carbohydrate food reserves are used, the second part of the investigation will be uneventful. There will be little or no net volume change in the respirometer.

Questions and answers

Calculate the respiratory quotient of the seeds.

a –

What is the respiratory substrate most likely to be present in seeds? What tests could you perform to discover the nature of the substrate? Does the R.Q. correspond with your expectations?

b Students should perform food tests on the seeds used to discover the nature of their reserves.

What would you expect the R.Q. of living yeast to be (see Chapter 6)?

c The quotient has no real meaning with anaerobic organisms which absorb no oxygen. As oxygen absorption decreases, so the R.Q. tends to infinity.

Are question (c) *and its answer in any way relevant to the respiration of germinating seeds? Give your reasons.*

d Yes; many germinating seeds are known to respire anaerobically and their R.Q. will thus depend not only on the substrates respired but also on the type of respiration; the greater the fraction of anaerobic respiration, the larger the R.Q. will become.

Suggest three different hypotheses to account for a respiratory quotient of unity (1·00) found by experiment.

e Aerobic respiration of a carbohydrate substrate.

Aerobic respiration of two substrates each with R.Q.s below and above unity, respectively.

Aerobic respiration of a substrate with R.Q. less than unity and anaerobic respiration of another, thus raising the R.Q. to give an experimental result of 1·0.

In 1905, C. R. Barnes wrote: '... This respiratory ratio (R.Q.) has proved a veritable will o' the wisp leading investigators into a bog where their labours and their thinking were alike futile ...'. Explain one use of R.Q. which you think would be futile and one which might be fruitful.

f The question provides an opportunity to summarize the pros and cons of R.Q. derived from reading and discussion.

E3.3 Investigation of an intermediate respiratory reaction

Principles

The aim of this investigation is to focus attention on the enzyme succinic dehydrogenase and provide an insight into some of the techniques used in research on complex enzyme systems, including the use of redox indicators.

Teaching procedure

Associated materials
S(M) 1.4, 2.4, 2.5, 6.2, 6.3, 6.6

Before this work, students should review the biochemistry of respiration. There is no need to consider the details of the Krebs cycle but the class should discuss its role in energy production and the kinds of molecule involved in it. Particular reference should be made to succinic acid. The class should also review the organization of cell contents, particularly the mitochondria, as revealed by electron microscopy.

Students should be aware of the inaccuracies in results which can be obtained by using homogenized tissues for biochemical investigations.

Practical problems

The directions given for enzyme extraction are a compromise between those adopted by biochemists equipped with elaborate equipment and a pestle and mortar technique unlikely to produce any useful results.

It is essential to carry out an extraction reasonably fast. Once cells are disrupted, further metabolism is short-lived.

Questions and answers

Do your results support the idea that succinic acid is oxidized in an extract of mung bean seedlings? (Give your reasons.)

Do the results obtained when using succinic acid added in the medium further support this idea?

a and *b* The decolorization of dichlorophenolindophenol (dicpip) by an extract is not, in itself, a certain indication that succinic dehydrogenase enzyme is present. If the addition of succinic acid increases the reduction of dicpip to its colourless form, this can be taken as evidence of the enzyme.

How would you find out experimentally if the oxidation of succinic acid is enzyme-controlled?

c The simplest test is to apply heat to see if the agent responsible for dicpip reduction is thermo-labile. Alternatively, the literature could be consulted to find a poison for succinic dehydrogenase.

If dicpip is an indicator of succinic acid oxidation and this oxidation is a stage in the chemistry of respiration, do you think that dicpip solution could be used as an indicator of respiration as a whole? If so, design a simple experiment to test this idea.

d This is a reasonable proposition and can be easily tried with suspensions of yeast or bacteria. Methylene blue is another indicator of chemical reduction which works admirably when added to yeast suspensions in a test-tube. (Students may then ask why there is any need to take trouble to make an extract. The point of extraction is to try and isolate that part of the metabolic complex which is specifically responsible for dicpip reduction.)

The reduction of dicpip is not specifically connected with the oxidation of succinic acid. What steps could be taken to avoid decolorization of dicpip by agents in the tissue extracts other than succinic acid?

e There are a number of naturally occurring substances which reduce dicpip, including ascorbic acid and glutathione. It is best to consult the literature before interpreting results. 'Feeding' additional substrates, as suggested in *Laboratory guide (M)*, is probably the best way of indicating that one enzyme system rather than another is responsible for dicpip reduction.

E3.4 Chloroplast activity in photosynthesis

Principles

A most important step forward in discovering the mechanism of photosynthesis was made in 1940 when Hill and Scarisbrick showed that chloroplasts can be isolated, more or less free of other material, from ground-up leaves. When illuminated, these isolated chloroplasts can reduce certain substances and produce oxygen. The capacity of the chloroplast suspensions to reduce and evolve oxygen in the light, which has come to be called the Hill reaction, was shown to be similar to that of photosynthesis. A variety of treatments had similar effects on both processes. Incidentally, carbon dioxide itself was not reduced by the chloroplast suspensions.

Teaching procedure

Associated materials
S(M) 6.2, 6.3, 6.6, 6.7, 7.3, 7.4, 7.6, 7.7, 8.3

Students should be well aware of the importance of the Hill reaction before they undertake these experiments. However, these make no provision for the detection of oxygen as this is technically difficult.

The substrate to be reduced is, as in the previous investigation, 2:6 dichlorophenolindophenol (dicpip). This raises the interesting point that photosynthesis and respiration reactions are, in fact, similar although we normally stress the opposite nature of the two processes. Succinic acid (E3.3) was oxidized and, since as one compound is oxidized another must be reduced, the dicpip was reduced. Illuminated chloroplasts also reduce dicpip. We could say that, at the same time, water is oxidized by having a hydrogen atom removed from each molecule. However this form of words is seldom used. The reaction can be described as follows:

$2H_2O \longrightarrow 2[H]+2[OH]$

Blue dicpip $+ 2H \longrightarrow$ reduced, colourless dicpip

$2[OH] \longrightarrow H_2O+\frac{1}{2}O_2$

The square brackets in the above equations indicate that H and OH are not free but in combination with some other substance.

Through considering these ideas, students may come to discuss the relationship of respiration to photosynthesis.

In this investigation, the Procedure gives directions for extraction but only *suggests* the design and number of experiments to be used through the Questions which follow.

Practical problems

This method of extraction is somewhat rough and ready. It is intended to be the simplest which will give useful if not perfect results. Speed of operation is important. Lettuce gives reasonable results and is available all the year round, spinach is probably better.

Questions and answers

Design and carry out an experiment to compare the effects of different light intensities on a chloroplast suspension containing dicpip as an indicator of chemical reduction. Record and discuss the results obtained.

a Suggested experimental procedures: expose tubes of chloroplast suspension with dicpip to bright light; put some at different, measured distances from the light source, others in total darkness; set up a control with dicpip alone to see if light 'fades' the dye.

What other factor or factors, associated with light, are likely to affect such an experiment? How would you eliminate such factors so that light intensity is the only one which differs?

b Heat from the lamp will affect temperature. Introduce heat filters or immerse the tubes in a temperature-controlled water bath.

How would you find out if the green suspension in fact contains chloroplasts?

c Examine a drop of suspension under a microscope.

Describe experiments you could perform to see if enzymes are involved in the reduction of dicpip by chloroplasts.

d Use a sample of chloroplast suspension which has been heated to about 70° C for five minutes and allowed to cool. Add small quantities of well known enzyme poisons.

Additional bibliography

General reading

Baldwin, E. (1947) *Dynamic aspects of biochemistry*. Cambridge University Press. (Describes the uses of redox indicators.)
Dixon, M. (1951) *Manometric methods*. Cambridge University Press. (A full account of the respirometers used in this section with much additional information.)
James, W. O. (1953) *Plant respiration*. Oxford University Press. (Many examples of respiratory measurements, Q_{10} and R.Q.)
Thomas, M. (1949) *Plant physiology*. 3rd edition. Churchill. (Includes information on redox indicators and the effects of ascorbic acid and glutathione.)

References

Hill, R. (1939) *Proc. Roy. Soc. (London)* **127 B**, 192.
Hill, R. and Scarisbrick, R. (1940) *Proc. Roy. Soc. (London)* **129 B**, 238. (Two original papers on the Hill reaction.)
Syrett, P. J. (1951) *Sch. Sci. Rev.* **32**, 387. (Describes a simple respirometer and its uses.)

Chapter 8

Metabolism and the environment

Chapter review

This final chapter of *Maintenance of the organism* is intended to direct the attention of students back to the first, and to the investigation of model communities. To find out how organisms maintain themselves it is necessary to study, separately, their metabolic processes and associated organs. The work of the present chapter again involves model communities and focuses attention on whole organisms living together and interacting with one another and their environment.

This rather difficult undertaking is attempted by simple methods. We examine the counteracting effects of two metabolic processes by investigating the compensation periods of plants. We then consider the influence of animals by introducing them into a plant community.

The use of enclosed and isolated model communities leads to the concept of chemical (element) cycles in nature.

The sequence of topics is:

1 Compensation period.
2 The interaction of plants and animals.
3 Isolated communities and chemical cycles.

Assumptions

This concluding chapter is largely retrospective and no new background knowledge is required. It refers to the use of – radioactive tracers, so students should, if necessary, revise the terminology and methods of detecting radioactivity.

8.1 Compensation period

Principles

The aim of this investigation is twofold. As stated above, the teacher should warn students of the consequences of thinking that metabolic activities are isolated, independent processes. Photosynthesis and respiration are taken as examples of interacting physiological processes with strong ecological implications. The second aim is to suggest that differences in photosynthetic activity may affect the distribution of plants in their natural habitats (see question *f*). Through this study, students can relate an important aspect of ecology to its physiological background.

Teaching procedure

Associated materials
S(M) 1.1, 1.3, 1.4, 1.5, 1.8, 7.1, 8.3

The apparatus illustrated in *Laboratory guide (M)* is only one example of a range of suitable containers. There is an opportunity here for students to devise their own apparatus from materials most readily available.

Practical problems

To obtain the greatest difference in compensation periods, one sample should consist of 'shade' or indoor plants and the other of 'sun' plants. Pretesting is advisable.

Questions and answers

By what means can you ensure that the quantities of plants in both containers are equal?

a By weighing them.

Is it better to stand the plants in soil or water? Give your reasons.

b In water. Soil contains micro-organisms which respire and so affect the carbon dioxide content of the air.

Should steps be taken to maintain constant temperature in the containers and if so, why?

c Yes. Temperature affects the colour reaction of the indicator; comparisons made at different temperatures are invalid.

The colour change of bicarbonate/indicator is gradual. It is difficult to assess the time it takes to become a certain shade of red again, accurately. What steps can you take to make the measurements more precise?

d If colour is judged by eye, the amount and quality of light entering the indicator solutions must be the same for each observation. The use of some form of colorimeter is preferable. Arrangements can be made to withdraw samples of indicator at intervals and measure their optical density. Whichever method is adopted, the thickness of the sample must be the same whenever an observation is made.

Do the two or more species of plants used have the same compensation period? If there is a difference, is it greater or less than the limits of accuracy of the timing method?

e Compensation periods can only be *relative* measurements comparing the contents of one container with those of another.

Suppose, regardless of the answer to question (e), *that some plant species differ in their compensation periods. Do you think that this would be important in a natural situation?*

f Yes. A plant with a long compensation period, i.e. one that is slow in reaching its compensation *point*, will tend to be outgrown and at a disadvantage in competition with neighbouring plants with shorter compensation periods. (The latter, 'shade' plants, are usually unable to use high light intensities as efficiently as 'sun' plants.)

Is the size of the container, in relation to the number of plants used, important? Would you expect different results using large containers with a few plants?

g No. The compensation period is the time required for plants to absorb whatever carbon dioxide may have been produced in the dark. In theory, the size of the container is of no consequence. In practice, a few plants would have little effect on the atmospheric composition in a large container and it would therefore be difficult to detect changes in carbon dioxide.

How could you modify this experimental method to suit aquatic plants?

h Fill the container with water. Take small samples of water at intervals and test with bicarbonate/indicator. Or set up small aquaria containing bicarbonate/indicator solution in place of water.

8.2 The interaction of plants and animals

Principles

There is unlikely to be any surprise in store for students undertaking these exercises qualitatively; introducing animals increases the equivalent compensation period of the whole community. But it is possible to go further and get some idea of the effect of a relatively small animal population in a larger biomass of plants. Much will depend on the type of animals chosen and their rate of metabolic activity.

Teaching procedure

Associated materials
S(M) 1.1, 1.4, 1.5, 1.8, 8.1, 8.2, 8.3, 8.4, 8.5
S(P) 8.1, 8.4, 8.5

This practical work should stimulate discussion about the proportions of animal and plant life in natural communities and in the world as a whole. It should become clear that animals not only produce carbon dioxide continuously but do so to a greater extent than plants, weight for weight. Though they are not studying oxygen experimentally, students should also realize that though animals consume oxygen continuously, plants produce it intermittently, i.e. only when illuminated.

Practical problems

If this investigation is not pretested, it is quite easy to introduce so many animals that the indicator, having turned yellow in the dark, never returns to red in the light. If this happens, the microaquaria should provide an explanation even though these are continuously illuminated and compensation periods are not investigated.

Questions and answers

What is the proportion of animals to plants used in stages (1) and (2), as determined by fresh weight?

a –

Was the indicator restored to its red colour when the container was illuminated? From this observation, state whether the community contained too many animals for continued survival or whether it could accept more.

b If the compensation period is nearly a whole day, even under intense illumination, this indicates that there are probably more animals present than can be supported by the plant community. If compensation never occurs, then there are too many animals present. It must be remembered that only carbon dioxide is being considered here. 'Support' does not include the provision of food, which lies outside the scope of this investigation. But in nature, it is a far more pressing factor than carbon dioxide.

What proportions of animals and plants, by weight, form a balanced micro-aquarium community in terms of carbon dioxide concentration?

c An exact figure cannot be expected from this technique.

Suppose that you wanted to set up a balanced aquarium community, would stages (3) to (7) above form a useful method for determining the proportion of animals and plants to be used? State the limitations of this technique and suggest improvements.

d They would help, if the aquarium were to be sealed and illuminated continuously (both are unlikely conditions). The technique used is concerned only with the maintenance of constant pH, due mainly to carbon dioxide concentration. Information about other factors such as the supply of food is more important; thus, the realistic answer to the question is 'no'.

From these investigations, can you propose hypotheses concerning the proportions of animals and plants which form large, natural, balanced communities?

e Only in the most general terms. For example, that the biomass of plants must far outweigh that of animals if available oxygen supplies are to be maintained. As mentioned above, other factors such as food must be taken into account when considering balanced communities.

8.3 Isolated communities and chemical cycles

Principles

As in the work of Chapter 1, organisms have been investigated in isolated, artificial environments. Though small and sealed, they can sustain life indefinitely and are in this respect like the whole biosphere in that material neither enters nor escapes. The aim of this section is to encourage students to consider the implications of the fact and to realize that if life is to continue on this planet or in a sealed tank, chemical elements such as carbon, hydrogen, oxygen, nitrogen, and phosphorus must perpetually recombine as generations of organisms succeed one another.

Teaching procedure

Associated materials
S(M) 7.5, 7.6, 8.2, 8.3
S(P) 6.6, 8.1
S(C) 1.2

The idea of element cycles may already be familiar from an elementary study of the carbon and nitrogen cycles. Two lines of discussion could be profitable here, namely, to consider the fates, whether cyclic or not, of elements other than carbon and nitrogen, and to formulate methods for testing hypothetical cycles experimentally. To assist in this, students should refer to techniques described previously, particularly in Chapter 7.

Practical problems

Radioactive tracers are an obvious means of investigating the carbon cycle in an isolated, model community but such experiments raise considerable practical difficulties. Although ^{14}C, once introduced, would spread rapidly through such a community, precise chemical analysis would be required before a well-defined cycle could be demonstrated. Quite elaborate means of detecting radiation would also be necessary. In *Laboratory guide (M)*, the matter is therefore left in the form of questions calling for experimental design rather than specific procedures.

Questions and answers

A method of tracing the entry of radioactive carbon atoms from the atmosphere into plant leaves has been described in Chapter 7. Describe how, if you were provided with a sealed container, plants, animals, soil, and a source of radioactive carbon, you would attempt to demonstrate a carbon cycle.

a In brief outline, the procedure might be as follows: Introduce $^{14}CO_2$ into a sealed container of illuminated plants. Divide the plants into three lots. Carry out chromatography and autoradiography of a leaf extract. Remove all the $^{14}CO_2$ from the atmosphere, leave the plants in the dark, and then test the air for the presence of $^{14}CO_2$. Bury some leaves in a small quantity of soil and incubate for a prolonged period to allow decay. Remove any remaining leaf fragments and mix the soil with water. Separate the solid and liquid fractions and measure the radioactivity of each. Place both in sealed containers with air and test this at intervals for the presence of $^{14}CO_2$. Use small invertebrates to explore this aspect of the cycle.

Describe how, with apparatus and materials similar to those listed in (a), *but using radioactive phosphorus in a solution as phosphate, you would investigate a phosphorus cycle. Radiophosphorus (^{32}P) has a short half-life of about 14 days; it emits more radioactivity, atom for atom, than ^{14}C. How would you modify your method accordingly?*

b Radiophosphorus as a solution of phosphate could be introduced to plants through their roots. Once it was inside plants, it would be difficult to decide whether it has been incorporated into organic molecules or was merely present as phosphate ions in the cells; quite elaborate chemical analysis would be required. Its return to the soil from decaying plants would also present similar problems. The short half-life of ^{32}P would make it necessary to introduce large initial doses into plant tissues in order to detect its return to the soil after several months of decay.

Refer to textbooks for details of the nitrogen cycle. There are no sources of radioactive nitrogen available. What techniques would you employ to investigate the nitrogen cycle?

c Without radioisotopes, observing a cycle of atoms becomes a formidable task and evidence, at best, is circumstantial. In principle, one must assume that if, in an isolated system, nitrogen in place A decreases at the same time as it increases in place B, then it has actually passed from A to B. For example, if plant material containing nitrogen decays and the nitrogen content of the soil increases, it may be assumed that this has come from the plant. It is a different type of problem to show that most plants accept nitrogen only in the form of nitrate ions. This requires a series of separate experiments, providing plants with nitrate, nitrite, ammonium salts, and other sources of nitrogen. However large the variety of nitrogen sources, such experiments can never be absolutely conclusive. A third series of techniques would be necessary to work out the sequence of bacterial reactions in the cycle.

Of the many elements found in living creatures, five are often set apart as playing a prominent role, namely, carbon, hydrogen, oxygen, nitrogen, and phosphorus. Describe hypothetical oxygen and nitrogen cycles. Is there any reason why the two should appear similar?

d An oxygen cycle could be set out as shown in figure 12.

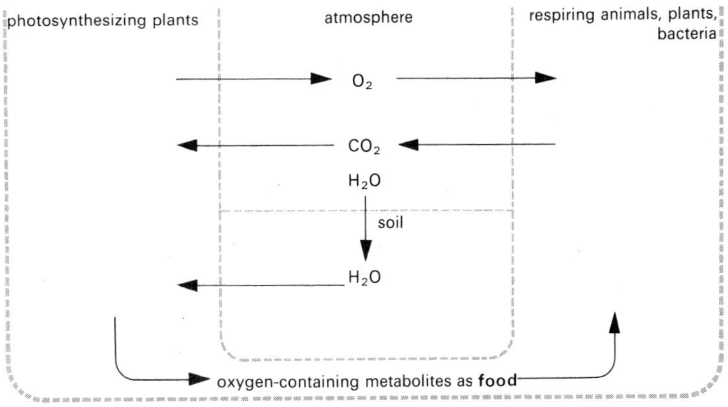

Figure 12
Diagrammatic summary of the oxygen cycle.

The hydrogen cycle is essentially part of the oxygen cycle but there is no free hydrogen. It is always combined with oxygen as water or in the more complex organic molecules of metabolites.

'The outer layers [of the earth] in their melted form, must have contained in addition to silicates much water and carbonate in solution, the whole being originally surrounded by atmosphere of hydrogen and hydrides, CH_4, NH_3, H_2S *and* H_2O *though in far less quantities than now. This original atmosphere must have been modified in two particular ways. The actual crystallization of the crust must have forced into the atmosphere vast quantities of water vapour and carbon dioxide. . . .' (from* The physical basis of life, *1951, by J. D. Bernal, F.R.S.). Supposing this to be an accurate description of the earth's original atmosphere, propose hypotheses to account for the change to its present constitution.*

e The short answer to this question is that once green plants had evolved they must have photosynthesized, thus absorbing carbon dioxide and producing oxygen in its place. In addition, the absence of CH_4, NH_3, and H_2S from our present atmosphere must be explained. The passage is quoted to stimulate thought and further reading on the subject; it contrasts the stability of the present atmosphere with the changes which took place millions of years ago.

Additional bibliography

General reading

Fogg, G. E. (1963) *The growth of plants.* Penguin.
Simon, E. W., Dormer, K. J. and Hartshorne, J. N. (1966) *Lowson's textbook of botany.* University Tutorial Press.

References

Hosokawa, T. and Odani, N. (1957) 'The daily compensation period and vertical ranges of epiphytes in a beech forest.' *J. Ecol.*, **45**, 901.
Nuffield O-level Biology (1966) Text and Teachers' Guide Year III *The maintenance of life.* Longmans/Penguin.
Thomas, A. K. and Field, J. A. (1966) 'Estimation of daily compensation period.' *Sch. Sci. Rev.*, **43**, 711.

Organisms and populations

Chapter 1

Variation in a community

Chapter review

The first part of the chapter focuses attention upon the idea of variation. By studying a freshwater community, it illustrates some of the problems of identification and shows how to describe continuous variation.

The second half attempts to find some explanation for the variety and patterns of variation occurring in populations, communities, and species. In particular, it explores the consequences of cultivating different organisms together by beginning three long-term experiments whose results will be used in later chapters.

The sequence of topics is:

1 Identifying organisms.
2 Describing continuous variation.
3 Intra-specific interaction between two varieties of clover.
4 Intra-specific interaction in insects.
5 Inter-specific interaction between plants.

Assumptions

– That students know how to use a hand lens, and also a monocular and a stereomicroscope.

1.1 Identifying organisms (preliminary)

Principles

The principles behind this investigation and the next one are closely linked. Variation is a common characteristic of all living things and of the environment in which they live. It may be *discontinuous* or *continuous*.

Some examples of variation are:

1 Height in man (continuous).
2 The production of seeds by daisies (continuous if measured by weight, discontinuous if measured in numbers of seeds).
3 Size of shell in snails (continuous).

4 The concentration of oxygen in pond water (continuous).
5 The distribution of clover in a lawn (discontinuous).

It will be apparent to students that it is important for the taxonomist and systematist to understand variation and its causes. However, some of the other ways in which variation is important to a biologist will not be so obvious; it is a purpose of this investigation to explore them.

Teaching procedure

Associated materials
S(P) 1.1, 1.7
Key to pond organisms

Students who have done similar work already may find it best to turn straightaway to the making of a key. The average student should be able to work through the exercises as suggested.

For less able students and those who have done little previous biology, it may be better to follow this sequence:
1 Pose the question, 'what species are represented in the community?'
2 Answer the question in terms of the large Algae, using the key.
3 Describe the binomial system of nomenclature and discuss the principles of taxonomy sufficiently to make the work easier.
4 Make a key to a group of animals such as the snails or planarians from the aquarium.
5 Discuss the practical aspects of compiling keys and complete the elementary discussion of taxonomy.
6 Identify some of the large and common organisms, noting their distribution in the aquarium.

Using a key
The *Key to pond organisms* explains how to use this key and includes a bibliography of publications which will enable the student to identify organisms outside its scope.

Making a key
This exercise gives practice in examining material carefully, searching for similarities and differences, and classifying into categories. Compiling a key is also an exercise in logic.

Whilst performing the exercise, students will discover a hierarchy of groups based upon different degrees of resemblance. Some may suggest that a system of relationships such as that shown below is not only a matter of convenience to the taxonomist, but also indicates phylogeny;

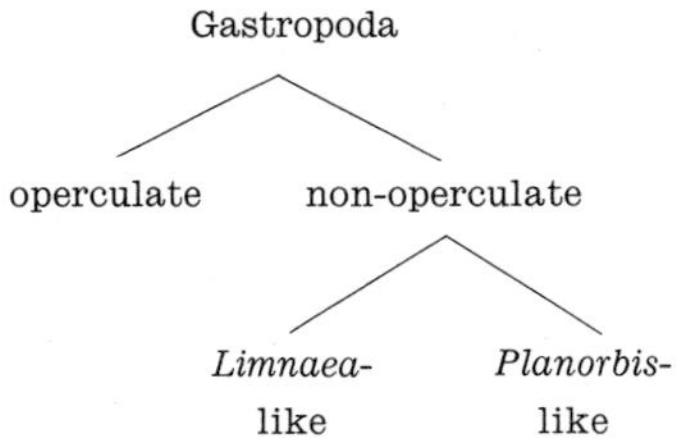

The exercise helps to make the concepts of genus and species more real. The difficulty of making a key depends upon the kinds of organisms involved and the range of variation they display. For able students, the Gastropoda will serve well. With less able students, try a small group of highly contrasted organisms, such as the *Hydra* species together with the planarians.

Students will need some help in choosing criteria but they gain most from this exercise if they are left to work on their own. The variety of classificatory systems they devise will provide good material for discussion. The teacher will need to introduce into any subsequent discussion an authoritative view on the criteria used on taxonomists. Comparing the students' systems with a conventional key and the recognized classification of the group can lead into the next topic. It will also help to correct any wrong ideas which may have arisen.

Practical problems

Aquarium communities are convenient for this sort of work, and they compensate for whatever may be lacking in realism by making it easier to conduct genuine ecological and other work. The communities in tanks can be regarded as models, representing a sound teaching device.

In order to have as few organizational difficulties as possible, we can start with an aquarium specially prepared to suit our purpose. Such an artificial community serves as a much simplified version of the situation existing in a natural locality such as a pond.

Aquarium communities are easy to establish and manage. They are easy to investigate and, if kept over a long period, demonstrate succession and competition. They also serve as a reservoir of organisms for other investigations.

Questions and answers

Did you succeed in identifying all the species of snails? If not, what were the principal causes of difficulty?

a Possibly not. The most likely difficulties arise from variations in the size and shape of immature animals and the students' lack of familiarity with the terms used in the key. There is some overlap of characters between species.

What other characteristics, besides structural variation, could be useful in constructing a key?

b Behavioural, cytological, chromosomal, and biochemical characters. Any of these suggestions has merit, but students would not be expected to know them all.

Did you encounter any groups of organisms whose variation was of a kind which was of little use for key-making, e.g. a continuous gradation of colour? If so, which species were they and what characteristics were involved?

c The question arises from the difficulty of using keys which depend upon parameters that cannot be accurately defined. It is not, in itself, a disadvantage that a character shows continuous variation. The key could include an expression of the modal value and the permissible spread. It might also take account of the effects of age, accident, and disease, but only in so far as is practicable within reasonable limits.

What other characteristics besides external features might have been useful for identification?

d Biochemical, chromosomal, cytological.

1.2 Describing continuous variation (preliminary)

Principles

Discontinuous variation, with which we shall be much concerned in the next chapter, is relatively easy to describe and quantify. Continuous variation is also common but is harder to describe and to explain in genetic terms. Where key-making is concerned, continuous variation is far less useful than discontinuous because differences are often so finely graded. A study of colour variations in planarians such as *Polycelis nigra* and *Dugesia lugubris* illustrates the point well.

Teaching procedure

Associated materials
S(M) 1.4
S(P) 1.2, 1.3

The variation of a parameter within a population can be investigated and recorded graphically (in a histogram) and arithmetically (by representing mean and modal values). This work can be given more meaning if it is related to some real situation. For instance, study of variation within a species (e.g. of snails) might serve to show whether selection by a predator favoured a group of individuals of a particular size and could also provide information for making a key.

Practical problems

Students will need help in choosing a species and a parameter. Suitable examples are,
Chironomus sp.: length of larvae
Asellus sp.: length
Limnaea sp.: width of shells
Lemna sp.: length of roots
Callitriche sp.: length and breadth of submerged or floating leaves.

It does not matter much at this stage if the variation is determined chiefly by the age structure of the population, and not by its genetic diversity. It is more important to give practice in measuring and recording variation. It will be necessary to discuss the errors that arise through measuring too small a number of individuals. If there are too few in each tank, then the results from all tanks could be combined.

Questions and answers

In what circumstances might the modal class midmark differ from the arithmetic mean (average)?

a When the distribution is markedly skew. Further analysis might show that, for example, there are no small, young animals, and that mortality occurs at all ages with equal proportions dying in each age (size) class.

If you found two modal classes adjacent on the histogram, what would this tell you?

b That perhaps the class intervals were small in relation to the range of sizes which are particularly well represented in the population. Such a case often arises. Other answers may be valid.

If you found two modal classes of equal or nearly equal size well separated on the histogram, what would this denote?

c The possibility that the population contains two groups of individuals which differ in typical size, perhaps due to differences of age or sex.

1.3 Intra-specific interaction between two varieties of clover

Principles

It has been said that two closely related species cannot occupy the same ecological niche, and even though this statement does not stand up to examination in such a simple form, it reminds us that members of a species have common needs and it is likely that, if two variants of a species exist together, one is likely to be more successful than the other in the struggle for vital resources. This could be true, whether or not variation were heritable, but for our purposes it is much more interesting to examine cases where differences are genetically controlled. In such instances, selection may act to promote evolution which may become evident in the course of several generations.

The clovers demonstrate an important facility which plants use under stress conditions. They change their shape by differential growth and thus place their leaves and flowers advantageously.

This investigation uses commercial strains of clover species ('cultivars') partly because each contrasting form will grow in a predictable and uniform way, and partly to illustrate how ecological and genetic studies are relevant to this aspect of farming. The particular features which are observed here in clovers can be seen also in wild communities, so this investigation also helps to establish a more general understanding of the influences which may affect the composition of a community.

Teaching procedure

Associated materials
S(P) 1.4, 1.6, 2.6, 4.1, 4.4, 6.2

The Latin square

Students should appreciate the merits of a Latin square arrangement, and should learn a simple method of treating the data produced from one.

The results of the investigation are likely to be fairly clear cut, so a detailed statistical analysis may be unnecessary. However, the most competent students may like to analyse their data more rigorously.

The imaginary data supplied to students are:

			Average per sub-plot row:
S100 160	S100 105 S184 32	S184 75	$\frac{372}{3} = 124$
S184 70	S100 145	S100 97 S184 30	$\frac{342}{3} = 114$
S100 85 S184 27	S184 60	S100 140	$\frac{312}{3} = 104$
$\frac{342}{3} = 114$	$\frac{342}{3} = 114$	$\frac{342}{3} = 114$	

Average per sub-plot column

It is important to notice that the figures relating to sub-plots carrying mixed strains are the actual weights of the crops of each strain. Since the density of sowing was the same in every sub-plot, the total weight of the plants of each strain in a sub-plot of mixed strains is produced by half as many plants as in the sub-plots of pure strains.

We are interested in the performance of the strains undergoing each of the experimental treatments, and the most helpful aspect to measure might be the average weight of the plants of each strain in each treatment. This would, however, involve counting the plants, which would be very time-consuming. It is much more convenient to work in terms of weight of crop per unit of area, assuming an equal density of plants. It is therefore necessary to double the values obtained in the sub-plots of mixed strains. The procedure outlined below could be followed:

1 Set out the field data:

Grown separately		*Grown combined*	
S100	*S184*	*S100*	*S184*
160	75	105	32
145	70	97	30
140	60	85	27

Table of unadjusted weights of crop

2 Adjust the field data to give values in weight per unit of area. Take the area of a sub-plot as a unit of area.

Grown separately		*Grown combined*	
S100	*S184*	*S100*	*S184*
160	75	210	64
145	70	194	60
140	60	170	54

Table of adjusted weights of crop

3 Students can now calculate the means for each strain and each treatment from the adjusted weights of crop.
4 By inspecting the means, it is possible to see whether S184 performs differently in the two circumstances.

The imaginary data suggest the existence of a gradient of fertility. This can be demonstrated more clearly by calculating the mean crop per sub-plot in each row and each column as shown in the table below.

			Rows Mean crop/sub-plot
S100 160	S100 170 S184 30	S184 75	$\frac{435}{3} = 145$
S184 80	S100 150	S100 150 S184 40	$\frac{420}{3} = 140$
S100 150 S184 30	S184 70	S100 155	$\frac{405}{3} = 135$
$\frac{420}{3} = 140$	$\frac{420}{3} = 140$	$\frac{420}{3} = 140$	Mean crop/ all sub-plots $= 140$

Columns Mean crop/sub-plot

The data also show how S100, when grown in combination with S184, performs better (per plant) than when grown pure. This is probably because of the available extra resources which the S184 is not using. The S100 spreads its leaves over the rows of S184.

The establishment and maintenance of field trials will be found worth while if there is time and space. Where circumstances are restricted, the relevant information can be obtained from 1.6 in *Study guide (P)*, which considers Black's work on *Trifolium subterraneum*.

The experiment is not easy to administer and in some areas it may be best for several schools to conduct it as a co-operative enterprise. It is possible to carry it out on a small scale in seed trays or plastic bowls. This will yield reliable results, but the edge effects are considerable when small plots are sown, and there is a great risk of drought when the crop becomes tall in proportion to the depth of soil.

Practical problems

At the beginning of the summer term, it is advisable to decide upon procedure to be used and to start with a small group of students who can begin the operation, bringing in the rest of the class later on.

List of matters to be decided and recommendations
1 Choice of species and strains – T. repens; S100 and S184.

2 Choice of lay-out – Boxes or field plot. Latin square arrangement of 3×3 sub-plots. Adequate replication. Labels. Map.

3 Choice of soil – Sterilized loam or John Innes Compost, or garden soil.

4 Seed planting pattern – Plants approximately 2 cm apart in rows 2 cm apart. A high density will promote early competition. Perforated hardboard or 'comb' is helpful for spacing. Broadcasting is practicable but difficult.

5 Control of lateral illumination – Border rows of mixed seed, or adjustable screens to reduce 'edge effects'.

6 Culture – For an even tilth, it is necessary to prepare the seed bed carefully. This is most important. Soil must be well levelled for effective use of hardboard or comb.

7 Obtaining evidence of interaction – The ideal way is to determine the dry weight of aerial portions at harvest and also the number of surviving plants of each strain. More rough and ready methods may prove adequate.

8 Measuring light intensity – Photographic light meters have a logarithmic scale. This may be plotted directly onto log-normal graph paper, or first converted to antilogarithms and plotted on conventional paper. It will be necessary to practise taking light readings in a low canopy such as clovers provide.

9 Measuring canopy composition – Mark off the sampling area in each sub-plot by temporary string or tape lines.

10 Mechanism of interaction–Canopy composition–record the number of leaves visible from above in, say, 20 cm × 20 cm area of each sub-plot. It might be possible to estimate leaf areas similarly, but this would probably be tedious. Data such as Black's involve much work and serious disturbance of experimental plants. Light profile–use the smallest available light meter and take readings at 2 cm vertical intervals at 5 (random) stations in each type of sub-plot.

Questions and answers

What conclusions can you draw from this investigation into the interaction between the two varieties of clover? In the light of experience, what improvements would you make in experimental design in order to determine more exactly the nature of any interaction?

a The answer depends upon results. The expected conclusion is that S100 grows at least as well in combination with S184 as in pure culture. The better performance of S100 could be due to extra resources (light, nutrients). These are not taken up by S184 where the two are grown together because the S184 dies or remains low, and does not offer as much competition for resources as S100 plants would in its place. S184 grows better in pure culture than in combination with S100.

Improvements:
1 A Latin square with more sub-plots.
2 Eliminate root interactions, to identify more clearly the expected competition for light and to detect any consequence of root interaction.

Would it be worth doing the same experiment for a longer time, perhaps until after the seed has been shed? What changes would you need to make to the experimental procedure?

b Yes. Some (not all) possible modifications are:
1 Control or prevent any cross-pollination of strains.
2 Leave the plot to seed itself, or collect the seed and re-sow.
3 If leaving the plants to shed seeds *in situ*, arrange to preserve the sub-plot boundaries by shielding.

On the basis of the information you have obtained from your experiment, what are the possibilities of using a combination of S100 and S184 in a ley which serves two purposes?

c The answer depends on results. The expected answer is that it is possible to sow a mixture, but it is necessary to adjust densities of sowing to produce a suitable mixture of herbage. In fact, S100 gives an early crop but S184 may come in for hay or silage, or as a late grazing crop. It persists for several years, whereas S100 tends to die out.

1.4 Intra-specific interaction in insects

Principles

The interactions detectable among different strains of animals, resulting from differences in vigour, reproductive capacity, and behaviour in courtship are less obvious than those in a mixed population of clover. They are no less important to the species concerned.

For such studies, population chambers containing pure and mixed populations of *Drosophila* will be convenient. The class should use easily recognizable variations; vestigial wing, dumpy wing, and ebony body have been found to be suitable competitors with the wild type. The essential differences between this experiment and the last arise, not from the fact that one concerns animals and the other plants, but rather because in this experiment the organism has a short generation time. Thus, numerous generations can be raised in a comparatively short period.

In competition with wild type, most of the easily recognizable mutants disappear after 5 to 10 generations. Ebony body, however, tends to establish equilibrium at about 3 per cent of the population or roughly one-fifth of the gene pool. For this reason, ebony body should be one of the mutants chosen for this experiment. It is characteristic of populations such as these that the recessive character promptly disappears (in F_1 heterozygous individuals), then reappears and finally becomes rare or extinct after a longer period.

Teaching procedure

Associated materials
S(P) 1.6, 2.1, 2.3, 2.6, 4.1, 4.4, 5.2, 6.1
Film loop 'Handling *Drosophila*' NBP–70
Film loop 'Mating behaviour of *Drosophila*' NBP–53

The experiment gives results which can be used in subsequent discussions of genetics (Chapters 2 and 3), growth of population and mechanisms of selection (Chapters 4 and 5), and of evolution (Chapter 9).

After preliminary discussion of procedure and design of the experiment, we suggest the following laboratory sequence.

1 Practise handling *Drosophila*. This takes time and is an essential preliminary to any quantitative work. Each student can make up reference cards for sexes and mutants. These allow the teacher to check that the sex identifications are reliable.

2 Set up population chambers. The teacher could delegate this work to a group of students who could be responsible for maintenance and census records. They should be encouraged to watch for courtship behaviour since the failure of the vestigial winged flies to complete the courtship dance puts them at a selective disadvantage and thus accelerates the disappearance of the gene concerned.

3 Results will usually become available within the term.

4 After a year, there will be records from previous groups (and perhaps from the chambers with extant populations) for comparison. In some years it may be unnecessary to set up fresh cultures.

Practical problems

Drosophila cultures are fairly hardy and can live at room temperatures. A warm situation away from intense sunlight is desirable and the higher the temperature, the quicker will be the life cycle. Advanced students might cross two mutants–for example ee × dpdp

Questions and answers

What do you conclude from comparing the performance of the two pure cultures?

a That flies of both types can breed successfully in the conditions provided.

In the mixed population, did the proportion of vestigial winged flies fall at first? Did it increase afterwards? If there were such changes, what can you deduce from them?

b There will be a fall in the proportion of the recessive character in the F_1 and a subsequent increase in the F_2. Students will need to exercise caution, so that they make fair deductions which go no further than the facts warrant.

The F_2 should emerge within three or four weeks, depending on temperature.

What fundamental differences are there between this experiment and the one with two strains of Trifolium repens*? Is it true to say that interaction occurred in both cases, and that in each, one variety succeeded at the expense of the other?*

c In the *Trifolium* experiment some individuals suffered as a direct consequence of competition with other individuals of the same species. In this case it is a population that appears to suffer when in competition with a different population. Yes, interaction occurs in both.

1.5 Inter-specific interaction between plants

Principles

This experiment is a long-term one, providing a source of information for Chapters 5, 7, and 9 also.

Many lawns and pastures have *Trifolium repens* growing in patches and the persistence of the mixture suggests that the community is fairly stable. Clover does not usually die out in a neglected lawn; it may become even commoner when the lawn is neglected, and when nitrogen is lacking. Patches of clover may travel across a lawn, as can be confirmed by mapping over a few years. The explanation is as follows. Grass grows well in the presence of a good supply of nitrogen but many soils lack nitrogen, especially compacted ones.

Where the grass is mown with a box on the mower, the loss of nitrogen is continuous and debilitating to the grass. Clovers help to re-introduce nitrogen and thus aid grass so that, immediately next to the clovers, the grass flourishes. Indeed, it often flourishes here at the expense of the clover which, however, is able to spread into neighbouring areas that are deficient in nitrogen. The few grass leaves which penetrate a patch of clover are green and long. Since it is evident that both species can flourish separately in most lawn soils, a simple way to investigate the situation is to watch what happens when one of the components is mechanically removed at the boundary. Where one member is persistently removed, the other member usually spreads to colonize the bare ground.

Thus we can confirm that there is an interaction, but the mechanism remains in doubt. Adding nitrogenous fertilizer makes the grass grow well, and clover dies out. Evidently nitrogen is an important resource and it is demonstrably in short supply at the start. It seems that the nitrogen supply is affecting the general vigour of the plants, and we may suspect that it affects the success in competing for water, mineral nutrients, space, or light.

An obvious idea that could come from considering the combined growths of clover and grass in a lawn is that they may be competing for some resource such as light or water. Students will find that the situation is not so simple, and will need to reconsider the idea of competition.

Teaching procedure

Associated materials
S(P) 1.4, 1.5, 2.6, 5.2, 6.2, 7.1, 7.2

The investigation could start with a brief class discussion. The teacher could delegate the operations to one or two small groups of students who could keep the records for presentation when the class undertakes the work of Chapter 5.

It will probably be best to let the investigation run for some weeks and then arrange a class discussion with the evidence at hand.

The experiment is essentially simple and to exploit it fully the class should consider it with other experiments and exercises in *Study guide (P)*.

Practical problems

The most likely source of difficulty is the content of nitrogen in the soil, and the quality of drainage. Since clover is inhibited by high concentrations of nitrogen, fertile soils may not have vigorous growths of clover. Such conditions are fairly rare. They can be overcome by lifting some turves with clover in them, transferring these to seed boxes or kipper boxes, and leaving the boxes on cinders or gravel.

Rain generally leaches the excess nitrogenous materials fairly quickly, and it is possible to start experiments within a few days. This treatment is also good where the soil is heavy clay. If no turves are available, then sow grass and clover seed in loam. Allow the mat to form – this will take about five weeks, and should be started early in March.

If *Trifolium repens* is absent, other legumes will probably behave in similar fashion, but perhaps less dramatically.

If lawn space is limited, run the experiment as a demonstration. If no lawn is available, use turves in seed boxes in the laboratory or greenhouse.

Ammonium sulphate is a convenient nitrogenous fertilizer. Suitable controls could use potassium sulphate and potassium nitrate, also tap water. Local circumstances will dictate what can be attempted.

Mapping should be kept to the absolute minimum which is sufficient for the present purpose.

It is desirable to make quantitive measurements of growth, but the changes that occur are usually so striking that mapping and a visual or photographic record are convincing enough.

Questions and answers

Does the evidence suggest that in the absence of one species the other might eventually cover the lawn?

a If one species is removed mechanically this normally permits the unhampered species to invade the territory and suggests that either could colonize the whole lawn. Evidently the soil and climate are suitable for both species.

What sort of changes do you suppose could prevent this happening?

b There is some sort of interference in the process, but it is not possible to answer the question fully until the investigations are complete.

Does grass grow more vigorously when additional nitrogen is supplied? If so, what advantages could the increased growth confer on the grass?

c Yes; lusher, greener. By inference, this produces greater wet and dry weights than untreated grass. Nitrogen permits better growth of root and leaf. *Excessive* nitrogen makes the grass grow so luxuriantly that lawns become very susceptible to drought, probably owing to extreme transpiration.

Does clover grow better with additional nitrogen? How do you explain the results you have obtained?

d Not usually; the bacteria seem to provide adequate nitrogen for the clover. This topic is studied further in Chapter 5.

What evidence is there that grass responds in the same way to added nitrogen and to being near clover? If there is similarity, can you put forward any hypothesis to account for it?

e Same appearance. Clover perhaps supplies extra nitrogen.

Is there any evidence of competition between clover and grass? If so, what might they be competing for?

f This question cannot yet be answered completely. Students should ask themselves how much they can say for certain from the evidence available.

Do the results of your experiments justify the conclusion that clover and grass are competing for a limited supply of nitrogen in the soil?

g No; this is not proved. It is, however, a sensible suggestion and probably true to some extent. In times of drought, the relative extent of the root system might be significant. This question is intended to emphasize the problem of defining competition and the following points are relevant:
1 There is always enough nitrogen for the clover.
2 There may be adequate nitrogen for the grass.
3 Nitrogen is a resource which both require.
4 There *could* be competition for nitrogen, and clover is the likely winner, since most nitrogen is fixed endogenously. The grass will tap this source only when the clover releases it (dead roots and discarded nodules). The grass can also tap other small reserves of nitrogen in the soil.

There is no clear evidence that there is competition for the nitrogen in the *soil* and this would probably not be important.

Additional bibliography

General reading

Bailey, N. T. J. (1959) *Statistical methods in biology*. Edinburgh University Press.
Brookes, B. C. and Dick, W. F. L. (1953) *Introduction to statistical method*. Heinemann. (Arithmetical treatment of Latin square results, for advanced students only.)
Browning, T. O. (1963) *Animal populations*. Hutchinson.
Chancellor, R. J. (1959) *Identification of seedlings of common weeds*. Ministry of Agriculture, Fisheries and Food Bulletin No. 179. H.M.S.O.
Dawson, R. B. (1960) *Lawns*. Penguin.
Loveday, R. (1958) *Statistics*. Volumes I and II. Cambridge University Press.
Moroney, M. J. (1953) *Facts from figures*. Revised edition. Pelican.
Morton, J. E. (1964) *Mollusca*. Hutchinson.
Salisbury, E. (1962) *The biology of garden weeds*. The Masters Memorial Lectures. The Royal Horticultural Society, London. (A good summary of facts on common weeds around schools, and obtainable from The Royal Horticultural Society, Vincent Square, London S.W.1.)
Savory, T. (1962) *Naming the living world*. Edinburgh University Press.
Shorten, M. (1954) *Squirrels*. Collins. (Chapter 13, for discussion of interactions between species.)

References

Milthorpe, F. L. (Ed.) (1961) Proceedings of symposium of the Society for Experimental Biology No. XV. *Mechanisms in biological competition*. Cambridge University Press:
Donald, C. M. 'Competition for light in crops and pastures.'
Grummer, G. 'The role of toxic substances in the relationship between higher plants.'
Harper, J. L. 'Approaches to the study of plant competition.'
Mather, K. 'Competition and co-operation.'
Milne, A. 'Definition of competition among animals.'
Milthorpe, F. L. 'The nature and analysis of competition between plants of different species.'
Salt, G. 'Competition among insect parasitoids.'

Black, J. N. 'The significance of petiole length, leaf area, and light interception in competition between strains of Subterranean Clover (*Trifolium subterraneum*) grown in swards.' *J. Aust. Ag. Res.* **11** (3), 277–291.

Proceedings of Symposium Number 1 of the British Ecological Society (1960). Blackwell's Scientific Publications:
Bunting, A. H. 'Some reflections on the ecology of weeds.'
Lieth, H. 'Patterns of change within grassland communities.'

Chapter 2

Inheritance and the origin of variation

Chapter review

The main aim of this chapter is to establish the following principles: there is a pattern in the manner by which similarities and differences are transmitted from one generation to another; chance also plays a part in inheritance; the genetic mechanisms of recombination and gene mutation create new combinations of character and new characters respectively; and the environment influences the mode of expression of a gene.

The sequence of topics is as follows:

– Inheritance of variation.

1 Inheritance in the fruit fly, *Drosophila melanogaster*. Mathematical and physical models are shown to be helpful in interpreting the results of crosses.

– Mendel's work on peas.

2 The action of genes and the environment. A simple demonstration shows that the genetic potential of an organism may not find full expression, except in a favourable environment.

– The origin of variation.

3 Mutation in yeast.

4 Artificial induction of mutations in yeast by ultra-violet radiation. We study 3 and 4 as examples of the way in which novel characteristics are produced.

Assumptions

– That students have performed the work of the preceding chapter.

Inheritance of variation

2.1 Inheritance in the fruit fly, *Drosophila melanogaster* (preliminary)

Principles

In this investigation, the life history of *Drosophila* is explained, so that pupils can interpret breeding behaviour and inheritance in terms of the organism's natural history. The investigation considers different aspects of inheritance so that in conjunction with Chapter 3 it will establish the gene theory of inheritance.

Teaching procedure

Associated materials
S(P) 1.1, 1.7, 2.1, 2.2, 2.3, 2.4, 2.5, 2.6, 3.1, 3.4, 4.1, 4.7, 9.3
S(D) 5.1, 5.2, 5.3, 5.4, 6.1
Film loop 'Handling *Drosophila*'
NBP 70

L(P) 2.1 outlines the techniques for handling *Drosophila* and provides procedures for investigating monohybrid and dihybrid inheritance and autosomal and sex linkage. The most economical plan is for students to undertake one of these practical investigations and to study the others by using secondhand data. If they have previously investigated a monohybrid cross they could undertake one of the other practical investigations here. For students new to genetics the monohybrid cross is suggested as the best practical investigation around which to build a course.

If time and facilities are available different students (or groups) could perform different investigations so that the class as a whole will have covered all the crosses by practical work. This requires careful organization. Ensure that the class obtains an adequate number of progeny from reciprocal matings and replicates for each investigation undertaken. Only apply the chi-squared test if there are plenty of progeny.

While waiting for the results of the investigation proceed with the rest of this chapter and Chapter 3. The conclusions drawn from the investigations in Chapters 2 and 3 should be considered together.

Practical problems

Cultures may be kept in small containers such as 3 in × 1 in tubes to reduce the space needed for storage. Room temperatures are generally acceptable, especially in summer. Incubators can be used to speed up the life cycle, which lasts 10 days or slightly more.

Questions and answers

B Monohybrid cross

How many kinds of colour of body appeared in the F_1?

a One – grey.

Was there any difference between the results of the first cross and its reciprocal?

b None.

How many kinds of colour of body appeared in the F_2?

c Two – black and grey.

If there were more colours than one represented in either generation, in what ratio did the colours occur?

d 3:1 (expected).

Did the colour ratio among the males differ from the ratio among the females?

e No (or if it did, not much).

How did your group's results compare with those of other groups, and with those of the whole class?

f Small samples approximate less frequently to the expected ratio, and less accurately than the group average.

C Model of an F_1 and an F_2 generation

Was there more than one genotype in the F_1 generation?

a No.

How many genotypes occurred in the F_2 generation?

b Three.

To what extent is the model inadequate for explaining your breeding results?

c It is only a model and has no logical connection with the reality. Resemblances in the performances of model and fly are significant in that the former suggests that there is a material basis for inheritance. The model is a useful aid in constructing hypotheses about underlying mechanisms of the behaviour of gametes and in portraying heterozygotes and homozygotes. Some students may suggest the idea of dominance and recessiveness as a result of using the model. 'Dominant' and 'recessive' describe characters, not genes.

Dominance

How could you interpret the experimental results?

d A 3:1 ratio indicates that both homozygotes and heterozygotes are present in a generation and that a dominant-recessive relation exists between the characteristics.

D Backcross

What genotypes will be produced by the two crosses and in what ratios?

a ++ × +e gives ++, ++, +e, and +e.
ee × +e gives +e, +e, ee, and ee.

What phenotypes will result and in what ratios?

b From the first – all wild type.
From the second – wild type: ebony, in proportion 50:50.

Which of these crosses is the more useful for determining the genetic constitution of a fly which could be either ++ or +e?

c ee × +e, the backcross to the double recessive.

E Dihybrid cross

Can you construct a model to predict the results of this kind of cross? If in difficulty, look this up in any elementary genetics book (see Bibliography).

a Students could use a bead model. Two containers are required and each zygote would be represented by four beads, a pair from each container.

If you carried out a breeding experiment, did your observed results agree with expectation? If not, can you account for the discrepancy?

b Students should use the chi-squared test.

They may need reminding of the following points concerning the chi-squared test and its application:

1 The chi-squared test is used by an experimenter after he has obtained results which may or may not fit with his hypothesis. The first job is to decide what results the hypothesis makes most likely. These constitute the *expected results*. In most cases, the *observed results* are not the same as the expected ones because of the influence of chance during the experiment.

The question arises: How likely are the observed results to have occurred if the hypothesis is correct?

If the chi-squared test tells the experimenter that he is extremely unlikely to have obtained such results if the hypothesis is good, then clearly the hypothesis must be changed. The results cannot be changed.

2 The chi-squared test presents the experimenter with a value (P) which expresses in quantitative terms the likelihood of getting the observed results.

A value of 0·9 implies that the observed results are very likely indeed to have been observed if the hypothesis is correct. A value of 0·1 suggests that chance has affected the observations, but not sufficiently to cast real doubt on the validity of the hypothesis. Values of 0·05 and less are sufficiently low to suggest that the results are not in accordance with the hypothesis, which must be altered.

3 The number of degrees of freedom is calculated by counting the number of terms which must be added together and subtracting one. Thus $n = 4 - 1 = 3$.

4 For the chi-squared test to be applicable, each expected value must be at least 5. This means that if very few flies hatch from the dihybrid cross there will be very few ebony bodied, dumpy winged flies expected. For example, with ratios of 9:3:3:1 expected, there must be at least 80 experimental flies to permit an expectation of 5 in the smallest category. It would be technically incorrect to embark on a chi-squared test of an F_2 smaller than 80. The more flies the better.

5 In the case of the dihybrid cross the hypothesis suggests that the expected ratio of phenotypes is 9:3:3:1. These are the expected values. The problem is to discover whether the observed values are sufficiently like the expected ones to allow the hypothesis to stand unamended.

Where chance plays a part, it is true that almost *any* results are possible and, indeed, it is conceivable that a dihybrid cross such as the one in question *might* produce an F_2 generation consisting entirely of double recessives in respect of both characters. Such an outcome would in practice raise doubts about the hypothesis but this might, nevertheless, be allowed to stand because of the other occasions on which it has been shown to be valid. The test, when applied to our data, will tell us how to interpret the deviations of our results from the expected ones. If they differ so widely that there is very little likelihood of their having arisen by chance, it is best to regard the hypothesis as an inadequate explanation of the results. Then, if we have confidence in the administration of the experiment, it is necessary to construct a better hypothesis by modifying the original.

F Autosomal linkage

Crossing-over occurs in female *Drosophila* but not in the male. If, instead of making the F_1 backcrosses as suggested, the experimenter uses the *reciprocal* crosses (i.e. uses F_1 *males* in place of F_1 females) then all the progeny resemble the grandparents. This is a simple result which clearly demonstrates linkage. It is suggested that less able students should use this simpler cross.

For more advanced students, the females should be used, as suggested in *Laboratory guide (P)*. The work on *Sordaria* in Extension Work I could supplement it. In this case all four combinations of the two pairs of characters appear in the offspring.

The crossover value is determined by calculating

$$\frac{\text{Number of recombinations}}{\text{Total number of offspring counted}} \times 100$$

The loci for ebony body and curled wing are both on chromosome III.

Backcrosses in which the investigator is looking for linkage are sometimes called testcrosses.

Students may use the conventions suggested below to help them analyse results. It may be a good idea to remind them that the female is always mentioned first and that the sign + refers to the wild type of whatever character is in question. Here it may stand for wild type wings or wild type body colour.

In Cross 1 (i.e. wild type body, wild type wing × ebony body, curled wing) the mutants are coupled.

In Cross 2 (i.e. ebony body, wild type wing × wild type body, curled wing) the mutants are in repulsion.

Cross 1

P $\quad \dfrac{++}{++} \times \dfrac{e\ cu}{e\ cu}$

$F_1 \quad \dfrac{++}{e\ cu}$

Phenotype – wild type

Backcross A – $\dfrac{++}{e\ cu} \times \dfrac{e\ cu}{e\ cu}$

On the simplest hypothesis (no crossing-over), the progeny will be as shown below.

♀ \ ♂	$\underline{e\ cu}$	$\underline{e\ cu}$
$\overline{++}$	$\dfrac{e\ cu}{++}$	$\dfrac{e\ cu}{++}$
$\overline{e\ cu}$	$\dfrac{e\ cu}{e\ cu}$	$\dfrac{e\ cu}{e\ cu}$

Phenotypes

Ebony body wild type wings	Ebony body curled wings	Wild type body wild type wings	Wild type body curled wings
0	2	2	0

On the assumption that crossover is complete, *but in the female only*, the progeny will be as shown below.

♀ \ ♂	e cu	e cu
+cu	$\frac{e\ cu}{+cu}$	$\frac{e\ cu}{+cu}$
e+	$\frac{e\ cu}{e+}$	$\frac{e\ cu}{e+}$

Phenotypes

Ebony wings wild type wings	Ebony body curled wings	Wild type body wild type wings	Wild type body curled wings
2	0	0	2

Cross 2

P $\quad \frac{e+}{e+} \times \frac{+cu}{+cu}$

$F_1 \quad \frac{e+}{+cu}$

Phenotype – wild type

Backcross B – $\frac{e+}{+cu} \times \frac{e\ cu}{e\ cu}$

Assuming no crossover the progeny will be

♂ / ♀	e cu	e cu
e+	e cu / e+	e cu / e+
+cu	e cu / +cu	e cu / +cu

Phenotypes

Ebony body wild type wings	Ebony body curled wings	Wild type body wild type wings	Wild type body curled wings
2	0	0	2

Assuming 100 per cent crossover the progeny will be

♂ / ♀	e cu	e cu
e cu	e cu / e cu	e cu / e cu
++	e cu / ++	e cu / ++

Phenotypes

Ebony body wild type wings	Ebony body curled wings	Wild type body wild type wings	Wild type body curled wings
0	2	2	0

Questions and answers

What was the phenotype of the F_1 offspring?

a Wild type in respect of both pairs of characters.

How do your results differ from those of the previous dihybrid cross? Were any of the expected phenotypes absent?

b See above.

Was there any difference in the results from the two sexes?

c This will be unanswerable in so far as the sex of the parents and backcrosses are concerned, unless the reciprocal crosses have been set up. There should be no sex difference in the F_2 proportions according to sex and phenotype.

Were there any differences between the progeny of backcrosses A and B? If so, how do you account for them?

d Assuming no crossover, the results will be in complete contrast. Some evidence of crossover will, however, appear in both backcross progenies.

With the aid of a book on genetics (see Bibliography), construct a model to account for the results you have obtained.

e This is an invitation to read up about linkage and crossover. Wire models of chromosomes could be used. This question is best left until Chapter 3 has been completed.

G Sex linkage

To what extent are the phenotypes for eye colour in the F_2 associated with sex?

a Cross white eye × wild type: Expected results:

	Wild type eye		White eye		Ratio
	♀	♂	♀	♂	
P		+−	ww		1:1
F_1	+w			w−	1:1
F_2	+w	+−	ww	w−	1:1:1:1

Cross wild type × white eye: Expected results:

	Wild type		White eye		Ratio
	♀	♂	♀	♂	
P	++			w−	1:1
F_1	+w	+−			1:1
F_2	++ and +w	+−		w−	(1+1):1:1

Construct a model to explain the experimental findings (use a book on genetics to help you, if necessary).

b A model can be constructed using beads, wire models of chromosomes, or diagrams. This question can be used as a basis for class discussion on sex linkage.

Mendel's work on peas

The selection of appropriate organisms and characteristics enabled Mendel to discover the fundamental explanation of inheritance. His work was a significant example of carefully executed scientific enquiry and seems outstanding when one considers the period in which it was undertaken. The time between the generations of *Drosophila* provides an opportunity to discuss this. As a focus for such discussion it is helpful to have two modern strains of garden pea plants (living or herbarium specimens) to show the fruit characters. Examples of Mendel's characters are shown by plants of *Pisum sativum*, Cambridge Line 1 and Pellew's group strains.

Choosing organisms and characters for breeding investigations
The following points are generally relevant.
The organisms should:
1 Have a short life cycle.
2 Be easy to rear or grow under fairly standardized conditions.
3 Allow easy control of mating and fertilization.
4 Be of a kind in which the experiments can protect the female parent from foreign sperm or pollen.
5 Be prolific.
6 Have forms with several pairs of contrasting characters.

Furthermore, organisms which are small and easily reared take up less space and will normally be cheaper to use. The characters should be known to be inheritable and little affected by the environment. It is also necessary to ascertain that populations of the organisms can be obtained which breed true for each of a pair of characters and for combinations of characters.

Mendel's investigations
After discussing their own suggestions students could refer to the studies of inheritance before Mendel which were concerned with the inheritance of a complex of characters many of which, like height or weight, were examples of continuous variation. Mendel's success arose from the fact that he restricted each of his studies of inheritance to only one or two markedly contrasting characters.

At this point students might examine the Cambridge Line 1 and Pellew's group peas and be asked to find the pairs of contrasting characters. Seed and fruit characters can be demonstrated by dried specimens, and colour transparencies of flowers may be useful if flowers have not yet appeared.

Table 1 shows the characters that Mendel used, together with the gene symbols now assigned to them, and additional characters to be found in Cambridge Line 1 and Pellew's group.

The characters Mendel used in his experiments

	Mendel's description of character	Dominant	Symbol	Recessive	Symbol
1	difference in form of ripe seed	round	R.R.	wrinkled	r.r.
2	difference in colour of cotyledons	yellow	I.I.	green	i.i.
3	difference in colour of testa	coloured	A.A.	white	a.a.
4	difference in form of ripe pods	inflated	Pe.Pe.	constricted	pe.pe.
5	difference in colour of unripe pods	green	Gp.Gp.	yellow	gp.gp.
6	difference in position of flowers	axial	Fa.Fa.	terminal	fa.fa.
7	difference in length of stem	long (tall)	Le.Le.	short (dwarf)	le.le.

Additional characters found in Cambridge Line 1 and Pellew's group

8	difference in shape of wing	normal wing	K.K.	keeled wing	k.k.
9	difference in nature of leaf	normal leaf	Ac.Ac.	Acacia leaf	ac.ac.
10	difference in shape of ripe seed	drum/ round		drum/ round	

Table 1
Characters of the garden pea, *Pisum sativum*

Cambridge Line 1 has round, green, white-coated seeds; white, terminal flowers; green, constricted pods; and a short stem. Thus it is recessive for all the characters except seed shape and pod colour for which it is dominant. In addition, it has normal wings to its flowers and its leaves bear tendrils.

Pellew's group has drum shaped, yellow, brown-coated seeds; coloured axillary flowers; yellow, inflated pods; and a long stem. Thus it is dominant for all the characters except seed shape and pod colour for which it is recessive. It has keeled wings to its flowers and the normal tendrils are replaced by three leaflets.

Other points which can be usefully brought out in discussion are that the colour character (3) is expressed not only in the seed coat but in the flowers and the leaf axils. Thus, it is *pleiotropic*. The colour character (5) is expressed in the stalks, leaf veins, and the calyx. Mendel mentioned both.

The inheritance of the drum shape in the seeds deserves notice because this character appears to be inherited maternally: the seeds of the offspring have the form of those of the female parent, and this points to *cytoplasmic inheritance*.

Several genes with varying degrees of interaction are known to affect seed colour and seed shape. The foregoing account is therefore somewhat simplified.

If F_1 plants (from crosses between Line 1 and Pellew's group) are available, it is possible to show convincing examples of dominance and recessiveness. The pea is self-pollinated, and this renders artificial pollination in the production of the F_2 generation unnecessary.

On the other hand, pollen is liberated at quite an early stage of the bud's growth so that, for the original crosses, the experimenter must emasculate the flowers a day or two after the colour of the petals can first be seen. Fortunately it is possible to pollinate at the same time and enclose the flowers in Cellophane bags to prevent foreign pollen contaminating them when the flower opens. Geneticists need large stocks that breed true for the characters in question. Mendel was alive to this and he examined and bred for two years up to thirty-four varieties, obtained from commercial seedsmen, before he selected twenty-two for his experiments.

2.2 The action of genes and the environment (preliminary)

Principles

This investigation is intended to dispel the assumption that the phenotype is a sure guide to the qualities of the genotype and to show that the expression of genes depends on there being an appropriate environment both within the organism (including neighbouring genes) and outside it.

Teaching procedure

Associated materials
S(P) 2.1, 2.3
S(D) 5.1, 6.1, 6.2, 6.3, 7.2, 7.3, 7.4, 7.5, 7.7

It is probably best to treat the investigation as a demonstration which can serve as a good focus for a discussion of the influence of the environment on the expression of genes. The selective disadvantages of the character are obvious and can be referred to also. It is necessary to take care not to get drawn into a detailed consideration of Mendelian ratios or of the method of maintaining and identifying the barley plants. Other examples of this phenomenon are:

1 The genetically distinct strain of sheep called Merino produces the best wool when kept on a poor diet.

2 The pink colour of flamingos is not expressed unless the diet contains certain crustaceans – a fact which the keepers in zoological gardens need to take into account if the birds are to keep their 'natural' colour.

3 Rust-susceptible antirrhinums only express their susceptibility in the presence of a rust infection.

4 The spore colour of the fungus *Aspergillus niger* is black unless magnesium is withheld from the culture. (See *Laboratory guide (P)*, E1.4.)

Questions and answers

What differences are there between the plants kept in the light and those in the dark?

a

	In the dark	In the light
Normal strain	all pale	all green
Xantha strain	all pale	pale:green 1:1

Other aspects of etiolation may be seen in plants which have been in the dark.

How do the plants deficient in chlorophyll differ from the normal ones?

b Even if kept in the dark, plants of the strain deficient in chlorophyll are paler than those of the normal strain. The seedlings do not survive for more than a week or so and gradually become noticeably more thin and weak than the normal plants.

What conditions are required before a plant is able to produce chlorophyll?

c

1 Light (environmental factor).

2 The presence of a factor in the plant itself, presumably inherited (genetic).

In the light of this experiment, what conclusions can you draw regarding the influence of the environment on the phenotypic expression of a genotype?

d This experiment has not shown that the characteristic of chlorophyll production is inherited. Given this information it can be deduced that the expression of genotype in producing the phenotype depends on the influence of the environment.

The origin of variation

Associated materials
S(P) 2.7, 2.9
S(D) 1.1

It will probably be thought desirable to fill out the brief introduction by discussion. A small collection demonstrating mutant forms, either of living specimens or illustrations, might be a useful starting point. Examples showing the economic applications of mutation would be particularly valuable. For this, it is possible to obtain illustrations of breeds of domestic and farm animals and of plants from the breed societies or biological supply agencies. It might be helpful to mention other examples such as the inheritance of haemophilia in some lines of European aristocracy. A collection illustrating mutant mice, *Drosophila* etc., also affords good illustrative material. Collections of plants are also valuable for demonstrating mutations. The Additional Bibliography refers to somatic mutations, chimaeras, and mosaics. Examples of plants with unstable genes are: *Antirrhinum* ('Bizarre'), *Aquilegia clematiflora*, *Zinnia elegans striata* (peppermint stick), and *Barbarea vulgaris* var. *variegata*.

It is worth also pointing out that recessive mutations are difficult to detect and require close inbreeding to bring them out. Furthermore it is often difficult to distinguish between the recombination of rare genes and mutation. A decision will have to be taken on the use of the term *mutation*. Since it is detected in the phenotype before its causes are known, we suggest that it should be used to cover *all* cases of changes in the hereditary material giving rise to changes in characteristics; thus it includes changes in the structure of a gene, change in the structure of a chromosome (inversions, translocations, and deficiencies), and changes in the numbers of chromosomes (polyploidy). Some geneticists think its use should be restricted to mutation of genes.

2.3 Mutation in yeast (preliminary)

Principles

Studies with micro-organisms which breed profusely and quickly enable students to observe mutation taking place. Mutation is seen to be a rare but continuing source of variation.

The introduction of an experiment on micro-organisms also helps to maintain a balance between work on plants, animals and micro-organisms, and acts as a reminder of the way in which micro-organisms have been used extensively for research.

Teaching procedure

Associated materials
S(P) 2.7, 2.8
Film loop 'Inoculation with a loop'
NBP–48

Here, students might consider how closely *Saccharomyces* approaches the ideal organism for genetic work. It will be necessary to explain any terms new to the students in the life cycle illustrated in *Laboratory guide (P)*, figure 16. Diploid cells are less likely to show the effect of a mutation, unless it produces a dominant character. It would require two mutations to produce the homozygous state for any recessive character in order that it could be detected. In this investigation and the next, the fact that yeast has a haploid stage in its life cycle is thus most important.

Before beginning the investigation make sure that students are reasonably competent in using the sterile techniques required. A 'dummy run' using, say, milk instead of a yeast suspension can provide suitable training.

At the end of the investigation, it might be wise to stress that this is a case of *back-mutation* – mutation which involves a reversion to the wild type character. It is less common than mutation from the wild type.

Practical problems

Students may need help in using top (reflected) light in order to distinguish red and white cells under the microscope. The substage mirror should be turned so that no light comes from below; alternatively, the iris diaphragm should be closed. Then the user can direct strong side light onto the suspension at a suitable shallow angle of incidence. He should focus the microscope up and down as it will probably be easier to distinguish the cells when they are just out of focus.

Questions and answers

Are any white yeast colonies which appear sufficient evidence that mutation has occurred? If not, what further information is required and how would you set about obtaining it?

a In itself the investigation does not give sufficient evidence that mutation has occurred. It has to be shown that the white characteristic is inherited. Thus it would be necessary to breed through several generations.

Is there any other explanation for your observations? If so, how would you decide which explanation is correct?

b Some white cells may have been present in the suspension and then have outgrown the red cells. However, note that the appearance of white colonies on the edges of the red colonies at different stages in their development supports the hypothesis that there was mutation.

It would be necessary to carry out a further systematic check on the suspension. Put out several samples of roughly equal numbers of red cells on plates at daily intervals and calculate the percentage of white cells produced. If the percentage increases in a similar manner in each there is *prima facie* evidence that mutations are occurring.

How often do you think mutation (or some other kind of change) is occurring?

c This is a straightforward calculation from the number of red colonies that produce white colonies. If possible calculate the percentage of mutations per generation in preference to the percentage of mutations per day. However, this is not so easy.

2.4 Artificial induction of mutations in yeast by ultra-violet radiation

Principles

The mutation rate in yeast increases through the influence of ultra-violet radiation. This experimental procedure resembles the classical work of Muller, who worked with *Drosophila*.

Radiation and other mutagens are used nowadays to induce random mutation in seeds, spores, and other structures in the hope of producing an occasional beneficial mutation of commercial or medical significance. This has led, for example, to the production of higher yielding strains of *Penicillium*.

Teaching procedure

Associated materials
S(P) 2.7, 2.8

The procedure for handling the yeast is similar to that of the previous investigation. All that is necessary before starting the investigation is a demonstration on the use of the u/v lamps. In fact, it is best if this part is undertaken under the strict control of the teacher, or demonstrated by him, especially if any glass filter has been removed.

If possible, the percentage of cells killed by the radiation should be determined. To do this, spread out equal measured volumes of yeast suspension on four or five plates of culture medium. Aim to spread about 1000 cells evenly on each plate. Keep one plate as a control and subject the others to varying dosages of ultra-violet radiation. The difference between the growth of the populations on the control and that of populations exposed to radiation will make it possible to calculate the percentage 'kill'.

Students might be apt to confuse the red colour of the adenine-requiring mutant yeast, used in the previous investigation, with the red dye (Magdala red) employed in this one. There is no known connection between the two.

Mutation rates

Organism	Mutation rates	
	From	To
Bacterial virus (bacteriophage)	10^{-9}*	10^{-3}
colon bacillus	10^{-9}	10^{-5}
maize	10^{-6}	10^{-4}
Drosophila	10^{-7}	10^{-5}
man	10^{-6}	10^{-4}

Table 2
Mutation rates found in various organisms.

* (10^{-9} means one mutation occurs among every 10^{9} individuals. The other figures should be interpreted in the same way.)

Figure 13
The relation between irradiation level and number of mutations produced.

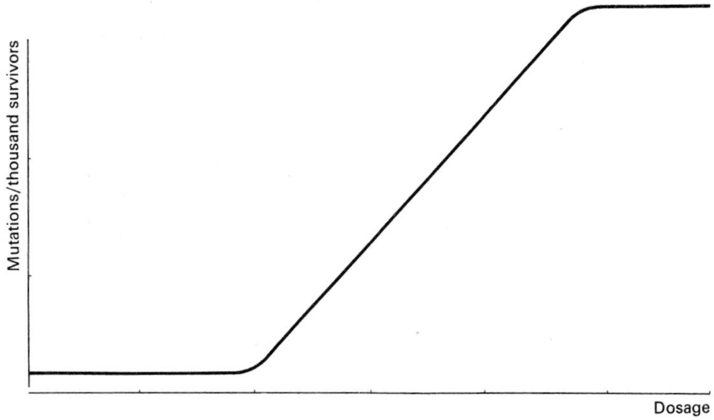

Students may wish to know more about mutation rates. The topic is important because of its bearing upon evolution. It is, however, difficult to estimate mutation rate and the information available is fragmentary. Points to bring out in teaching are:

1 The rate of spontaneous mutation is low; about one in a million per gene per generation. The rate varies considerably between different genes in the same species, between species, and under different environmental conditions.

2 Special methods have been developed for measuring mutation rates. Impetus was given to the study of mutation frequency by J. B. S. Haldane's work on haemophilia.

3 Mutation rate might limit evolution but the interplay of rates of mutation, rates of selection, and size of population is very complex and it is not possible to draw reasonable general conclusions in the present state of knowledge. There may have been periods of high mutation rate and rapid evolution under certain favourable physical conditions during the earth's history.

Practical problems

Much of the success of this experiment rests upon determining beforehand the most effective range of dosages. This will depend not only upon the distance of the suspension from the lamp and how long it is irradiated, but on the strain of yeast used and the qualities of the lamp. In preliminary experiments to determine the best range of dosage it will probably be convenient to keep the distance constant and vary the time of exposure. Allow colonies under different doses of radiation to develop at 30° C for 24 hours. Keep one plate as a control.

The haploid prototrophic strain, 188, of *S. cerevisiae* is suitable. It is important to point out that the relatively long wavelength of ultra-violet radiation makes the penetrating powers of these rays slight and thus they can only be used for producing mutations in small organisms or thin layers of cells. Students also need an additional warning about the danger of ultra-violet radiation to eyes.

The Magdala-red technique was used originally for the rapid detection of respiratory-deficient mutants. The method does not detect *all* mutants and therefore can only be used to show that mutations have been induced or to compare the rates of mutation under different conditions. To show that the deeply stained cells and colonies are indeed mutants, it might be worth while transferring some of the mutants to minimal medium. Many of them are unable to survive, whereas the wild type prototroph can. Some students might determine more precisely what the mutant deficiencies are.

Questions and answers

What relationship is there between how long the yeast cells are exposed to u/v radiation and the percentage of mutations induced?

a The higher dosages produce more mutations per thousand surviving cells but more of the original cells are killed. If mutations per 1000 survivors are plotted, this usually produces a curve somewhat like the one shown in figure 13.

Is the evidence provided by this experiment adequate to prove that mutations have, in fact, occurred? If not, what other experiments would you perform to establish this?

b The evidence is conclusive if the Magdala-red identification is accepted. The experimenter can check this by transferring deeply stained cells to minimal medium and then working through a series of nutritional supplements.

Additional bibliography

General reading

Auerbach, C. (1965) *Heredity, an introduction for O-level students*. Oliver & Boyd.
Bateson, W. (1913) *Mendel's principles of heredity*. Cambridge University Press.
Darlington, C. D. and Mather, K. (1949) *The elements of genetics*. Allen & Unwin.
Gabriel, M. G. and Fogel, S. (1955) *Great experiments in biology*. Prentice-Hall.
Head, J. J. and Dennis, N. R. (1968) *Genetics for O-level*. Oliver & Boyd.
Mackean, D. G. (1968) *Introduction to genetics*. John Murray.
Peters, J. A. (1959) *Classic papers in genetics*. Prentice-Hall.
Winchester, A. M. (1964) *Heredity. An introduction to genetics*. Harrap.

References

Alexander, P. (1957) *Atomic radiation and life*. Pelican.
Alexopoulos, C. J. (1962) *Introductory mycology*. 2nd edition. John Wiley. (Basic reference book on morphology, classification, and biology of fungi.)
Auerbach, C. (1966) *Genetics in the atomic age*. Oliver & Boyd.
Barker, W. B. (1952) 'The production of coloured sweet maize "seeds" for illustrating Mendelian segregation.' *Sc. Sci. Rev.*, **120**, 219–223.
Crane, M. B. and Lawrence, W. J. C. (1954) *The genetics of garden plants*. 4th edition. Macmillan.
Darlington, C. D. and Bradshaw, A. D. (Eds.) (1966) *Teaching genetics*. Oliver & Boyd.
Fincham, J. R. S. and Day, P. R. (1965) *Fungal genetics*. 2nd edition. Blackwell.
Glass, B. (1965) *Genetic continuity*. B.S.C.S. Laboratory Block and Teachers' Supplement. D. C. Heath.
Haskell, G. (1961) *Practical heredity with* Drosophila. Oliver & Boyd.
Horn, P. and Wilkie, D. (1966) 'Use of magdala red for the detection of auxotrophic mutants in *Saccharomyces cerevisiae*.' *J. Bac.*, **91**, 3, 1388.
Iltis, H. (1932) *Life of Mendel*. Allen & Unwin.
Lawrence, W. J. G. (1951) *Practical plant breeding*. Allen & Unwin.
Lewis, K. R. and John, B. (1964) *The matter of Mendelian heredity*. Churchill.
McKelvie, A. D. (1963) 'Studies in the induction of mutations in *Arabidopsis thaliana*.' *Radiation Botany*, **3**, 105–123.
Mather, K. (1959) Modern Science Memoirs 31. *Genetics for schools*. John Murray.
Mather, K. (1964) *Statistical analysis in biology*. University Paperbacks Methuen.
Stadler, L. J. (1942) 'Frequency of spontaneous mutation in corn.' *Spragg Memorial Lectures* 3rd series. Michigan State College.
Strickberger, M. W. (1962) *Experiments in genetics with* Drosophila. Wiley.
De Vries, H. (1903) *Die Mutations Theorie* I and II, translated 1910 and 1911 by Farmer, J. B. and Darbishire, A. D. and published as *The mutations theory* by Kegan Paul.
Wallace, B. and Dobzhansky, T. (1963) *Radiation, genes and man*. Holt Library.
Wallace, M. E., Gibson, J. B. and Kelly, P. J. (1968) 'Teaching genetics: the practical problems of breeding investigations.' *J. biol. Educ.*, 2, **4**, 273–303.
Weaver, W. (1964) *Lady Luck*. Heinemann.
Williams, W. (1964) *Genetical principles and plant breeding*. Blackwell.

Department of Education and Science Notes (obtainable from D.E.S. Laboratories, Ivy Farm, Knockholt, Sevenoaks, Kent):
'Notes on the use of *Antirrhinum* for biological studies in schools.'
'Notes on the use of two chlorophyll mutations of barley in the teaching of genetics.'
'Notes on the use of groundsel (*Senecio vulgaris*) and some associated species in school biology courses.'
'Notes on the use of sweet maize for genetical experiments in schools.'
'Notes on the use of mice for genetical work in schools.'
'Demonstrations on the genetics of the edible pea (*Pisum sativum*).'

Chapter 3

The cell nucleus and inheritance

Chapter review

The main aim of the chapter is to show how it is possible to relate the evidence from cytological investigations of meiosis to the evidence from breeding experiments, in an analysis of the mechanism of inheritance.

The breeding experiments of Chapter 2 can be undertaken in parallel with the work of this chapter. Students could deal with this work whilst the *Drosophila* progeny are hatching.

The knowledge derived from Chapters 1, 2, and 3 is used in the next two chapters. These cover some of the ecological consequences of variation and its inheritance. Chapter 9 uses this knowledge in a study of the mechanism of evolution.

The sequence of topics is:

– Gametes and inheritance. The gametes unite in the zygote to form the chief physical link between one generation and the next. This suggests that there might be a genetic substance or a physical basis of heredity that is likely to be found in the nucleus of the sex cells.

1 Formation of pollen in a plant (*Tradescantia*). Preparations of pollen mother cells and spermatocytes are observed and interpreted. Male gametes are used because, unlike female gametes, they lack reserve food material and accessory structures, and can thus be seen clearly. The essential features of meiosis can be analysed by a composite study of cytological preparations, photographs, and the results of breeding experiments.

2 Gamete production in an animal (locust).

– Restatement of the problem of inheritance.

Assumptions – An elementary knowledge of flower and insect structure, sufficient to allow the stamens and testes to be located.

This chapter does not assume that students have any knowledge of cell structures and cell division.

3.1 Formation of pollen in a plant *(Tradescantia)* (preliminary)

Principles

Investigations L(P) 3.1 and L(P) 3.2 can be regarded as alternative. However, it is important to point out that gametogenesis is a process which occurs, with similar features, in all sexually reproducing organisms. Some students might use only prepared slides and/or photographs of meiosis for analysis and answering the questions.

The practical work provides the student with firsthand experience of cytological methods, but it is unlikely that a complete range of meiotic figures will be observed. For this reason it is necessary in any case to provide photographs of the stages of meiosis; these will help students to analyse the nature and sequence of the behaviour of chromosomes.

The argument running through the chapter can be put in the form of a series of statements and questions.

1 The results of the breeding experiments and the common pattern they reveal suggest that there may be some physical basis for inheritance. Where should we look to test this broad hypothesis?

2 The physical link between one generation and the next resides in the gametes, which fuse in the process of fertilization to form the zygote from which the new organism develops. What will a closer examination of the processes of the formation of gametes, and possibly those of fertilization, reveal?

3 It appears that, with some minor exceptions, the contributions of the male and female parents are roughly equal. As the male gamete is almost entirely made up of the nucleus should we begin by studying the formation of male gametes?

4 Our observations reveal some well marked structures (chromosomes) in the dividing cell nucleus in what are different stages of an orderly process. What properties have these structures and what is the order of the stages?

5 How can we relate the behaviour of the chromosomes to the results of breeding experiments, in an analysis of the mechanism of inheritance?

6 This question can lead to the notion of linearly arranged genetic particles (genes) on the chromosomes which form linkage groups.

Teaching procedure

Associated materials
S(P) 2.1, 3.1, 3.2
Film loop 'Squash preparation' NBP–46
Film loop 'Meiosis' NBP–50
Photographs 'Meiosis'

Students will probably need help in using the microscope. They should be shown how to gain a three-dimensional picture by focusing up and down carefully. It is also necessary to demonstrate the squash technique for preparing slides of cells, following the procedure in *Laboratory guide (P)*. A film loop of a demonstration is suitable. Students should be able to consult it whilst they are doing the work, to check on possible errors.

It is possible to combine the practical work with the use of secondhand evidence in the form of a film loop of meiosis, photographs, or a *Study guide* investigation. The balance between firsthand and secondhand experience that is most suitable will depend on the students' abilities and background. It would be possible to put bright students with some experience of this type of work in the position of a researcher who has only his own preparations to depend on. Students requiring more help should use secondhand evidence in a logical sequence. The practical work can then be used in an ancillary way to add realism to their studies.

Tradescantia is used because its chromosomes are relatively large and distinctive and the chromosome number is usually small. For this particular investigation it is best to use *T. paludosa*, *T. bracteata*, or *T. brevicaulis*. *T. virginiana*, the commonest species, is less suitable because it has a large number of chromosomes.

The points that should emerge from this investigation are:
1 The number of chromosomes in the cells of one species is normally constant.
2 Some cells in the reproductive organs contain a half complement of chromosomes (haploid). Most body cells are diploid.
3 The gametes are derived from cells with the haploid number.
4 Chromosomes exist in pairs in the diploid condition. The members of a pair come together at a certain stage in meiosis.
5 The separation of the paired chromosomes occurs in such a way that one from each pair passes into each of two gamete (daughter) cells. It is best to study further details of meiosis in photographs. Students could construct models of stages in meiosis using wire, pipe cleaners, or Plasticine to help them visualize the processes involved. A flick book of drawings of stages in meiosis (see figure 14) will demonstrate the process in a dynamic way.

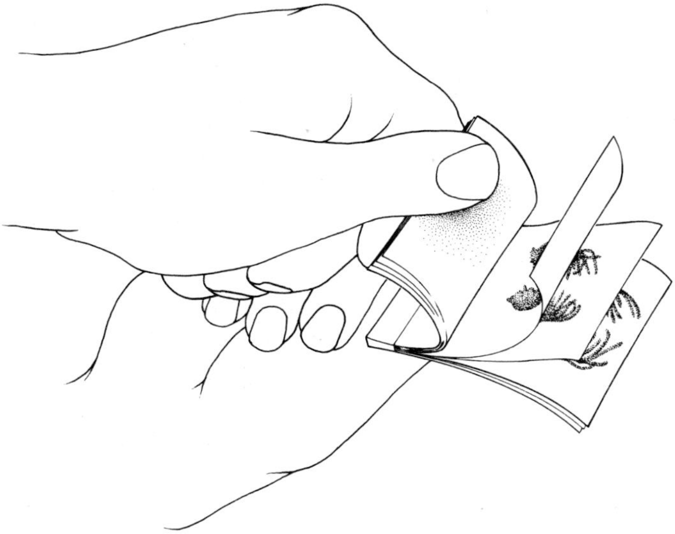

Figure 14
A flick book demonstration of meiosis.

Practical problems

Temporary preparations will normally serve well enough. They can be stored for a week or so in a refrigerator if ringed with rubber solution or other sealing compound, for example, Copydex. Propionic orcein stain may prove better than acetic orcein.

If air bubbles appear in the preparation after it has been macerated and squashed, it means that it was not macerated sufficiently and must be tapped further or, that there is too much material on the slide.

If the material is not sufficiently spread out or appears in different focal planes, then it has not been macerated sufficiently and must be tapped further or that there is too enough. *Crocus balansae* ($2n = 6$), *Paeonia* ($2n = 10$), *Allium ursinum* ($2n = 16$) and *Lilium regale* ($2n = 24$) can be used as alternative material to *Tradescantia* spp.

Additional practical
Pollen from *Tradescantia* can be induced to form pollen tubes which grow into a sugary agar medium. Then the chromosomes pass along the tube in file and can be readily seen and counted.

The questions for L(P) 3.2 can be used with investigation 3.1.

3.2 Gamete production in an animal (locust) (preliminary)

Principles

As L(P) 3.1.

Teaching procedure

As L(P) 3.1.

Associated materials
S(P) 2.1, 3.1, 3.2
Film loop 'Squash preparation' NBP–46
Film loop 'Meiosis' NBP–50
Photographs 'Meiosis'

Practical problems

Propionic orcein may be preferable to acetic orcein. It stains the cytoplasm less.

Specimens of fifth (penultimate) instar or young adults of either *Locusta migratoria* or *Schistocerca gregaria* can be used. The chromosomes are generally not so clear as in *Tradescantia*, and patience may be needed in searching the squashes for follicles of testes in suitable stages of development. Different follicles and different parts of each follicle undergo meiotic divisions in sequence. If the base of a follicle proves unsuitable, students should look near the apex.

Grasshoppers (*Chorthippus*) and froghoppers (*Philaenus*) provide alternative material. Grasshoppers are said to give the best meiotic figures when killed early in the day, but this assertion requires more careful testing. Grasshoppers have lower chromosome numbers (e.g. $2n = 17$, compared with $2n = 23$ in *Schistocerca gregaria*), but are difficult to collect and the young males seem to be available only in July and August. Preserved specimens might be used.

In Orthoptera the male is typically the heterogametic sex, there being no Y chromosome.

Questions and answers

What effect does aceto-orcein have on the contents of a cell nucleus?

a It stains chromosome material but not the rest of the nucleus nor cytoplasm. It also fixes the material. The question can introduce a discussion of the processes involved in making microscopic preparations if students have not considered these earlier.

Estimate the proportion of gamete-producing cells in your preparation which showed chromosomes.

b The answer depends on the preparation and on the care with which the student examines it. It is likely that most cells will be in prophase. The number of actively dividing cells at any one time is relatively small.

Did the behaviour of chromosomes in different cells indicate some kind of orderly sequence of events?

c This also depends on the preparation. It is necessary at this stage to establish the idea that the chromosomes divide into ten equal groups during meiosis.

What part could cells with no recognizable chromosomes be playing in the sequence?

d Resting, not dividing.

Count the number of chromosomes in any cells where this is possible. How do your estimates compare with those of the class as a whole?

e It is important for students to realize how difficult it is to get a complete count of chromosomes. It might be a good idea to point out that the correct chromosome complement of man ($2n = 46$, not 48) was established by Tjio and Levan and by Ford and Hamerton as recently as 1956.

Is there any common pattern of behaviour of chromosomes in Tradescantia *and a locust, in spite of their distant relationship?*

f Although the number of chromosomes involved is different the process of meiosis is similar in all species. This is illustrated by the two species studied.

The process of cell division we have been studying is called meiosis. *What function could it serve in the formation of gametes and in the life cycle of the organism?*

g Reduction division. If two sets of chromosomes are put together at fertilization there must be some mechanism for reducing the number which a gamete contributes. The joining together of two sets of chromosomes enables new combinations of inherited material (genes) to be produced. In this way variation is increased. (The importance of variation in evolution could be considered here or left to later chapters.)

Additional practical:
Examination of living testis cells of locust

Preparations such as those suggested in *Laboratory guide (P)* give no idea of the time taken for nuclear division. By using phase contrast equipment it is possible to see meiotic activity for an hour or more in locusts' or grasshoppers' testes, prepared from the living animals and squashed but not stained.

If no phase contrast equipment is available, it is worth while for students to explore the tissue under a variety of conditions of lighting. The best effects are usually obtained by reducing to a minimum the light passing through the substage condenser and by varying the direction and intensity of the illumination from above.

Procedure

1 Make a ring of Vaseline about 5 mm in diameter round a drop of insect saline solution containing a testis follicle. Place a cover-slip over it and press down gently, using pieces of filter paper between the thumb and the cover-slip. This should flatten the follicle sufficiently to make an examination under high power possible.

2 Find cells with some recognizable structure to their nuclei. The structures may not appear distinct. Make a sketch to indicate the relative positions of any light and dark patches and the outlines of the cells in question so that they can be identified later. Note the time.

3 Leave the preparation for fifteen minutes and examine it again, being careful not to move the slide at any time.

4 Make another sketch without referring to the previous one. If no changes have occurred, leave it for another fifteen minutes and try again.

It is not easy for students to make such observations. However through them they can acquire direct evidence about the *rate* of nuclear division. Details of the stages of meiosis are unlikely to be detected.

Restatement of the problem of inheritance

Associated materials
S(P) 2.1, 3.1
S(D) 3.1, 3.2, 3.3, 4.1, 4.2, 4.3, 4.4, 4.5
Film loop 'Removing and exchanging nuclei in Amoeba' NBP–3

Evidence derived from practical investigations should be combined with evidence at second hand.

During discussion, consider the inheritance of both similarities and differences, though it is perhaps simpler and easier to stress the latter when working with less able students.

To avoid confusion, it might be advisable to consider continuous variation separately. It is also best to avoid a too detailed discussion of the influence of the environment. This can be condensed later. Concentrate on the essential features of monohybrid and dihybrid inheritance and their cytological concomitants.

Through the review and discussion of the work of Chapters 1, 2, and 3, students should acquire not only an understanding of the fundamental concepts of genetics. They should also come to appreciate the evolution of genetics during the last hundred years and the complexity and logical beauty of genetics itself. Perhaps they may catch some of the excitement and sense of achievement geneticists have felt during the last twenty years – a period of advance in biology comparable to the advance in mechanics associated with the names of Galileo and Newton in the seventeenth century.

Questions and answers

To what extent are your experimental results consistent with the following assertions? (Take care to avoid jumping to conclusions – some of the assertions are not wholly true.)
1 *Gametes carry inheritable material.*
2 *The zygote carries inheritable material from both parents.*
3 *The zygote carries all the inheritable material that the parents carried.*
4 *The zygote carries about half the inheritable material that the parents carried.*
5 *Chromosomes exist in pairs in most cells of an organism. Members of a pair resemble each other in appearance.*
6 *Gametes carry half the number of chromosomes that is found in most of the cells of an organism. Each member of this half-complement is selected by chance from amongst the chromosomes of the gamete-producing cells in such a way that the gametes contain one member of each chromosome pair.*

a Answers must depend on the experimental results. (*1*) and (*2*) will have been shown to be true. (*3*) will have been shown to be untrue. (*4*), (*5*), and (*6*) will not have been completely substantiated although the evidence acquired points to them being probably true. Note, however, that in *(6)* the half-complement does contain one member of each pair.

What evidence have you for supposing that the inherited material exists as indivisible units?

b The appearance of discontinuously variable characters is of an all-or-none nature.

What part of the behaviour of chromosomes during meiosis could correspond to the segregation of units of inherited material (genes)?

c When the members of chromosome pairs separate.

Account for the genetic constitution of a heterozygote, in terms of chromosomes and allelic genes. Say which evidence comes from your own investigations.

d On each member of a pair of chromosomes there are genes. The genes at corresponding points (loci) on each of the two chromosomes influence the same feature, for example, wing shape, and each could be acting to produce the same wing shape. However, the genes may be different, so that one may be acting to produce a normal wing, the other a vestigial wing. In this case the organism is a *heterozygote* in respect of this character, and the genes at this locus. Heterozygotes when crossed produce typical 3:1 or 1:2:1 ratios of characters in their offspring. The 3:1 ratio of normal wing to vestigial wing *Drosophila* in the F_2 of a monohybrid breeding investigation is an example of this.

Genes which may occupy the same point on a chromosome (and its partner) are said to be *alleles*, or members of an *allelic series*. It is possible for a feature of an organism to be under the influence of many genes, and these need not all be members of one allelic series; indeed, they rarely are. The commonest situation is where a feature (such as eye colour or hair colour in humans and mice) is controlled by members of several allelic series, only two members of each series being present in any particular individual).

We can explain linkage by supposing the linked alleles are on the same chromosome. It has been found that there are generally as many linkage groups as there are pairs of chromosomes. Does this explanation accord with what you deduced about the mechanism of inheritance?

e The deductions drawn from the practical investigations do not provide direct evidence that a chromosome carries a linked group of genes. However, they do not contradict the hypothesis (secondhand evidence can be provided to support it).

Suppose that the sex-linked characters were determined by genes on the same chromosome as those which determine sex. Would this adequately explain the inheritance of sex-linked characters that you have observed?

f In part. The contrast between the sexes will depend essentially on the X chromosomes. Y, in *Drosophila* and man, seems to be almost void.

Additional bibliography

General reading

Barrass, R. (1964) *The locust*. Butterworth.
Darlington, C. D. and La Cour, L. F. (1962) *The handling of chromosomes*. 4th edition. Allen & Unwin.
Duddington, C. L. (1961) *Practical microscopy*. Pitman.
Mackean, D. G. (1968) *Introduction to genetics*. John Murray.
Nuffield O-level Biology (1967) Text and Guide Year V *The perpetuation of life*. Longman/Penguin.
Shaw, G. W. (1959) Modern Science Memoirs No. 40 *Modern cytological techniques*. John Murray.

References

Barker, W. B. (1942) 'Note on meiosis in pollen mother cells.' *Sch. Sci. Rev.*, **92**, 86–89.
Burd, L. H. (1942) 'Note on meiosis in pollen mother cells.' *Sch. Sci. Rev.*, **90**, 227–228.
Savage, J. R. K. (1967) 'Demonstrating cell division with *Tradescantia*.' *Sch. Sci. Rev.*, **48**, 166, 771–782. (Details of chromosomes in pollen tubes.)

Extension work I

Biochemical genetics

Review

This chapter examines the mechanism of inheritance more closely, using biochemical evidence to investigate the events of meiosis and the relationship between genes and biochemical pathways leading to the production of certain phenotypes.

The sequence of topics is as follows:

1 Segregation of alleles for waxy and non-waxy in maize.
2 Tetrad analysis in meiosis of *Sordaria fimicola*.
3 Gene segregation and biochemical effects in *Coprinus lagopus*.
4 Influence of the environment on the expression of a gene in *Aspergillus*.
5 Multiple gene expression in the coat colour of mice.

Assumptions

- An elementary knowledge of probability and the use of a chi-squared test.
- Experience in the use of sterile techniques.
- An understanding of the principles of enzyme action in biosyntheses.
- Sufficient experience of laboratory work to plan the various investigations.
- That enough time is allowed for the experiments to be carried out. Mice breeding programmes usually require a month or more, so they must be started near the beginning of term.

E1.1 Segregation of alleles for waxy and non-waxy in maize

Principles

It is not easy to present, convincingly, direct evidence that heterozygotes produce two kinds of gametes in approximately equal numbers. Nevertheless this is a basic assumption underlying the explanation of Mendelian ratios.

The haploid genotype of maize pollen grains determines the nature of the carbohydrate reserve. Therefore, the distinction between 'waxy' and 'non-waxy' grains can be easily recognized.

Teaching procedure

Associated materials
S(P) 2.1, 2.2, 2.3, 3.1

The practical aspects of this investigation take very little time to complete, provided a stock of hybrid male inflorescences is available. Only one anther is required for each student. The work can probably be done most profitably while the F_2 of other breeding experiments is awaited, or as revision, once a student has realized that an untested assumption is involved in explaining Mendelian ratios.

Practical problems

Faulty scoring is rather common, due to the presence of empty grains which are usually counted as 'waxy'. The difficulties are increased by poor illumination, or if the iodine solution is too strong. Staining takes a few minutes to give the clearest contrast between the blue-black 'non-waxy' grains and the brown 'waxy' ones.

Questions and answers

Do your results support the hypothesis that alleles segregate as you assumed in your explanation of the Drosophila *breeding results? Use the appropriate statistical techniques, combining your results with any others that are available.*

a A chi-squared test is appropriate, and if total scores based on successively larger samples are tested the value of P should increase. Reasons for unusual ratios are:
1 Faulty scoring.
2 Inflorescence of non-hybrid origin.
3 Differential viability of pollen genotypes.

To what extent can you explain in biochemical terms the nature of the dominance and recessiveness of the two characters in this experiment? Compare your explanation with that used in the experiment involving Aspergillus *(E1.4).*

b A simple explanation involves the suggestion that the non-waxy plants have a mechanism (perhaps an enzyme) which promptly converts the 'waxy' material (amylopectin) to starch. Another explanation is that, whenever the mechanism which causes the production of a blue-black staining material is active, the pale brown colour, although present, is obscured, so the heterozygote will not show both characters phenotypically.

E1.2 Tetrad analysis in meiosis of *Sordaria fimicola*

Principles

The evidence presented during the analysis of spore colours in *Sordaria* provides rich material for discussion. Students will not be able to explain the results they obtain unless they have properly understood the sequence of events in meiosis. The evidence from crossing-over suggests the possibility that genetic information is located at particular places on chromatids and leads into a discussion of linkage maps and their construction.

Teaching procedure

Associated materials
S(P) 2.1, 2.2, 2.3, 3.1, 3.2, 3.3, 3.4

If hybrid asci are already available, it is possible to complete the practical aspects of this investigation within an hour.

For some students the operation might form a revision exercise, valuable partly because the results are incomprehensible unless they have properly understood meiosis. For others, the material, set out as a demonstration, could serve to corroborate previous cytological evidence.

If hybrid asci are not already available, it could be a valuable exercise for a student keen on microbiology to set up a cornmeal agar plate with white- and black-spored strains of *Sordaria*. Sterile techniques are desirable but contamination does little harm.

Most students are greatly helped in understanding meiosis by constructing models, made of two or more colours of pipe-cleaners or plastic coated wire. The model is generally sufficient when $2n = 2$ ($n = 1$), which is unrealistic but simple.

It will be necessary to make clear the distinction between the point of crossover and the position of the chiasma which works its way to the ends of the chromatids during the process of terminalization. The region in which portions of the maternal and paternal chromatids have exchanged allegiance does not move at all, once the join has been made. It may also be important to check that students have understood that this investigation can give evidence about the frequency of crossing-over only in the region between the centromere and the locus of the gene which determines colour of spores. There can be no evidence about crossovers in regions distal to the locus or on the opposite side of the centromere.

Practical problems

Plates with hybrid asci can be kept for months in a refrigerator if sealed against desiccation. Students may assume that the spore colour shows through the opaque, black wall of the perithecium. They should be encouraged to examine up to a dozen perithecia from the zone of hybridization before concluding that hybrids are absent. Even in this zone, there will be 'pure line' perithecia, the hyphae not having united in every case. Students should take care to examine the large perithecia because the small ones may be immature, with spores that are not yet fully coloured.

Questions and answers

Explain why the many asci which have both white and black spores are usually like (c) *and* (d) *in figure 22. Why are they unlikely to resemble* (e), (f), (g), *and* (h)?

a The displays in (*c*) and (*d*) of figure 22 of *Laboratory guide (P)* arise when there is no crossover between the centromere and the locus. (There could be crossing-over distal to the locus, or on the opposite arms.) The fact that (*c*) and (*d*) are present in equal numbers suggests that the maternal and paternal centromeres are equally likely to go to each pole of the ascus.

Did you find any asci with an arrangement unlike (c) *and* (d)*? Can you explain your findings? (Remember the possibility of chiasma formation during the first meiotic prophase.)*

b If a crossover has occurred between the centromere and the locus, then one of the displays in (*e*), (*f*), (*g*), or (*h*) will result. It is to be expected that these four categories will be in approximately equal numbers and a chi-squared test can be applied before making deductions. The fraction

$$\frac{e+f+g+h}{b+c+d+e+f+g+h}$$

gives a measure of the frequency with which crossovers occur in the region between the centromere and the locus. If we were to assume that crossing-over is equally likely to occur in each small part of the chromatids, and only once in each meiosis, then the fraction gives an estimate of the distance between the locus and the centromere, in terms of the length of the chromatid. Perhaps the majority of students who embark on this work may appreciate that the value obtained from the fraction

$$\frac{e+f+g+h}{b+c+d+e+f+g+h}$$

could be halved to take account of the fact that, even when a crossover has occurred, half the progeny will nevertheless be like their parents. This is because the other chromatids in the bivalent are not involved in crossing-over. The value can be multiplied by 100 to give a figure for the length of the chromatid between the centromere and the locus as a percentage of the total length.

In fact, it seems possible that crossovers may involve any member of the two pairs of chromatids in a bivalent, that each may form a chiasma with any other, and that two chiasmata might involve three different chromatids.

E1.3 Gene segregation and biochemical effects in *Coprinus lagopus*

Principles

Coprinus has been chosen because of the range of phenomena which can be studied through using its mutants. It is relatively easy to cultivate and its generation time is not much greater than that of *Drosophila*.

The main themes which students can explore through the suggested practical investigations and associated reading are:

1 The idea of mating types – These are genetically distinct variants corresponding to sexes and thus promoting outbreeding. An investigation of mating types might lead into the topic of physiological, anatomical, and behavioural mechanisms which promote outbreeding, also the corresponding mechanism for inbreeding. It will be necessary to discuss the advantages and disadvantages of in- and outbreeding in terms of the amount of variation and variability to which each might give rise. If there has been no other opportunity, it might be a good idea to lead from such a discussion into the topic of vegetative reproduction and its genetic and ecological implications.

2 *Segregation*–The determinants of mating-type characters can be traced through analysis of the quartet of basidiospores. These spores can sometimes be picked from a basidium and grown separately on agar, so that the experiment can determine the mating type of the resultant mycelium by testing against known genotypes.

3 *Gene complementation*–The example suggested is a simple one, in which a haploid strain deficient in the ability to make adenine is mated to produce an effectively diploid organism by union with a different haploid strain–one which lacks the ability to make para-amino-benzoic acid. The investigation leads well into a discussion of the biochemistry of the action of genes.

4 *Biosynthetic pathways*–by which, for instance, a complex organic substance may be constructed by stepwise alterations of a simpler one.

5 *The idea of a vitamin*–seen from a biochemical and genetical point of view.

6 *A biochemical basis for the occurrence of dominance*–If an allele were responsible for the production of an essential enzyme, then it is reasonable to assume that such an allele might be dominant to one that failed to lead to the production of that enzyme.

Teaching procedure

Associated materials
S(P) 2.1, 2.2, 2.3
S(D) 5.5

Students would be well advised to read around the topics thoroughly before commencing the practical investigations since, unless they understand these, many days' work may easily be lost. On the other hand, there will certainly be those for whom the series of investigations may present an appealing challenge which would be spoiled by overmuch reading. The technique of collecting spores from the gills is not easy.

Practical problems

1 Sterile techniques are necessary, not so much to ensure freedom from bacterial infection, as to contaminate the laboratory as little as possible with spores and fragments which may confuse later workers. The entry of wild type *Coprinus* propagules into experimental cultures can vitiate a long-term programme.

2 Students can be helped to recognize the difference between monokaryon and dikaryon colonies if plates of each are kept as sealed cultures in a refrigerator, or through preliminary work before the full-scale experimentation is started.

3 Ordinary daylight is necessary for the growth of fruiting bodies. Otherwise, the cultures may be kept in an incubator. Stocks can be stored in a refrigerator at 4° C for many months.
4 Many students will have difficulty in using the very fine, pointed needles to remove the four tiny basidiospores from a gill surface. An alternative method is as follows:
Lay the gill flat on the surface of a slide in the lower half of a Petri dish. Place nearby a few crystals of silica gel to desiccate the gill. Cover and leave overnight. Stroke the gill when it is dry with the smooth end of a glass rod. This causes the tetrads of sticky spores to spring clear of the gill onto the slide, where they can be picked up and separated under a stereomicroscope, using the fine needles.

There are several common species of *Coprinus* and despite the composition of the recommended culture medium, it is not true that *Coprinus* is mostly found near dung.
Clamp connections are seen best in the thick, young hyphae near the margin of a growing colony. After a while they disintegrate and the hyphal thread becomes slender. Oidia are only rarely encountered.
As a result of the investigation of mating types (Section B) it is to be expected that the results will be as follows:

Code name	$A_5\,B_5$	$A_5\,B_6$	$A_6\,B_5$	$A_6\,B_6$
$A_6\,B_6$	much	none	none	none
$A_6\,B_5$	none	much	none	
$A_5\,B_6$	none	none		
A_5B_5	none			

The *chol-1* mutant lacks the enzyme which converts monomethyl ethanolamine to dimethyl ethanolamine. The *chol-2* mutant lacks the enzyme which converts the latter to trimethyl ethanolamine (choline). Growth is therefore to be expected as shown in Table 1.

Variant	Medium					
	Complete	Minimal	Minimal + ethanolamine	Minimal + monomethyl ethanolamine	Minimal + dimethyl ethanolamine	Minimal + trimethyl ethanolamine (choline)
Wild type	much	much	much	much	much	much
Chol-1	much	none	none	some often occurs, though not expected	much	much
Chol-2	much	none	none	none	none	much

Table 1

It should, perhaps, be emphasized that there are, in the wild (and in culture collections), a large number of mating types. The allelic series at the loci A and B are both large, amounting to a score or more forms for each locus.

The culture conditions for identifying the mutants referred to in Section D are complete media except for the absence of the compound in question. Since it is usual to work with so-called 'minimal' media, they can be described as 'minimal plus adenine' and 'minimal plus para-amino-benzoic acid'.

The *chol-1* and *chol-2* mutants (also the *ad* and *paba-1* strains) must, of course, be of different mating types. Otherwise the fusion upon which the experiment depends will not occur.

Quite often it is found that the mutants grow unexpectedly well. Such forms are said to be 'leaky' and their performance is due, not so much to the inadequacy of the medium, as to the fact that alternative pathways may exist within the organism which permit the production of vital compounds such as choline. If the media are not completely devoid of the appropriate intermediate compounds, then growth will occur to an unexpected degree.

Incubation temperatures are given in *Laboratory guide (P)* as a standard 30° C. However, it may be best to vary this where administratively possible. For mating strain investigations, use 37° C. For work on *ad* and *paba-1* strains and on choline mutants, use 30° C.

It may be noted in passing that many experiments in microbiological genetics can be run at room temperatures with no hindrance, except that development is slower. If life cycles are not completed, or if the expected results are not obtained, then it would be wise to revert to the recommended temperatures.

Questions and answers

What general deductions can you make concerning the interactions between the so-called mating types in Coprinus?

a Taking the labels of the mating types at their face value, there appear to be two sets of variables: the two genes and the allelic forms of each. Unless the contributing haploid parents are different at both loci, a dikaryon cannot be formed. If the parents have a common allele, monokaryotic growth is all that can be expected, and no fruiting body. Dikaryotic growth appears only from the matings $A_6B_6 \times A_5B_5$ and $A_5B_6 \times A_6B_5$.

What light do your experiments with Coprinus *throw on the nature of gene action and the inheritance of non-allelic nutritional deficiencies?*

b Gene action can be explained, in part at least, in biochemical terms. The details which students can be expected to give will depend upon how far they have experimented and read around the topic. The question could be answered in essay form.

In what circumstances could adenine play the part of a vitamin in Coprinus? *What advantage in normal circumstances would the wild type* Coprinus *have over the* paba-1 *mutant?*

c Adenine will count as a vitamin for any variant that cannot make it. The wild type is at an advantage over the *paba-1* mutant whenever para-amino-benzoic acid is in short supply.

Would you expect the character chol-1 *to be dominant or recessive to the wild type? Give the reasons for your answer.*

d Recessive, since a single allele (*chol-1*) which led to the production of no enzyme would have its influence subordinated to the effect of the wild type allele. The latter would lead to the production of the enzyme and hence the viability of the heterozygote would be assured at a level comparable to that of the wild type homozygote.

From your experience with Coprinus, *say what is meant by 'gene complementation'?*

e Genes act together. Unless the allelic constitution (genotype) is complementary, the organism will not grow or exhibit a particular character. This is a very simplified form of the concept. It should be possible for a student to understand at least that it may be necessary for two or more genes to exist in particular allelic forms in order that a particular character shall be manifested.

Section E (choline biosynthesis) provides a better example of complementation than Section D because it is concerned with one feature, the ability to produce choline. Section D is concerned with only two out of the numerous genes which must complement each other to make an organism viable.

E1.4 Influence of the environment on the expression of a gene in *Aspergillus*

Principles

The reaction of the fungus to mineral variations is so sensitive and specific that it is used to detect, and even assay, deficiencies in soils. This has important economic implications since some animal and plant diseases are due to absence or shortage of trace elements obtained from the soil at first- or secondhand. For example, boron deficiency leads to 'heart rot' in mangolds and sugar beet, while cobalt deficiency causes 'pining sickness' in sheep. For *Aspergillus niger* magnesium is generally required at the comparatively high rate of 200 μg per 50 cm^3 of culture medium, the deficiency signs being the retarding of mycelial growth and pale brown spores instead of black ones.

Teaching procedure

Associated materials
S(P) 2.1, 2.2, 2.3, 3.4
S(D) 5.1

This investigation can be used to lead to more wide-ranging discussion of the extent to which the environment may influence the expression of inherited characteristics. Such an approach can help to correct any idea that the genotype is all-important.

Questions and answers

What differences in spore colour were visible?

a Brown spores are expected to occur on a medium deficient in magnesium, in contrast to the usual black spores.

To what extent were these differences attributable to the influence of magnesium?

b On the assumption that the plates were made up correctly, magnesium must be implicated. An alternative suggestion arises from the fact that the medium deficient in magnesium lacks some sulphate, by comparison with the full medium. Students might suggest how this idea could be tested.

Would you say that the variations you observed were genotypic or phenotypic, or both? How would you test the validity of your views?

c Most probably phenotypic. Replicate, using material from one stock culture. Results should confirm that the variation persists even though the genotype is uniform.

Compare your findings in Aspergillus *with any others of a similar kind that you have encountered elsewhere. What are the requirements for describing adequately the expression of a particular gene?*

d It is sometimes necessary to specify the environment in which a gene is acting before the effects of the gene can be stated simply. This leads on to the next investigations, using mice.

E1.5 Multiple gene expression in the coat colour of mice

Teaching procedure

Associated materials
S(P) 2.1, 2.2, 2.3
S(D) 5.2, 5.3, 5.4

The programme, which need not be undertaken as a whole, can lead to a much fuller understanding of the action and interaction of genes. It is essentially a long-term undertaking unless a number of students can combine their efforts. Students should not begin the work of this investigation until planning is complete and it is realized how much work is involved. The demands on equipment may be greater than is customary, even at sixth form level, and it is best to check supplies and costs in advance.

It will, of course, be necessary to ensure that adequate care and attention can be given to the mice during the holidays and in cold or very hot weather.

The work can be greatly eased if the programme is taken in stages, and the results (records and pelts or corpses) are kept for reference by subsequent classes.

Questions and answers

What differences are there between the heterozygotes in F_1 and the homozygous agouti (AA)? Continue your observations until the coat colour is fully developed – at about the fourteenth day.

a Agouti (A) is the wild type, with a^t producing a glossy black back and a tan coloured belly.

Dominance is incomplete, so the heterozygotes show a mixture of parental characters: the hairs on the back are black near the base and pale near the tips, whereas the belly hairs are cream or tan.

What results were you expecting? Give reasons. Did the results obtained deviate from expectation? If so, can you explain why?

b

Genotype	Body colour	Eye colour
cc	white	pink
c^ec^e	pale coffee	black
c^ec	white	black

Table 2

From Table 2 it will be seen that eye colour and body colour behave unexpectedly in the heterozygote – it might have been expected that, if white body colour were recessive, pink eye colour would also be. In fact it is dominant, a useful reminder of the distinction between a character and its determinant.

Combine your results with any other comparable ones. Do they raise any doubts about the existence of a 3:1 ratio in the F_2?

c See above.

What change in your ideas about dominance and recessiveness is necessitated by these experiments?

d See above.

Combine your results with any other comparable ones available. Is there any evidence of a 2:1 ratio? Is there any justification for expecting this ratio?

e It will be an advantage to have plenty of progeny for this cross, since the 2:1 ratio (which arises because A^yA^y dies *in utero*) would not otherwise be distinguishable from a 3:1 ratio. A chi-squared test is appropriate, provided there are sufficient progeny to make the number expected in the smallest category more than five.

What component of the F_1 is absent? Can you explain its absence?

f See above.

Does the sex of the living progeny at birth have any bearing on the results? Could there be a differential viability? Dissect a weak male and a healthy female and report on your findings.

g Dissection reveals kidney abnormalities – far more frequently in the male. Thus it may be seen that the se gene is affecting more than one system – an example of pleiotropy as well as sex-limitation.

Pg 39 Recomb + variation

Pg 45 Squad

Restatement of problem of inheritance

Then 46

Agouti = + black back + tan belly

Dominance incomplete

→ hairs one back = black near base
Pale near tips

Belly cream/tan

STAFF CIRCULAR

Week beginning Monday, May 20th 1985

Monday	May 20th	City & Guilds Exams begin.
Tuesday	May 21st	Cambridge Exams begin
Wednesday	May 22nd	London Exams begin
Thursday	May 23rd	
Friday	May 24th	Last C.S.E. Written Paper. Official Leaving Date for 5th Year.

Half-Term: 27th May to 31st May

** ** ** ** ** ** ** ** ** **

New Appointments

Mr. J. Thomas and Mr. J. Gee will be joining the staff in September to teach P.E. and Geography respectively.

H.M.

Mini-Bus Driving Test

There will be a Mini-Bus Driving Test on Wednesday, May 22nd from 9.30.a.m.- until 12.00. noon.

9.30.a.m.	–	Mr. Fee
10.00.a.m.	–	Mr. Jervis
10.30.a.m.	–	Mr. Fluskey
11.00.a.m.	–	Mr. J. Bell
11.30.a.m.	–	Mrs. Cozens

C.P.V.E. Course

This will continue on Wednesday May 22nd.

H.M.

Staff Absences

Mrs.Miles	-	All week
Mr. Austin	-	Wednesday
Mr. Walsh	-	Friday
Mr. Jervis	-	Friday.

E.A.B.

Examination Clashes

Individual candidates have been informed as to the procedure regarding clashes of subjects, and instructions will be left for Invigilators concerned. It is essential that absolute security is maintained and candidates involved in clashes must not be left unsupervised under any circumstance.

E.A.W.

It may be helpful if students score separately for coat colour and ear character, since the combining of two 3:1 ratios will then give 9:3:3:1.

Additional bibliography

General reading

Darlington, C. D. and Bradshaw, A. D. (Eds.) (1966) *Teaching genetics*. Oliver & Boyd.

Gruneberg, H. (1957) Medical Research Council Memorandum 33. 'An annotated catalogue of the mutant genes of the house mouse.' H.M.S.O.

Michie, D. and McLaren, A. (1955) 'The importance of being cross bred.' New Biology, **19**, 48–69. Penguin.

Whitehouse, H. L. K. (1969) *Towards an understanding of the mechanism of heredity*. Arnold. (Contains a good glossary.)

References

King, R. C. (1968) *A dictionary of genetics*. Oxford University Press. (A valuable guide to terminology.)

Lange, M. and Hora, F. B. (1968) *Collins guide to mushrooms and toadstools*. Collins.

Wallace, M. E. (1965) 'Using mice for teaching genetics' Parts I and II. *Sch. Sci. Rev.*, **160**, 646–658, and **161**, 39–52. (Keeping mice, genetics of coat colour with photographs, chromosomes.)

Chapter 4

Population genetics and selection

Chapter review

This chapter introduces the idea of a gene pool together with an investigation into some of the influences which determine its composition. It also includes the concept of polymorphism as a subsidiary theme. This leads to a study of mechanisms of selection and some consequences in human and other populations. The genetic make-up of populations is seen to be the outcome of interactions between organisms and their environment.

The sequence of topics is:

1 Genes in laboratory populations.
2 Models of a gene pool.
3 Distribution of cyanogenesis in a white clover population.
4 Slugs as biotic selective agents on clover.
5 Frost as a physical selective agent on clover.
– The concept of polymorphism.

Assumption

– Knowledge of previous chapters.

4.1 Genes in laboratory populations (preliminary)

Principles

If selection acts on *inheritable* variation, then the consequences extend beyond the time scale of a single generation. Its action will promote either change or stability, but which of these actually occurs depends upon the extent to which the population concerned is adapted to its existing environment.

There is bound to be an element of insensitivity in the action of selection because:

1 It can act only in existing environmental conditions. Yet the future holds the key to the eventual survival of a species or population.

2 Selection acts on the phenotype and not directly on the genotype, yet it is the latter which persists.
3 Chance plays a part in survival, especially in small populations.

Teaching procedure

Associated materials
S(P) 2.1, 4.1, 4.4, 4.7, 5.1, 6.1
S(D) 6.1
Film loop 'Handling *Drosophila*' NBP–70
Film loop 'Mating behaviour of *Drosophila*' NBP–53

Since the population chambers will have been set up for only a few weeks at the most, results will not be forthcoming for some time, so students will have to rely temporarily upon secondhand data from *Study guide (P)*. The population chambers are not difficult to keep from year to year, so in future there may be little need to set up new ones.

Questions and answers

Have the Drosophila *populations changed in their constitution, judging by the appearance (phenotypes) of their members?*

a Yes, if the F_1 has emerged.

It is possible to say how far the populations have changed in genetic *constitution?*

b Students will need to view the consequences of cross-breeding at the population level, rather than to interpret the results of crosses between identifiable parents. Classical genetics deals with very unreal situations so far as the field naturalist is concerned. Unless they were already familiar with this topic, students would not be able to say, at this stage, to what extent the populations had changed in genetic constitution.

4.2 Models of a gene pool (preliminary)

Principles

The Hardy-Weinberg mathematical model provides a valuable means of determining the genetic constitution of a population in terms of gene-frequency. Pupils are sometimes put off by the quantitive reasoning involved, but this is not really difficult and is set out in detail in *Laboratory guide (P)*. Coloured beads will prove invaluable in simulating the breeding of populations and, also, situations involving selection.

Teaching procedure

Associated materials
S(P) 2.1, 4.1, 4.2, 4.3, 4.4, 4.7, 9.3

Experiments in selection with beads tend to take rather a long time; fifteen generations of 'breeding' take about an hour. Therefore, it may be advisable to curtail the experiment somewhat, if only to avoid boredom. Frequently, five generations will be enough to indicate clearly the trend of results. A sound understanding of the Hardy-Weinberg principle is essential if pupils are to appreciate the basis of population genetics. They should be aware, too, of the limitations to its application.

Questions and answers

What is the effect on the proportion of the phenotypes and on the gene frequency of vg, of selecting against the homozygous recessives by removing 20 per cent of them at each generation?

If you continued selecting at this rate for some generations, would the vg gene eventually be completely eliminated from the population?

a and *b* The result will depend on the number of generations of breeding. The point that emerges is that while the frequency of the vg gene is progressively reduced, it will never be totally eliminated on account of its presence in the heterozygous state.

4.3 Distribution of cyanogenesis in a white clover population

Principles

The story of cyanogenesis in *Trifolium* is not yet understood in full. Perhaps the easiest account to consult is that of Pusey in Darlington and Bradshaw (1966). His standardized technique of testing for hydrogen cyanide is rather elaborate and students are provided here with a simpler version.

T. repens is an allotetraploid behaving as a diploid. The use of the symbols G, g, E, and e for both phenotypes and genotypes should be noted. A more complicated system would be more correct, but clumsy. Genes of several allelic series appear to be involved in the production of substrate.

Teaching procedure

Associated materials
S(P) 2.1, 4.7

Students could use either a set of 30 local wild plants or the same number of cultivated plants, in multipots. They could work either as a class or in groups, each with 30 plants. The plants must be tested to discover which are cyanogenic and which are not. They can then be subjected to the selective action of either slugs or frost. The results can be compared with the distribution of the genes in Europe. Populations are evidently adapted to their environments. From this point, discussions can move to the wider issues of population genetics in the final sections of the chapter.

Practical problems

The genetic constitution of clover populations near schools may be much influenced by the presence of various cultivars that are often sown in nearby fields. It is therefore advisable either to purchase stock or to obtain the plants from truly rural situations.

Questions and answers

What reasons can you suggest for the existence of two sorts of clover plants – acyanogenic and cyanogenic?

a Students may think of a variety of agencies which can act selectively. They might also suggest mutation.

Sometimes clover plants in lawns are nibbled by slugs or snails. Have you any evidence that they nibble the acyanogenic plants more than the cyanogenic ones?

b To be answered according to experimental results.

4.4 Slugs as biotic selective agents on clover

By feeding on plants, animals (a factor of the biotic environment) can act as selective agents favouring the evolution of plants possessing certain genes.

Teaching procedure

Associated materials
S(M) 1.4, 1.5
S(P) 1.4, 2.1, 2.3, 4.1, 4.4, 4.5, 4.6, 5.2, 6.2, 9.2, 9.3
S(D) 5.5

The cyanogenic properties of clover are confined to the leaf, which is surprising considering how often slugs can be seen severing leaves by chewing at the petioles. Hence the source of the practical problem. Students should be encouraged to devise their own style of investigation, but they may not anticipate the difficulty in scoring predation. Quite often the cyanogenic plant is found with the petiole nibbled; the leaf may then wilt and fall to the ground. As a result the enzyme and the substrate effectively come together, hydrogen cyanide is formed, and thereafter the leaf is left alone by the slugs. After a few hours the substrate is used up and the leaf becomes edible. Slugs sometimes reject a particular acyanogenic plant. The basis of this food choice is not known. The following procedure, for testing the clover populations and observing the effect of slug or snail predation, could be recommended to weaker students:

1 Obtain about 30 *young* clover plants with about 6–10 leaves per plant. These could be grown for about two weeks in multipots from New Zealand Certified Permanent Pasture seed (see figure 15). Keep well watered, thinning to one plant per pot as soon as two seedlings appear. Multipot trays must be kept level to ensure uniform irrigation.

2 Test all the plants for cyanogenesis and use a simple marking system to record their characteristics. Count the leaves left on each plant.

3 Put the plants in a large plastic bag and add a dozen fairly hungry slugs. The grey slug, *Agriolimax reticulatus*, which is common in gardens and produces a milky mucus, is satisfactory. Most other slugs and snails will do equally well.

4 Blow up the bag, tie it firmly, and leave it overnight.

5 Observe it as often as circumstances permit. This precaution helps to overcome the difficulty of detecting the eating of cyanogenic leaves after they have lain for a few hours.

6 Score the leaves eaten. It is advisable to use young plants as they have fewer leaves to count.

7 Often there is a clear cut result, but sometimes the distinction between cyanogenic and acyanogenic plants is less obvious. A χ^2 test may be necessary. Much depends upon the proportion of slugs to food, the duration of feeding, and the appetite of the animals. The role of cyanogenesis in promoting selective feeding is still the subject of research.

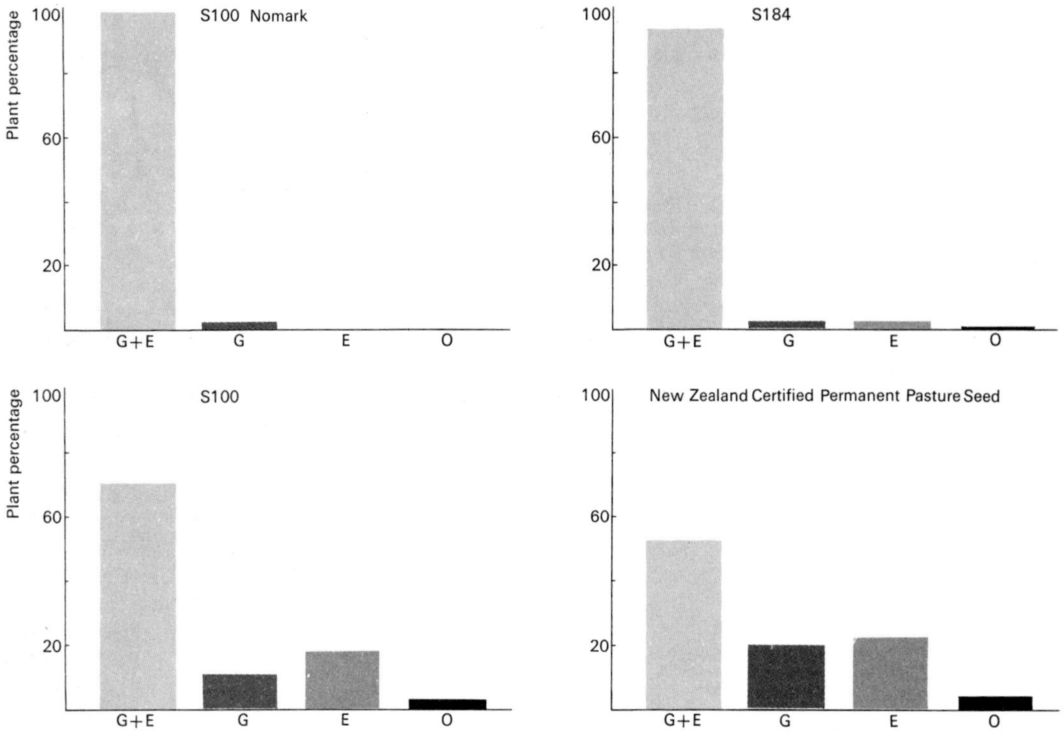

Figure 15
Frequencies of phenotypes in commercial strains of white clover (*Trifolium repens*).

4.5 Frost as a physical selective agent on clover

Principles

Factors in the physical environment can act as selective agents. The role of frost in favouring acyanogenic forms of clover has been established.

The precise action which frosting has on clover leaves is not known. It has been observed, however, that after a period of frosting, only the cyanogenic leaves become dark in colour and look wilted.

Teaching procedure

Associated materials
S(M) 1.4, 1.5
S(P) 1.4, 2.1, 2.3, 4.1, 4.4, 4.5, 4.6, 5.2, 6.2, 9.2, 9.3

Trials of this investigation suggest that only half an hour of frosting is necessary in the freezing compartment of a domestic refrigerator. Avoid temperatures below about $-1°$ C. The leaves do not appear to respond much during the treatment but evidently the enzyme is inhibited by low temperature. After a few hours at room temperature, a difference between the two sorts of leaves becomes apparent and it is easy to detect the release of hydrogen cyanide. Table 1 suggests a method of tabulating results.

Plants \ Treatment	4° C	0° C
Cyanogenic		
Acyanogenic		

Table 1
For recording the results of experiment in frosting. (Enter in each rectangle whether hydrogen cyanide was released.)

Figure 16 shows a suitable apparatus for investigating the effects of temperature on cyanogenic and acyanogenic forms of clover.

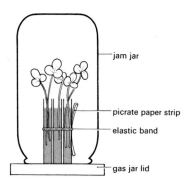

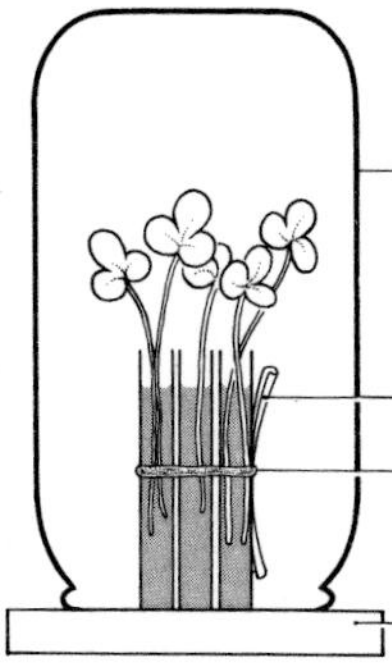

Figure 16
Apparatus for investigating the effects of temperature on clover.

Questions and answers

From the evidence available, how far can you explain why it is an advantage to white clover to be acyanogenic in one part of its geographical range and cyanogenic in another?

a There are at least some indications that, in regions where there is much frost, the acyanogenic forms are favoured. In places where there are slugs, the cyanogenic forms are at an advantage.

Suppose you were studying a small population of plants covering, say, 25 square metres, to what extent would the findings from the three previous investigations (4.3 to 4.5) enable you to calculate the gene frequency of G (gene for substrate present) and E (gene for enzyme present)?

b In the circumstances, we should be dealing with a typical Hardy-Weinberg population – one which was effectively circumscribed with no organisms being added or removed. We should therefore be justified in calculating the frequency of genes G and E from the data obtained previously (see 4.2).

The concept of polymorphism

Associated materials
S(P) 1.1, 1.7, 2.1, 2.2, 4.5, 4.6, 4.7, 9.2, 9.3

Polymorphic forms of plants and animals provide particularly good material for the study of selection, partly because the different phenotypes are usually easily discernible and also because the balance between them is often rather sensitive, and therefore responds rapidly to changes in environmental conditions. Much of the modern work on selection and evolution has been based on polymorphic species such as snails, insects, and, of course, man.

Laboratory guide (P) gives a definition of polymorphism so that students will not confuse this with the occurrence of rare variations such as haemophilia in man, which are almost certainly maintained by recurrent mutation. For a species to be polymorphic, the rarest form must exist at a level above what is judged to be a normal mutation rate. In a changing environment such as the Industrial Revolution brought about, when the countryside became progressively more polluted, polymorphic forms such as the peppered moth, *Biston betularia*, adjusted rapidly and the balance between the black (melanic) and typical forms must have been constantly changing. Such a condition of *transient polymorphism* contrasts with a situation when a species has struck an equilibrium with a more or less stable (or only slowly changing) environment. We can describe this as a *balanced polymorphism*, such as occurs today in the human A, B, O blood groups.

Cyanogenesis in clover provides a good example of balanced polymorphism. Other examples that could be introduced here are the A, B, O blood groups in man, sickle cell anaemia in man, industrial melanism in a wide range of moths including the peppered moth, and shell patterns and background colour in snails of the genus *Cepaea*.

In flax there is a similar polymorphism to that in clover, the cyanogenic roots releasing hydrogen cyanide into the atmosphere, thereby reducing the chances of infection by soil nematodes.

Additional bibliography

General reading

Darlington, C. D. and Bradshaw, A. D. (Eds.) (1966) *Teaching genetics.* Oliver & Boyd. (Cyanogenesis in *Trifolium repens.*)
Ford, E. B. (1945) New Naturalist Library. *Butterflies.* Collins. (Genes in natural populations.)
Ford, E. B. (1955) New Naturalist Library. *Moths.* Collins. (Genes in natural populations.)
Ford, E. B. (1964) *Ecological genetics.* Methuen. (Experimental studies of selection in polymorphic species.)
Harrison, G. A. *et al* (1964) *Human biology; an introduction to human evolution, variation and growth.* Oxford University Press.
Nuffield O-level Biology (1967) Text and Guide Year V *The perpetuation of life.* Longmans/Penguin. (Elementary models of selection in populations using beads.)
Peters, J. A. (Ed.) (1959) *Classic papers in genetics.* Prentice-Hall. (Includes original 'Hardy-Weinberg' paper.)
Smith, J. M. (1958) *The theory of evolution.* Penguin.

References

Berry, R. J. (1967) 'Genetical changes in mice and men.' *Eugenics Review*, **59**, 78–96.
Daday, H. (1954) 'Gene frequencies in wild populations of *Trifolium repens*.' *Heredity*, **8**, 61–78.
Demaine, C. (1964) 'Genetics in a school population.' *Biology and Human Affairs*, **29**, 2.
Haldane, J. B. S. (1955) 'Population genetics.' *New Biology*, **18**, 34–51. Penguin.
Karn, M. N. and Penrose, L. S. (1951) 'Birth weight and gestation time in relation to maternal age, parity and infant survival.' *Ann. Eugen.*, **16**, 147–164.

Chapter 5

Population dynamics

Chapter review

In this chapter, emphasis shifts from the genetic aspects of individuals and populations towards a more ecological approach.

The sequence of topics is as follows:

1 Growth of a population of yeast. This illustrates the way in which numbers can increase exponentially under favourable conditions.

2 Population dynamics in a plant community. Examples are grass and clover, which was investigated earlier (L(P) 1.5) in another context.

Assumptions

- A knowledge of sterile techniques for the handling of micro-organisms, such as will already have been used if students have performed the work of L(P) 2.
- That the work of L(P) 1.5 precedes L(P) 5.1 by at least three weeks.

5.1 Growth of a population of yeast

Principles

The yeast population usually grows well and will provide ample data for class work. The chief factor governing growth is food, supplied in bulk at the beginning. Most wild populations use a *continuing* supply of food so some caution must be exercised in regarding the yeast population as an entirely adequate model.

The investigation allows a strictly quantitative assessment of the rate of growth of a population, and demonstrates one influence (food) which must be taken into account in any explanation of the composition and structure of a community. It also introduces a thread into the argument for the theory of evolution by natural selection – the pressure which populations may exert on each other when a resource (such as light or food) is in short supply. This aspect, together with intra-specific competition, need not be emphasized unduly in this chapter as they are stressed later, when their relevance will be more apparent.

Schizosaccharomyces pombe has been chosen in preference to *S. cerevisiae* because the cells are larger and the presence of an obvious and rapidly formed cell plate is a reliable index of cell division. Another advantage of *S. pombe* is that it does not produce buds, which tend to complicate counting, and also, its cultures are usually devoid of dead cells and debris. If *S. pombe* is not available, *S. cerevisiae* will serve as second best.

The time between one cell division and the next is termed the *generation time* and its relationship to temperature is given in figure 17. Figure 18 shows typical growth curve for *S. pombe*.

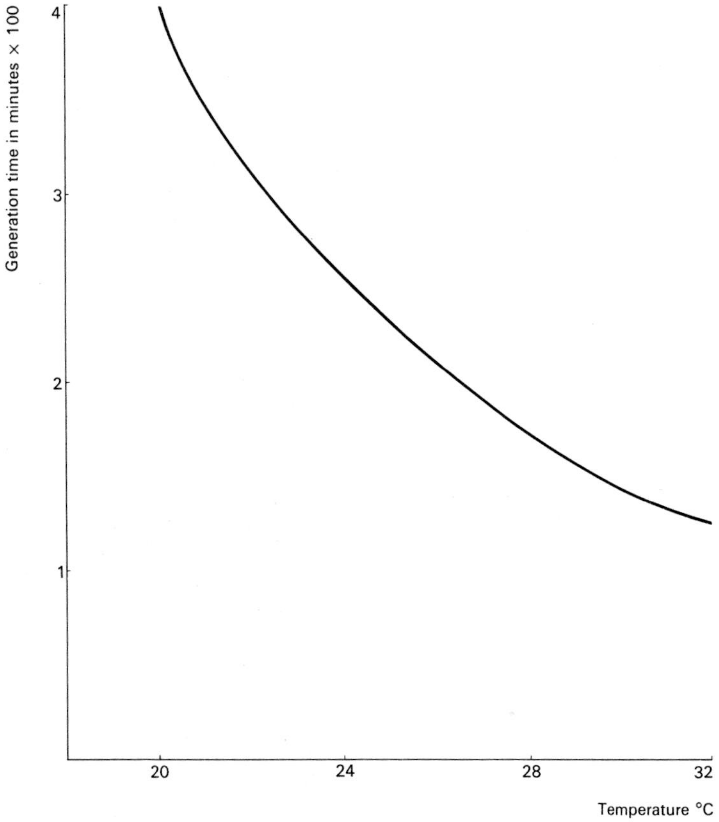

Figure 17
The relationship between generation time and temperature in yeast. *After Gill, B. F. (1965) Ph.D. thesis, University of Edinburgh.*

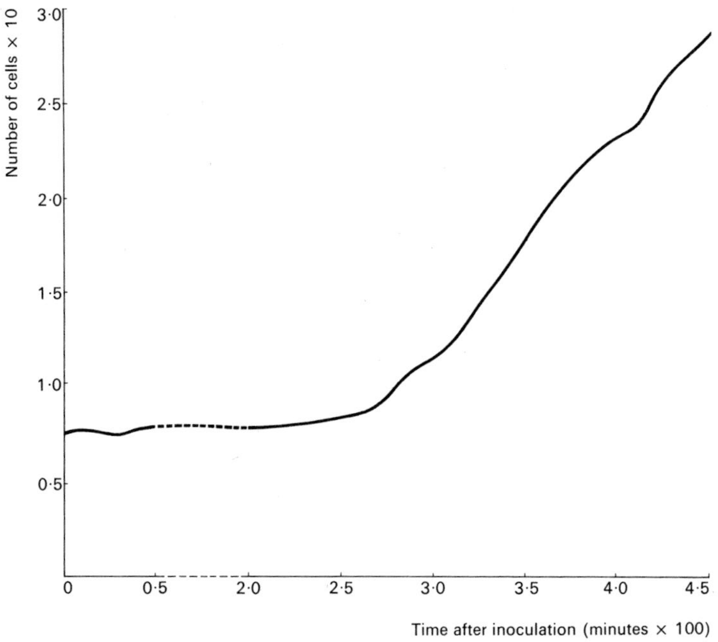

Figure 18
Growth of a population of *Schizo-saccharomyces pombe* following inoculation of fresh growth medium with resting phase cells. *After Gill, B. F. (1965) Ph.D. thesis, University of Edinburgh.*

Teaching procedure

Associated materials
S(M) 1.4, 1.5, 8.4
S(P) 5.1, 5.2, 5.3, 5.5, 5.6, 5.7
S(D) 2.1
Film loop 'Inoculation with a loop' NBP–48
Film loop 'The control of bacteria in food' NBP–67

It is necessary to take care in arranging a timetable lest important phases of growth of population occur when they cannot be observed. There may be some difficulty, since growth lasts for about 30–40 hours. Growth can be inhibited temporarily by keeping cultures in a refrigerator (not a deep freeze). This makes it possible to regulate the periods of growth to fit in with the students' timetable.

Clear evidence of logarithmic growth can be expected. The mathematical aspects of this are discussed in some detail in *Laboratory guide (P)* and *Study guide (P)*.

Students may suggest that the formation of alcohol could play a part in controlling growth of population. They can test this by adding alcohol to fresh cultures. The following facts are a guide to such an investigation.
1 *S. pombe* can tolerate 5 per cent ethanol in the culture medium, and this is a higher concentration than will ever be generated.
2 Most laboratory stocks of ethanol contain a poisonous impurity, so it is necessary to use Analar grade. This is expensive.

Those who wish to discover which component in the food mixture is most important could make up the medium with the individual components in varied concentrations. For its composition, they should consult the manufacturer's handbook. It seems likely that one of the carbohydrates is important, but this is not known for certain. The quantities of vitamins needed cannot be tested with ordinary school facilities.

Practical problems

The yeast cells are apt to enter a 'resting' stage when subjected to a change in environmental conditions such as temperature or pH, and when food supply becomes exhausted. Growth will only begin again after a period of about four hours. It is only possible to detect the resting phase by eye if the yeast is treated with toluidene blue, which is taken up only by active cells.

Generation times can be read off from the graph (figure 17), and it is worth while considering which temperature may suit the school timetable best. Choose a day when students are free to return frequently to make cell counts and when there is suitable time to prepare the stock culture. They can build up a composite picture of growth of population by running two sets of cultures, started at different times; one would show the first phase of growth, the other the second.

It is wise to have a rehearsal of the critical parts of the operation before committing the whole class.

Possible sources of difficulty are:
1 That students may not be familiar with haemocytometers and the appearance of *S. pombe*. Preliminary practice with both is essential. A useful teaching device, consisting of clear plastic overlays which simulate the appearance of a haemocytometer grid and a suspension of cells, is sold with the Teachers' Supplement to the BSCS Laboratory Block, *Microbes: their growth, nutrition and interaction*.
2 That the stock culture may enter the resting phase at a crucial moment. It is therefore desirable to have replicate stock cultures.
3 Failure to prevent temperature shock. A change of 2 degrees Centrigrade can be sufficient to delay the start of population growth by about four hours.

An alternative programme
1 During the early part of the day, add extra medium to an active stock culture to ensure that it is in the log phase of growth by afternoon.
2 During the afternoon prepare to set up the experimental cultures. Start half of these (half have double strength medium) as late as possible, allowing time for one one cell count before the end of school.

3 Late in the evening, or early the next day, prime another stock culture so that it is certain to be in the log phase four hours later, when the second half of the experimental cultures can be started.
4 Throughout this day make as many counts as is convenient on all the experimental cultures.

Growth of the cultures can be arrested by adding a drop of formalin. This offers an alternative solution to the difficult problems of timetabling, since it is a simple operation to add a drop of fluid, and counting can be done later.

The amount of glassware needed for running the experiment, as suggested in *Laboratory guide (P)*, can be much reduced. Culture the yeast populations in two large flasks, preferably flat bottomed ones, and withdraw small samples at intervals. The errors introduced by reducing the volume of medium are insignificant, and in practice it has been found that the amount of contamination is not serious.

It may be necessary to remind students to keep the cultures well shaken so that local concentrations of food are not exhausted nor toxic materials allowed to inhibit reproduction. This precaution is particularly important for cultures in test-tubes and it may be worth while to add a few glass beads so that shaking stirs the medium more effectively.

Questions and answers

Does the evidence suggest that the growth of the population was logarithmic, arithmetic, or of some other kind? Name the period during which growth was most nearly logarithmic.

a The answer depends upon results, but there is likely to have been a period of nearly logarithmic growth. If the curve of the graph is wavy, this may be due to:
1 inefficient sampling techniques,
2 failure to bring the inoculum to a stage of active growth.

What factors appear to be controlling growth in the conditions of your experiment?

b Some component of the food medium. Local inequalities might be important if shaking was not complete. Temperature might possibly exert some effect.

You might have expected that the tubes which contained twice as much food would support a population twice as dense as the other tubes. Give as many reasons as you can why this was not so. Assume that you started each tube with the same number of cells.

c The question leads into quite difficult topics, unless students are limited to simple answers.
1 Possible effects on *rate* of growth: a more concentrated medium is less likely to have local pockets of shortage. But growth is more rapid, so perhaps the demand is correspondingly greater. Perhaps cells in a richer medium are more wasteful of resources.
2 Possible effects on *ultimate* size of population: more food will produce more cells, but unless the food is utilized with the same efficiency it will be used up before the population becomes twice as dense. If growth is more rapid, a different pattern of utilization of energy is involved and, on average,

more cells are younger. Thus the terminal population is reduced, because earlier generations have utilized food that might have been used later to produce a final dense population.

3 S. pombe might have reproduced sexually – it can do so. Food conditions might affect the balance between sexual and asexual reproduction. In fact, this is rather unlikely in the conditions suggested, except that sexual reproduction is stimulated by the onset of unfavourable conditions.

In what way does the supply of energy to the yeast population differ from the supply of energy to most populations in the wild?

d It is supplied in bulk, not continuously. The contrast is not necessarily valid, since many yeasts do colonize isolated sources of substrate – rotten fruit, for example.

Does a study of population dynamics in yeast in the laboratory throw any light on the factors that control the size of human populations?

e This leads into the work proposed by *Study guide (P)*.

5.2 Population dynamics in a plant community

Principles

This investigation, begun in L(M) 1.3, involves the study of two components of a community growing densely together. Students are justified in assuming that there is likely to be some interaction, and will be able to explore the situation through a programme of investigations in the field, laboratory, and library. This provides an opportunity of studying the dynamics of a natural community, of linking ecological studies with horticultural and agricultural practice, and of showing that ecological problems are susceptible to investigation by experiment, both in the field and the laboratory.

Nitrogen is one of the major components of fertilizers and deserves the large amount of attention which farmers and horticulturists give to it. The element is equally important in wild communities.

This investigation can be linked with L(P) 1.3 and L(P) 7.1.

Teaching procedure

Associated materials
S(M) 1.4, 1.5
S(P) 1.4, 1.5, 1.6, 2.6, 4.1, 4.4, 5.3, 5.4, 5.6, 5.7, 6.1, 6.2, 7.1, 7.2

It may be helpful here to query the use of the terms competition and cooperation. It will be useful to cross-refer the work on two sorts of clover (L(P) 1.3) since the interactions to be found in the clover plots contrast to some extent with those occurring in a lawn.

Practical problems

The outcome of the lawn investigations may not yet be clear. Much depends upon the season and the fertility of the soil. If necessary, the work of this investigation can be deferred until later in the term, and dealt with at the same time as the clover investigation (L(M) 1.3).

Questions and answers

To what extent have the populations of the two species changed since you last examined them?

a This depends on the season and the fertility of the soil.

It is likely that grass grows well where the clover is removed, and that clover grows well where the grass is removed. Hence it may be deduced that the soil is good enough for both.

What, therefore, keeps each in check? Possibilities: interaction amongst the roots or shoots, the effect of symbionts – see L(M) 7.1 – nitrogen in the soil.

What evidence is there that the population dynamics of clover and grass involves competition, cooperation, and selection?

b The answer depends upon the amount of observation students have done in the field and the extent to which secondhand evidence has been introduced.

In what fundamental respects do the factors affecting the rate of growth of clover and grass in a lawn differ from those influencing a population of S. pombe *under laboratory conditions?*

c	Clover and grass	*S. pombe* in culture
Relations	inter- and intra-specific	only intra-specific
Resource supply	continuous	batch
Environmental conditions	seasonal fluctuations	few, if any, fluctuations
	not under close experimental control	under quite strict experimental control
	not closely monitored	monitored to some extent
Time scale	long, few generations	short, many generations
Mechanisms for escape from unfavourable conditions	seeds, rhizomes with dispersal and food reserve functions	resting stage cells with dispersal and food reserve functions

Additional bibliography

References

On populations:
Hazen, W. E. (Ed.) (1964) Symposium, *Readings in population and community ecology*. W. B. Saunders:
Gause, G. F. and Witt, A. A. 'Behaviour of mixed populations and the problem of natural selection.'
Frank, P. W. 'Coactions in laboratory populations of two species of *Daphnia*.'
Park, T. 'Beetles, competition and populations.'

On *Schizosaccharomyces pombe*:
Brachet and Mirsky (Eds.) (1961) *The Cell, III: meiosis and mitosis*. Academic Press.
Gill, B. F. (1965) Ph.D. thesis. Edinburgh University.
Hawker, L. E., Linton, A. H., Folkes, B. F., and Carlile, M. J. (1960) *An introduction to the biology of micro-organisms*. Edward Arnold. (Controls on population growth.)
Sussman, A. S. (1964) Laboratory Block, BSCS, Students' Book and Teachers' supplement *Microbes, their growth, nutrition and interaction*. Harrap.
Sussman, M. (1960) Foundations of Modern Biology Series *Animal growth and development*. Prentice-Hall. (Has a short section on population growth at a level suitable for the majority of students.)

Chapter 6

Organisms and their physical environment

Chapter review

The uneven distribution of organisms sometimes reveals a great deal about their ecological requirements. For instance, experimental investigation may link the peculiar distribution of a species with a corresponding unevenness in a physical factor such as heat, light, or humidity.

Conversely, a study of the environmental conditions in which organisms flourish best can be a useful guide to their optimum requirements.

The sequence of topics is as follows:

1 The ecology of woodlice. Cryptozoic organisms often have specific and clear-cut ecological requirements, and so provide good material for studying the effect of physical factors. The behaviour of woodlice under controlled conditions.

2 Laboratory investigations of the influence of physical conditions can throw considerable light on the behaviour of animals in the wild state.

Assumptions

– An elementary knowledge of methods of measuring temperature, humidity, and light, and of the meaning of relative humidity.

6.1 The ecology of woodlice

Principles

Students are first introduced to the distribution of animals in the field. Then follows a consideration of the possible influences which might determine that distribution and the construction of hypotheses by way of explanation. Finally, a series of laboratory investigations with choice chambers and balances are set up. These will test the field observations and see how experimental and theoretical studies in physiology and anatomy can help to explain behavioural and ecological characteristics.

Teaching procedure

Associated materials
S(M) 1.4, 1.5
S(P) 1.4, 2.3, 5.2, 6.1, 6.2, 6.6
S(D) 6.3
S(C) 1.6
Film loop 'Grain weevil *Sitophilus granarius*'

Many kinds of common invertebrates could be chosen for this study but cryptozoic forms such as woodlice are particularly suitable. It will be best to confine attention to one species only, since lack of time will almost certainly cut short an extensive study. It is necessary to stress the role of behaviour in determining distribution.

The techniques used in determining density should, in the first place, be as simple as possible. *Laboratory guide (P)* suggests a crude but quite effective method of using the quadrat principle. If time permits, more elaborate methods could be tried involving mark, release, and recapture (see Extension Work II). Woodlice vary somewhat in their wandering tendencies. Sometimes the method is a success, at others it can be a complete failure. The best results are obtained when the weather is wet.

Practical problems

References to works of identification are included in the Bibliographies of *Laboratory guide (P)* and at the end of this chapter.

Cobalt thiocyanate papers may be made up or bought. Standard reference colours can be established by putting papers over liquids known to give specific relative humidities. Such papers can be re-used many times until they become dirty.

If there are no woodlouse colonies close to the school, then students can make model communities, using the same tanks as were used for aquaria. Woodlice will usually remain inside, but it is wise to smear the walls of the tank with Vaseline or a silicone fluid such as Releasil, as a precaution against escape. The bottom of the tank should be lined with soil, stones, bark, and moss, while a little raw carrot or potato provides a good source of food. These dry tank colonies could be used in place of aquarium communities to provide a variety of organisms for other investigations such as those of Chapter 1. Behaviour in choice chambers is affected by previous treatment. Woodlice from very moist conditions show little preference for dry atmospheres. The tanks should be kept rather dry before the practicals.

Questions and answers

What kinds of microhabitat support the highest and the lowest densities of woodlice?

a Woodlice are most likely to be found in moist, dark crevices, close to a supply of food. Calcium (lime) is important as a resource, because quite large quantities are used in the cuticle, which is sloughed at ecdysis; after this the animal looks white for a few hours.

In what circumstances do woodlice come to rest and when do they move?

b Woodlice move most frequently at night, after physical disturbance, and in dry conditions.

To what factors of the environment do you consider woodlice to be most responsive?

c Responsiveness can only be assessed by complicated neurophysiological apparatus. A rough guide can be obtained by finding what stimuli cause a response – such as light and humidity.

Do woodlice tend to cluster, or to remain apart? Suggest hypotheses which account for the behaviour and distribution of woodlice.

d In atmosphere of low humidity they cluster, creating a moist microclimate and thereby reducing the rate of water loss. The response of woodlice to dorsal contact (a particular form of thigmokinesis), can be examined by placing them in a choice chamber in which one half has a low roof made of glass or Perspex resting on Plasticine, so that the dorsum of a woodlouse can just touch the roof. They tend to cluster in such crevice situations, as would be expected of cryptozoites. Earwigs behave in the same way. The response is not detectable in moist atmospheres, where it would be of little adaptive value and would inhibit foraging and other exploratory activities.

How could these hypotheses be tested experimentally?

e First check on the field evidence to ensure that the hypotheses are sensible. For instance, the humidity in the crevices could be measured. Then use choice chambers, with realistic humidity ranges.

6.2 The behaviour of woodlice under controlled conditions

Principles

Associated materials
S(M) 1.4, 1.5
S(P) 2.3
S(C) 1.6

The choice chamber experiments, which could be supplemented by others testing preferences for darkness and crevices, provide clear evidence of the requirements of woodlice. The answers to questions in *Laboratory guide (P)* can be amplified by reference to the Bibliography. Some additional data are included here for convenience, and in order to show the advantages to be gained from applying physiological analysis to ecological behaviour patterns.

Woodlice and water

Water is one of the most important factors that determine the distribution of small arthropods and this is particularly true of woodlice.

The success of terrestrial insects is due in large part to efficient structural adaptations which reduce transpiration. Woodlice, on the other hand, possess an exoskeleton that is readily permeable by water, so their methods of controlling loss of water are behavioural rather than physiological and anatomical.

Waloff investigated the survival of three common species of woodlice in various humidities and obtained the results shown in table 1.

Relative humidity per cent	Duration of life in hours Temperature 14° C–18° C					
	Oniscus asellus		*Porcellio scaber*		*Armadillidium vulgare*	
	average	limits	average	limits	average	limits
0	4·3	3–5	5·27	4–6	7·15	6–10
25	6·85	5–7·5	8·17	6·5–10	9·92	6–16
50	6·2	5–8	10·17	6–16	30·15	16–44
75	16·25	12–20	25·25	18–44	59·15	36–87
85	25·5	11–28	29·0	18–43	65·65	25–96
93	33·17	165–75	39·17	20–67	114·6	49–240
100	–	32–over a month	–	47–over a month	–	76–over a month

Table 1
Duration of life in three species of woodlice at different humidities.

If woodlice are exposed to unsaturated air, they lose water, and normally make this loss good by feeding on moist food. Edney showed that after desiccation, and when kept at 95 per cent relative humidity, all woodlice continue to lose water. Even at 98 per cent R.H., most species lose weight, except *Armadillidium*, which is capable of absorbing water provided the air is still. This is an interesting discovery and in line with field observations, for *Armadillidium* is usually found in drier habitats. Some species are capable of taking in water via the mouth and anus. This is an active process occurring only in live animals. Another means of absorbing water that some species have consists of a series of fine channels on the body surface. It is thought that water is picked up from the substrate and passes by capillarity onto the pleopods (gills), so moistening the respiratory surfaces.

Do woodlice prefer an atmosphere of high humidity?

Questions and answers

What preference, if any, do woodlice show in a humidity gradient?

a For the higher humidity.

Did all show the same response in the same conditions?

b Very likely. If not, differences may be due to previous treatment, some animals having been in wet conditions.

Do you need to use a χ^2 test, in order to analyse your results by testing the 'null hypothesis' that the woodlice show no preference?

c Most unlikely. The question is designed to help students make guesses from the unequivocal evidence that they are likely to have obtained. A statistical test could be used – either χ^2 if the numbers are large enough, or Student's *t* test.

How do woodlice locate and remain in a favourably humid atmosphere?

Questions and answers

Did the individual animals respond by a direct movement towards the preferred environment?

a Unlikely.

Having reached this environment, did they remain there?

b Probably.

If they remained there, did they move around or did they become inactive?

c Inactive.

Was there a difference between the amount of turning movement in each of the contrasting humidities?

d Probably more turning in the dry zone.

Did the animals generally move faster in one environment than in the other?

e Speed is likely to be greater in the dry zone.

Was there any evidence of an interaction of two or more patterns of activity?

f This depends upon observation but there could be.

What tentative deductions can you make regarding the behavioural mechanisms involved in the animals' responses to humidity?

g They turn more often and travel faster in the dry zone. They are thus more likely to arrive (by chance) in wetter regions, and then to move more sluggishly in them. Hence a hypothesis to explain their uneven distribution in natural conditions and the fact that they are commonest in moist areas.

Do clustered woodlice lose water less rapidly than isolated ones?

Questions and answers

Do your results suggest that clustered woodlice lose water more slowly than isolated ones? If so, what bearing has this finding on the ecology of the animal under natural conditions?

a A change in weight can be assumed to represent an equivalent loss of water, though this may not be strictly justified. The observations show the adaptive value of the habit of clustering.

If there was a change in weight can you assume that this was due only to a loss of water? The answer to this question depends partly on whether you were able to carry out instruction (6).

b It would not be strictly right to assume this. It would reduce errors if students collected faeces. The only way to account for losses due to respiration would be to investigate comparable organisms with a respirometer.

In what ways could you improve the design of the experiments suggested in this section (6.2)?

c Possibly by applying wax to identify the site of water loss. Also, by making some mechanical improvements to apparatus?

If woodlice are responsive to humidity and shun dry conditions, what further considerations are involved in explaining how they move around to find food in unsheltered places?

d Hunger drive increases and may reverse the hygro- and photo-responses. Mating drive does likewise, unless this occurs in damp conditions. Woodlice feed at night when the temperature is lower and relative humidity higher. They also feed more in damp weather.

Additional bibliography

General reading

Fraenkel, G. S. and Gunn, D. L. (1961) *The orientation of animals*. Dover. (General account of orientation mechanisms in woodlice.)
Hinde, R. (1967) *Animal behaviour*. McGraw-Hill. (A definition of kinesis and taxis in terms of behaviour.)
Nuffield O-level Biology (1966) Text and Guide Year III *The maintenance of life*. Longmans/Penguin. (Woodlice ecology and behaviour.)
Waterhouse, F. L. (1966) 'Alternative or choice chambers for the study of arthropod behaviour.' *Sch. Sci. Rev.*, **47**, 726–736. (A short account of the use of choice chambers.)

Chapter 7

Organisms and their biotic environment

Chapter review

This chapter is complementary to the last and is concerned with the close relationships that may exist between species where symbiosis, parasitism, and territorial behaviour are involved.

The sequence of topics is:

1 Interaction between clover and *Rhizobium*.
2 Interactions in clover and aphids.
3 Aggression amongst sticklebacks (*Gasterosteus* spp.).

Assumptions

- That students are familiar with the use of sterile techniques.
- That students know how to use an oil immersion lens for studying microscope preparations of bacteria.

7.1 Interaction between clover and *Rhizobium*

Principles

Associated materials
S(M) 1.4, 1.5
S(P) 1.5, 1.6
S(D) 6.3, 6.4
Film loop 'Biological control (1) *Apanteles* as a parasite' NBP–37
Film loop 'Biological control (2) whitefly and *Encarsia*' NBP–38
Film loop 'Potato blight *Phytophthora infestans*'

The symbiotic relationship between legumes and bacteria is well known. Distinct species of bacteria infect the different species of legume, though it seems possible that a certain measure of anomalous infection may also occur.

The seedlings take a week or two to show clear evidence of interaction, so it would be wise to start the cultures early.

Practical problems

Use red or white clover, lucerne, or any other convenient legume. We suggest clover because the evidence from this experiment can then be linked with that from the other clover experiments.

Instead of dipping the seeds into a suspension of *Rhizobium*, it is advisable to add the liquid when the root hairs begin to grow, since the bacteria enter the plant through these. It is best to get the right inoculum for the particular species of seed used; *R. trifolii* for red and white clover, *R. meliloti* for lucerne and white clover.

Students can collect *Rhizobium* from root nodules and extract it by crushing them with a little water and filtering them through ordinary filter paper. The preparation can be used to inoculate the same species of plant from which it came. Commercial preparations are produced as moist humus or dry powders which the experimenter should mix with a little water before inoculating the seeds.

As well as examining a nodule, students could cut sections across an infected root and see that the bacteria are found in the cortex but do not extend beyond the pericycle. They can inspect the contents of the nodule under an oil immersion objective which, with a $\times 10$ eyepiece, gives a magnification of $\times 1000$.

The students are left to choose the parameters for measuring growth. The following are suitable, in addition to those suggested in the text:
1 wet weight of shoot,
2 dry weight of shoot,
3 colour of leaflet.

Dry weights are very small and require the use of a delicate balance; the colour of a leaf is important in estimating nitrogen status, but it cannot easily be quantified. The question will arise whether colour standards are necessary, or whether some scale could be made by subjective estimates of differences between the palest and darkest leaves.

Seedlings grow best in moderate temperatures: the tubes can trap sunlight, acting as small greenhouses. Keeping the tubes in large beakers of water has also yielded good results.

Light seems to inhibit the formation of nodules, so it would be advisable to paint the tubes black up to the level of the agar, or enclose them in black plastic sheeting secured by rubber bands. Sheeting is much easier to remove for inspecting root growth.

Table 1 gives some typical results.

	Treatments			
Nitrogen Rhizobium	– –	– +	+ +	+ –
Mean number of leaves	1·5	4·0	4·75	5·0
Mean leaf area (m^2)	0·015	0·049	0·05	0·06
Mean shoot length (cm)	2·66	5·75	5·75	5·5
Mean number of roots	3·0	5·0	6·5	8·0
Mean number of nodules	0	3·0	1·5	0
Total dry weight (g)	0·1	0·3	0·2	0·2

(Set up 23 May; harvested 4 July)

Table 1
Data from an investigation of the effects of *Rhizobium* and nitrogenous fertilizer on the performance of clover seedlings (8 × 4 replicates).

Questions and answers

Do your results support the hypothesis that the Rhizobium *supplies nitrogen to the clover? What other explanations are possible?*

a See table 1 for a typical set of results. The compensatory action of *Rhizobium* when there is no nitrogenous fertilizer is highly suggestive. It may be wise to warn students about the common usage of the term 'nitrogen', when what is really meant is a compound which includes the element nitrogen.

Suggest how Rhizobium *may benefit from the association.*

b The *Rhizobium* seems to benefit from the association by obtaining carbohydrates from the legumes. The situation is more complicated than this because the *Rhizobium* cannot fix nitrogen when it is growing by itself, although it will grow if given nitrogenous compounds such as nitrates, ammonium salts, and amino-acids. The full mechanism is still unknown.

What agricultural value have legumes?

c This leads into the exercises in *Study guide (P)* on the nitrogen cycle and crop rotation.

Do the results of this investigation add anything to the conclusions you drew from investigating the lawn community (1.5, 5.2)?

d It is expected that they will do so. See also 5.2.

7.2 Interactions in clover and aphids

Principles

The feeding relationships between aphids and their host plants are sometimes considered to be so close that they almost amount to parasitism. This may be defined as an association between two organisms in which one lives on or in the other (the host). The association is usually detrimental to the host but does not lead to its immediate death.

From the work of this chapter students should arrive at definitions of the following associations: epibiosis, symbiosis, commensalism, and parasitism. They should consider the adaptive value of each association to the organisms concerned, and withhold judgment in cases where there is no clear advantage or disadvantage.

Teaching procedure

Associated materials
S(M) 1.4, 1.5
S(P) 1.5, 1.6, 7.1
S(D) 6.3, 6.4, 6.5
Film loop 'Biological control (1) *Apanteles* as a parasite' NBP–37
Film loop 'Biological control (2) whitefly and *Encarsia*' NBP–38
Film loop 'Potato blight *Phytophthora infestans*'

The investigation suggested here involves patient and careful observation. *T. repens* attracts several species of aphids but it is difficult to identify any with precision. It has been found that they are frequently parasitized.

If aphids or clover parasites are not available, students could see the film loops on *Apanteles*, whitefly and *Encarsia* or *Phytophthora* and potato. Alternatively, cultures of *Ephestia* and *Anagasta* could be demonstrated.

Questions and answers

In what way do aphids feed? How could their feeding habits be related to their capacity for carrying disease?

a The mouthparts are piercing and sucking. They are enclosed in a sheath (labium). The middle portion (maxillae) consists of a double tube – the food and salivary canals. The outer portions (mandibles) are two sharp stylets. This kind of feeding device provides ideal opportunities for viruses to infect the host plant through the lesions formed by the stylets.

Do you think the relationship of aphids and their host plant is mutually beneficial? How does it differ from that of clover and Rhizobium*?*

b No. The plant is harmed but the aphid is favoured. Harm to the host may be negligible if infection is small, but it can become serious if unchecked.

Do you regard the aphid as a parasite? If so, how would you describe an insect which parasitized the aphid?

c Hyperparasite.

Some aphids, when kept in favourable conditions, have a generation time of a few hours, comparable to that of S. pombe *(5.1). If such reproduction were to continue unhindered it would be catastrophic. What factors in nature could determine the size and density of an aphid population?*

d Factors such as temperature, moisture, and food, also the vitality and distribution of the food plant. Bugs, parasites, and hyperparasites bring about control of numbers.

7.3 Aggression amongst sticklebacks *(Gasterosteus* spp.*)*

Principles

Aggression provides a good example of a situation in which one member of a species constitutes part of the environment of another. Sir Julian Huxley first observed that certain patterns of movement, found among animals in courtship, had lost their original function and become purely symbolic in character.

Numerous examples of ritualized aggression are known in animals. The result of these conflicts is decided without either participant being badly injured. In fact, very few examples of intra-specific aggression where one contestant is badly injured are known in the wild. A clear example of ritualization is found in the male fallow deer. The animals first parade broadside on, nodding their heads up and down. Then they stop, turn at right angles to each other, and lower their heads so that the antlers collide. In the wrestling contest which follows, the victor is the one who can hold out longest. Sometimes one animal turns before the other, but instead of attacking the unprotected flank of his rival, he turns back and continues the broadside parade. The inhibition against injuring a member of the same species is very strong. With man the use of a white flag and a red cross are examples of established signals designed to inhibit aggression.

One of the functions of courtship is to reduce the aggressive tendencies of animals since the first response of an animal to a prospective mate may be one of aggression. Sticklebacks in an aquarium exhibit aggression and it is possible to demonstrate this quite easily.

Teaching procedure

Associated materials
S(C) 4.1, 4.2

It is easy to keep sticklebacks in aquaria, and they provide material for the study of courtship as well as aggression. Films or film loops can be used in place of live animals, if necessary.

A slightly more complicated sequence of experimental procedure than that in *Laboratory guide (P)* can give extra information. Start with a glass division in the tank which had an opaque sheet and observe again, now that the fish can see each other. Remove the glass and watch the fish when they are free to enter each other's territory.

Practical problems

The tank ought to be at least 60 cm × 30 cm × 30 cm. Silver paper and red pencil fragments make good mimics. It is not possible to observe aggression properly unless the males are in breeding condition. At other times students may observe a lack of aggression, but they will not recognize the situation for certain unless they identify the sexes correctly and keep them separately in labelled containers. Aggression does not occur between the two sexes and it is not easy to tell them apart, except in the breeding season.

Questions and answers

In what ways does the appearance of the fish change when it fights?

a It goes redder, raises its spines, swims vertically (threat posture). It may charge and attempt to bite.

Assuming the glass partition marked the territorial limits of each fish, what happened when one trespassed on the other's preserve?

b The other probably chased it back. There would have been a general rise in activity and excitement. The behaviour of the fish alters as it enters the opponent's territory. The fighting response changes to a fleeing one and it turns and swims back to its own territory. The opponent also turns and chases it back. Thus a fight/flight situation is set up. Which behaviour is in operation depends on the spatial position of the fish.

Did the two fish injure one another? If not, what kind of behaviour prevented damage to each contestant?

c Probably not, because the contestant was able to retire into his own territory. When wild animals are confined they often fight continually because it is impossible to establish a proper territorial system. This fighting may lose its ritual nature and result in the death of contestants.

What advantage is it to a species if its behaviour pattern allows one member to threaten another effectively and makes it less likely that either will hurt the other?

d It gains advantages of threat and potential aggression without the loss of life or limb and the waste that this would involve. Better to achieve the end result by the least wasteful means.

What is the advantage gained by a male in establishing a territory?

e This reduces interference with breeding activities.

Which feature of a male seems to be most significant as a stimulus to aggressive behaviour?

f The red colour. Tinbergen relates that some male sticklebacks reacted to the movement of a red mail van seen 90 metres away through a window.

What non-aggressive behaviour did you observe when the mirror was in use? Can you explain such behaviour?

g At first the fish attacks the image by charging at it. It may then indulge in displacement activity by digging sand.

Additional bibliography

General reading

Caullery, M. (1952) *Parasitism and symbiosis*. Sidgwick & Jackson.
Dowdeswell, W. H. (1966) *An introduction to animal ecology*. 2nd edition. Methuen. (Chapter on special animal relationships.)
Imms, A. D. (1947) New Naturalist Library. *Insect natural history*. Collins. (Natural history of aphids and their parasites.)
Imms, A. D. (1959) *Outlines of entomology*. Methuen. (Calculation of unchecked aphid population growth.)
Jones, M. G. (1947) Modern Science Memoirs No. 26 *The bean and beet aphis*. Murray.
Kennedy, J. S. (1951) *New Biology* 11 'Aphids and plant growth.' 50–65. Penguin. (Very readable and helpful account.)
Rothschild, M. and Clay, T. (1952) *Fleas, flukes and cuckoos*. Collins. (A study of parasitism.)
Step, E. (1932) *Wasps, bees, ants and allied orders of the British Isles*. Warne. (Aphid parasites.)
Stewart, W. D. P. (1966) *Nitrogen fixation in plants*. Athlone Press. (A full treatment of the biology of nitrogen fixation.)
Wilson, R. A. (1967) *An introduction to parasitology*. Arnold. (A general account of the subject.)

References

Postgate, J. R. (1968) 'How microbes fix nitrogen.' *Science Journal*, 4, 3, 69–74.

Extension work II

Experimental field ecology

Review

This chapter introduces a number of fundamental issues in ecology, using a study of spatial distribution as the starting point. One of the difficulties in investigating the distribution of plants and animals in the field, under the conditions of a school, is to show pupils that the undertaking is relevant, not just a purely academic exercise. It is important to understand the interactions going on in populations and communities, such as those which are considered elsewhere (for example, in L(P) 1.3, L(P) 1.5). Moreover, such knowledge can have important implications for man, for instance in the control of plant and insect pests.

The few investigations included here should be regarded as merely examples of a wide range of alternatives which could be adapted to local conditions and facilities. With the exception of L(P) E2.2, all the topics suggested would be suitable for study at a field centre or in any other suitably rural situation. On the other hand, provided a patch of soil is available, all the investigations except L(P) E2.4 could be adapted to urban conditions.

The sequence of topics is as follows:

1 Distribution dynamics in the daisy, *Bellis perennis*. A study of colonization by a plant and the influence of various ecological factors, including that of man.

2 Colonization and aggregation in the broad bean aphid, *Aphis fabae*. This investigation concerns the artificial situation provided by a pure stand of a crop plant.

3 Population density and environment in symphylids. The soil provides an excellent environment for the study of distribution and density, on account of the very large number of animal colonists and the ease with which some of them can be extracted.

4 Estimation of numbers by means of capture-recapture.

Assumptions – Knowledge of the contents of previous chapters, particularly Chapter 1.

E2.1 Distribution dynamics in the daisy, *Bellis perennis*

Principles

This fairly straightforward investigation of plant distribution could be adapted in a variety of ways to suit local circumstances. Its main purpose is to highlight the following points:

1 Plant distribution is discontinuous.

2 It is sometimes, but by no means always, possible to relate discontinuity to ecological factors.

3 Any investigation of this kind must be quantitative and make use of an appropriate sampling technique and method of statistical analysis.

Teaching procedure

Associated materials
S(M) 1.4, 1.5
S(P) 1.4, 1.7, 2.3, 5.2, 6.2, 7.1, 7.2, 7.3, 8.1, 8.3

Throughout this investigation and the others which follow, there will be ample opportunity for bringing in other aspects of ecology arising from a study of distribution. For this reason the introduction to this section in *Laboratory guide (P)* has been expanded somewhat in order to set the contents of the chapter in their broader ecological perspective.

We need add little here about the technique of carrying out the investigation because, as with all Extension Work, this should be left as far as possible to the pupils to work out for themselves. The method of using quadrats in sampling is dealt with in most ecology books. The Bibliography to EII, LG(P), refers to the use of the point frame.

Practical problems

There should be little difficulty over apparatus as this is easy to construct. If the area chosen for study is a lawn or playing field which is regularly mown, it may be as well to know when mowing is going to take place. It will then be possible to make some estimate of how effective the mower is in preventing daisies from dispersing further through cut flowering heads left lying on the ground. Since daisy plants adopt a rosette type of growth, they are unaffected by mowing and so can be sampled at any time.

Questions and answers

Do you consider the distribution of daisies to be random or non-random?

a Non-random. (See Bibliography. This answer will be based upon a guess unless complex analysis is attempted.)

How do you account for the distribution that you found? What further evidence would be required in order to test your hypothesis?

b The answer will depend on local circumstances. Sometimes there is no evidence to account for distribution. The most likely agencies of dispersal are wind and man. Further evidence would be proof of the action of particular agents in dispersing daisies and more precise information about it.

From everyday experience, we might conclude that the daisy is rather a successful weed. How can we judge ecological success? Using your own data, suggest a way of judging it in the daisy.

c Some possible criteria could be the number of individuals per unit area of *habitable* ground or per unit area of total ground, or per unit area of *inhabited* ground.

Can you compare the ecological success of the daisy with that of some other weed growing in your area? How do you account for any differences?

d The answer will depend on the previous ones and the species to be compared. In general, weeds have a high reproductive potential and growth, once started, is rapid.

E2.2 Colonization and aggregation in the broad bean aphid, *Aphis fabae*

Principles

The purpose of this investigation is to emphasize the important point that the distribution of plants inevitably determines the distribution of the animals that feed upon them. In circumstances where the range of food plants of a particular species is restricted, and where one or more of these is grown at a high density (as in a crop plant), then colonization by herbivorous insects may result in a rapid increase in numbers leading to large aggregations. This is particularly true in species capable of reproduction by parthenogenesis.

Teaching procedure

Associated materials
S(M) 1.4, 1.5
S(P) 1.5, 1.6, 6.1

There are opportunities here for introducing further ecological problems relating to *Aphis fabae*. For instance, what happens when numbers on the broad bean plants become excessive – if they ever do? How are dispersal and overwintering achieved (remember that the broad bean is an annual)? If conditions are particularly favourable for this experiment, it would be well worth while comparing the density of aphids in successive years.

Practical problems

The main problem likely to arise, apart from the availability of a suitable plot, is getting the beans to grow in time. The best plan is to plant them in their final positions in early April. Some gardeners plant broad beans the previous autumn and allow them to overwinter in the ground. This is rather a hit and miss approach – splendid if it comes off but disastrous if it does not. If conditions are restricted, the experiment could be carried out on a small scale with plants grown in containers such as orange boxes.

Questions and answers

How fast did the density of the Aphis *populations increase (measured as the number of insects per plant)? What was their maximum density?*

a The information will have been derived from experimental results.

Was the rate of increase linear, exponential, or of some other kind?

b Exponential, or something like it.

Was the rate of increase of Aphis *populations raised in the laboratory similar to that occurring naturally? How do you account for any differences?*

c Similar in pattern but with a higher survival rate. Differences are possibly due to absence of predators and more favourable environmental conditions. There may well be other local considerations which should be taken into account.

How did the proportions of winged and wingless forms vary at different times of the season?

d During the summer the population is mostly wingless. Later, winged individuals appear.

Was there any evidence of emigration from the Aphis *population? If so, when did it occur? Can you relate it to the life cycle of the host plant?*

e Yes; almost certainly. Whenever winged forms appear and are ready to fly. No; the winged forms may fly off at all stages in the plant's life cycle, especially during senescence and wilting.

E2.3 Population density and environment in symphylids

Principles

Just as it is necessary to determine the density of plant species, so the same is true for animals. It is fairly easy to sample slowly moving species. If they live above ground, it is fairly often possible to estimate their numbers, using methods developed for plants, such as a quadrat. Animals living below the ground present more difficulty for these must be extracted from the medium in which they occur. Since the amount of soil used is likely to be small, it is essential to use a valid method of sampling.

Teaching procedure

Associated materials
S(M) 1.4, 1.5
S(P) 1.5, 5.2, 6.1
Film loop 'The conservation of topsoil' NBP–32

This investigation involves estimating a population of animals that cannot be seen since they live below ground. It provides a good opportunity for students to appreciate the significance of a well-designed sampling procedure and the use of statistical methods in making comparisons of density in different areas. In general, it will be found that the greatest densities of symphylids occur in soils with a high organic content. Waterlogged soils and those with little humus tend not to be colonized, or only in small numbers. The results from different localities can be compared visually by means of a histogram.

Practical problems

The best times for carrying out practical work with soil animals are in spring and autumn, when they are most active. Avoid periods of drought and cold when the creatures are usually inert. Soil cores can be collected with a soil sampler which can be made in the school laboratory. When extracting soil samples, it is important always to take them to the same depth as there is a considerable difference in content of humus between topsoil and sub-soil. When selecting an area of soil for investigation, it is advisable to choose at least one locality which has been well cultivated and contains plenty of humus.

It is quite easy to extract symphylids by flotation on water and a shallow container such as a large photographic dish is ideal for the purpose. The animals float even better on concentrated salt solution (brine).

Questions and answers

To what extent did the density (number per unit volume of soil) of symphylids vary in different soil samples, both from the same locality and from different ones?

a Variations may well have been considerable both in the same locality and in different ones. This underlines the importance of calculating the standard deviation for any set of samples in which the mean will be used as a basis for comparing the numbers of animals present with those occurring elsewhere.

Could the differences in density as between one locality and another be regarded as statistically significant? What was your criterion of significance?

b Once we know the means and their standard deviations, we can make a comparison of the densities of animals in two different areas by calculating the standard error of the difference between them.

Did 5 samples per locality prove to be sufficient? What advantage, if any, would have resulted from doubling the number of samples?

What advantage would have resulted from doubling the size of the samples but keeping the number at 5?

c and *d* This will depend on the numbers involved. The two alternative treatments might have different effects on the standard deviation, depending on the number of animals occurring in each sample.

Is there any relationship between the number of symphylids inhabiting a soil and its humus content? If so, can you suggest a hypothesis to explain this relationship? How would you put your hypothesis to the test?

e Yes. A possible hypothesis might be that symphylids eat humus. To test the hypothesis students might estimate the humus content of the soil in an experimental situation before and after habitation by symphylids, and examine mouthparts and gut contents of the symphylids. There are numerous other possibilities.

To what other factors do you think symphylid numbers might be related?

f Possibly humidity (related to humus content); aeration (important in clay soils).

E2.4 Estimation of numbers by means of capture-recapture

Principles

Mobile species present peculiar problems if we wish to estimate the numbers of their populations. The method of capture-recapture was first devised by Lincoln in the United States for the determination of numbers in water-fowl, which were marked by coloured rings on their legs. Since then, it has been used widely in a variety of situations. The mathematics involved have been the subject of a great deal of discussion and a reference to a recent review is included in the Additional Bibliography.

Teaching procedure

Associated materials
S(P) 6.1

It is important that pupils should understand the errors inherent in this procedure, apart from purely physical mishaps such as damage by marking, which are discussed fully in *Laboratory guide (P)*. For this purpose it is instructive to set up a bead model when the number of the 'population' is known, and then proceed to estimate the number by capture-recapture. Suppose we have a population of 100 animals; should our samples be, say, 10 or 40? Using beads we can compare the results achieved by the two methods. If required, we can introduce other variables such as immigration, emigration, deaths, and hatchings. This necessitates a somewhat more complicated mathematical treatment.

Practical problems

This kind of investigation should be carried out in an area of about an acre or less. The most important requirement is that sampling should be relatively easy and that the species chosen for study should satisfy the four requirements enumerated in *Laboratory guide (P)*. Any kind of grassland or heath is suitable, but localities containing many bushes or trees should be avoided.

When marking animals, it is important to use only a small dot of harmless paint or other marking fluid. Too much can easily spread onto other parts of the body, impeding movement and so preventing proper random dispersal on release. It is wise to release the marked individuals from some central point or group of points and revisit these shortly afterwards to ensure that all the releases have dispersed successfully. Any that have not should be investigated for damage and if this has occurred they should be killed or removed from the area, and an appropriate adjustment made in the records.

Questions and answers

What was the density of the animal population that you studied? (Express this as numbers per unit area for land animals and number per unit volume of water for aquatic ones.)

a The answer will depend on the results obtained.

What were the principal errors involved in the method you employed? How could these have been reduced to a minimum?

b This depends partly on local conditions. Possible sources of error could be too small samples, releases not properly dispersed at random, emigration and immigration, deaths and hatchings.

If you continued your investigations for several weeks, to what extent did the density fluctuate? Can you account for these fluctuations?

c The answer depends on results. Fluctuations might be due to the death of one generation and appearance of a new one, fluctuating predation, climatic changes – to mention a few possibilities.

What do you consider to be the practical use of an investigation of this sort? Consult the literature and find one example where the estimation of animal numbers has had important consequences for man.

d There are numerous examples, for instance in the control of insect pests such as locusts, flour beetles, and cockroaches.

Additional bibliography

General reading

Kevan, D. K. McE. (1962) *Soil animals*. Witherby.
Kühnelt, W. (1961) *Soil biology*. Faber & Faber.
Nuffield O-level Biology (1966) Text and Guide Year III *The maintenance of life*. Longmans/Penguin. (Experimental approach to the study of distribution.)
Nuffield O-level Biology (1966) Text and Guide Year IV *Living things in action*. Longmans/Penguin. (Experimental study of soil organisms.)
Paviour-Smith, K. and Whittaker, J. B. (1968) *A key to the major groups of British free living terrestrial invertebrates*. Blackwell. (A cheap key for identification of symphylids.)
Russell, E. J. (1957) New Naturalist Library *The world of the soil*. Collins. (Excellent general account.)
Salisbury, E. (1961) New Naturalist Library *Weeds and aliens*. Collins. (Ecology of daisies and similar weeds.)

References

Cloudsley-Thompson, J. L. and Sankey, J. (1961) *Land invertebrates*. Methuen. (Identification of soil animals.)
Johnson, C. G. (1962) 'Aphid migration.' *New Scientist*, **305**, 622–625.
Jones, M. G. (1947) 'The bean *Aphis*.' *Sch. Sci. Rev.*, **106**, 357–364.
Lewis, T. and Taylor, L. R. (1967) *Introduction to experimental ecology*. Academic Press. (Experimental aspects of colonization by *Aphis*; estimation of population numbers.)
Parr, M. J., Gaskell, T. J. and George, B. J. (1968) 'Capture-recapture methods of estimating animal numbers.' *J. biol. Educ.*, **2**, 95–117.

Chapter 8

The community as an ecosystem

Chapter review

In previous chapters we have been concerned largely with the relationships of individuals within populations (autecology). Here, we are faced with the more difficult task of studying interactions within a community (synecology), using both a model and a natural situation. The concepts of energy flow and trophic levels are seen as underlying themes which together establish the pattern that exists within all communities, and the chapter allows a review of the main ecological theories of *Organisms and populations*.

The sequence of topics is:

1 Autotrophs in a model ecosystem, making use of the tank communities established earlier.
2 Heterotrophs in a model ecosystem. This follows naturally from the previous investigation.
3 A natural community as an ecosystem. The principles established in the two previous studies are applied outside.

Assumptions

- An elementary knowledge of energy and its conversion into different forms; of the principle of the conservation of energy; of units of heat – calories and kilocalories and related units.
- That students can use a stereomicroscope and know elementary techniques for examining small organisms alive under high power monocular microscopes (hanging drop, raised cover-slip and excavated slide methods); and how to stain to identify cellulose, using Schulze's solution (chlor-zinc iodide).
- That students can use keys for identifying pond organisms.
- An elementary understanding of photosynthesis and its significance for the individual plant as a means of capture and transmutation of energy.
- It will be an advantage if students have already covered Chapters 1, 4, 5, 6, and 7.

8.1 Autotrophs in a model ecosystem

Principles

Associated materials
S(M) 8.2, 8.3, 8.5
S(P) 1.1, 5.2, 8.1, 8.2, 8.3
Key to pond organisms

Trophic relationships constitute some of the most important and obvious interactions which exist between the members of a community. There are many aspects that might be studied and it is necessary to make a choice.

On the one hand, the diverse mechanisms that organisms use to capture energy provide rich material for the study of the relationship between structures and their functions. On the other, students might investigate the ecosystem as an economic unit, from the point of view of the flow of materials and energy through the system. This is the approach this chapter adopts.

The first investigation involves the capture of primary energy by plants through autotrophic feeding. Subsequently, the energy is passed on to carnivorous and other sorts of feeders, such as decomposers. By understanding this principle, students will realize that the availability of food inevitably plays an important part in influencing the distribution and abundance of species. The idea of a food chain and web should emerge from practical observation rather than from reading a book account.

Practical problems

Microscope slides or Petri dishes should be hung in pond water for some weeks prior to the class work, in order that the colonizing organisms may be seen in abundance. This will not be successful unless the tanks contain a good variety of species. If, for instance, fresh material is added in early spring and again later on, there should be ample for students to see at the beginning and end of the summer term, and the slides will be well colonized.

8.2 Heterotrophs in a model ecosystem

Teaching procedure

Associated materials
S(M) 8.2, 8.3, 8.4, 8.5
S(P) 1.1, 5.2, 8.1, 8.4
Film loop 'Predator/prey relationships in a pond' NBP–69

It is possible to waste a good deal of time and effort on this work and we suggest treating it only as fully as interest and time allow, and making full use of the relevant material in the *Study Guide*. The work on the model ecosystems could be useful as a lead to considering the world food problem.

The need for light becomes obvious if a tank community is kept in the dark.

Gut contents of herbivores provide good corroborative evidence for feeding habits which have been observed. The difficulty in deciding whether an animal is scraping epibionts from a leaf or eating the leaf itself can be resolved in this manner, and by examining the leaf with a stereomicroscope. Unfortunately, gut contents are rapidly broken up and degraded. For this reason, the foregut is the best part to examine. In any event, students will tend to over-estimate the proportion of plant material because it is more easy to recognize in a mixture.

Although tank communities are inevitably small, it will often be possible to show how the population of a single habitat (or even microhabitat) can occupy a particular niche as far as feeding is concerned. Pupils sometimes find difficulty in understanding that an ecological niche is a concept that covers all the factors that determine an animal's place in nature. By contrast, a microhabitat is essentially a biogeographical concept.

As far as scavengers and decomposers are concerned, ample food can usually be seen and the frequency with which *Asellus* and planarians are found on such material is suggestive. Gut contents are not likely to be instructive. Annelid chaetae are often found in *Asellus* guts, but these may have been picked up inadvertently. They decompose very slowly and are a common component of pond detritus.

The work of the investigation might well be rounded off with a discussion of applied aspects such as the maintenance of fish ponds, the stocking of rivers, regulating sea fisheries, and the problem of pollution. The films 'The river must live' (Petroleum Film Bureau) and 'Fish farming in Sarawak' (Concord Films Council) are examples of good illustrative material that might be used with this work.

Practical problems

Quite often the water in the tanks may become clear, due to the total disappearance of plankton, except for the truly microscopic organisms. It is wise to ensure that *Daphnia* or its relatives are present, and that at least some of the tanks have free-floating Algae in reasonable quantities. A little fertilizer together with ample light can stimulate growth.

It is well worth following up the suggestion that carrion be put in the tanks, but this must be done with great care in order to avoid too much putrefaction.

Questions and answers

Do the species of herbivores feed on a specific range of plants? If so, what can you deduce from this?

a Some may be observed to feed specifically. This would make a good discussion point leading to the idea of adaptation, which the next chapter studies. The idea of an ecological niche could also be introduced here.

In midsummer there is likely to be more than enough food for all the snails. What is the situation likely to be at other times of the year?

b This depends upon the relative proportions of herbivores and food plants. Snails are likely to decimate algal growth during the winter, especially if the tanks are kept warm indoors and not well illuminated. This question could lead to a discussion of the effects of seasonal variations in environmental conditions.

Do the herbivores tend to feed for a greater proportion of the time than the carnivores? Compare your observations in the tank with your experience of other herbivores and carnivores and the problems they face in feeding on plant and animal material. How do you account for any differences you observe?

c Yes. This links field observations with the physiological problem of digesting plant material, and its nutritive value for herbivores.

Would you expect a greater number of herbivores or carnivores in a natural community? In the tanks, how does the biomass of carnivores compare with that of herbivores? Does this reflect the situation likely to exist in a natural habitat?

d This question relates to the idea of a pyramid of numbers and biomass. See also section 8.4 in *Study guide (P)*. There are usually far more herbivores than carnivores, but parasites could be considered carnivores and this complicates the answer to the question.

Is there evidence that the carnivores might control the size of the populations of herbivores? Is this likely to reflect natural conditions?

e Unless the tanks are protected from predation by birds, the snails and some other organisms quickly disappear. Errant *Dytiscus* and other carnivorous insects may temporarily lodge in tanks kept outside. Such predators and their larvae can be effective in killing even fish.

8.3 A natural community as an ecosystem

Principles

Associated materials
S(M) 8.2, 8.3, 8.4, 8.5
S(P) 1.1, 5.2, 6.6, 8.1, 8.2, 8.4, 8.5
S(C) 1.2, 1.6, 2.3
Film loop 'Predator/prey relationships in a pond' NBP–69
Film loop 'Camp followers of man (1) Neutral and beneficial organisms' NBP–34
Film loop 'Camp followers of man (2) Harmful organisms' NBP–35
Film loop 'Camp followers of man (3) Woodboring organisms' NBP–36
Film loop 'Camp followers of man (4) Garden organisms' NBP–28
Film loop 'The conservation of topsoil' NBP–32
Film 'Mosquitos and Tourists'

This investigation is closely related to that based on the tanks and is intended to show how the basic principles governing an ecosystem apply under natural conditions but usually in situations which are far more complex than those encountered so far. The investigation could be carried out at any convenient time and might well provide part of a programme at a field centre. Any kind of ecosystem would be suitable, the most important considerations being that it should be relatively small and simple. Part of a small pond, a stream, or a rock pool would be ideal. Alternatively, a lawn or piece of waste ground, or part of a hedgerow could be equally suitable, although collecting animals on land is usually more difficult than it is in water.

Questions and answers

How do the trophic relations in a natural community compare with those in the tank model?

a Answers will depend on the systems chosen for study. In general, the relations in the tank are bound to be simpler than those in a natural community.

Would you expect the populations within the wild community to remain stable over a number of years?

b No; the numbers of a population always fluctuate but the annual changes can be quite small. Factors such as disease, unusual temperatures, and pollution can bring about rapid changes.

If numbers fluctuated, would you expect changes in gene frequency among the species involved?

c Yes. This would provide particularly good opportunities for the more variable species to evolve new and better adjusted forms. Such a situation has been recorded and analysed several times.

What are the chief causes of instability that might bring about changes in the genetic and ecological character of a community? What causes might have the reverse effect – of achieving stability?

d Causes of instability include fluctuating environmental conditions, alterations in numbers, immigration, and emigration. Causes of stability would, in general, be the reverse of those producing instability. In particular, a stable equilibrium results from an ecosystem which is well balanced trophically.

In the natural community, can you construct a sequence of steps to show how succession could lead to climax?

e Any example could be chosen, for instance the formation of a mud bank in a stream which would result in a hydrarch succession: submerged water plants→plants rooted in water, stems and leaves in air→roots in mud→true land plants. Agriculture is largely concerned with interrupted successions.

Additional bibliography

General reading

Bennett, D. P. and Humphries, D. A. (1965) *Introduction to field biology*. Arnold.
Carpenter, K. E. (1928) *Life in inland waters*. Sidgwick & Jackson.
Dowdeswell, W. H. (1966) *Introduction to animal ecology*. 2nd edition. Methuen.
Dowdeswell, W. H. (1967) *Practical animal ecology*. 2nd edition. Methuen.
Macan, T. T. (1963) *Freshwater ecology*. Longmans, Green.
Nicol, J. A. (1960) *The biology of marine animals*. New York: Interscience.
Nuffield O-level Biology (1966) Text and Guide Year III *The maintenance of life*. Longmans/Penguin.
Nuffield O-level Biology (1966) Text and Guide Year IV *Living things in action*. Longmans/Penguin.
Phillipson, J. (1966) The Institute of Biology's Studies in Biology No. 1 *Ecological energetics*. Edward Arnold.

References

Yonge, C. M. (1928) 'Feeding mechanisms in the invertebrates.' *Biological Reviews* 3, 21.

Chapter 9

Evolution and the origin of species

Chapter review

This chapter emphasizes the mechanism of evolution as well as the evidence for it. The contributions of Darwin and Wallace, and advances in our knowledge of evolution since their time, follow naturally from the work in earlier chapters where we were concerned with variation and the process of selection.

Evolution is a subject which is difficult to cover by a prescribed sequence of practical work, since the possibility of carrying this out depends so much on local circumstances and facilities. For this reason, we make extensive use here of secondhand evidence derived from a variety of sources. However, this in no way dispenses with the need for practical work if this is possible; for instance, the investigation of a polymorphic species such as a population of snails or the stratification of fossils in sedimentary rocks.

The sequence of topics is as follows:

– The mechanism of evolution. This refers particularly to Darwin's findings in the Galápagos Islands.

1 Evolution in action. This is revealed by the study of selection in polymorphic species such as snails of the genus *Cepaea* and flowering plants like *Primula*.

2 Evidence for evolution from geology. The study of stratified rocks and their contents, and the information that can be derived from it.

3 Evidence for evolution from comparative anatomy. This also considers the relative importance of homology and analogy.

– Other evidence for evolution. A brief treatment and summary.

Assumptions

– Knowledge of the previous material, particularly in Chapters 1, 2, 4, and 5.

The mechanism of evolution

Principles

Darwin's findings in the Galápagos Islands provide a classic example of evolution in action. In particular they show the powerful effect of isolation and how a community cut off from interchange with others can evolve along peculiar and divergent lines; these can give rise to forms of plants and animals quite distinct from their ancestral stock. Numerous similar examples, for instance, the marsupials in Australasia, can be found in other parts of the world.

The Galápagos plants and animals also illustrate the effects of selection and the adaptive role of behaviour patterns in animals. The evolution of the woodpecker finch provides a beautiful example of a species which has succeeded in playing the ecological role which would almost certainly have been filled by a woodpecker elsewhere.

Teaching procedure

Associated materials
S(P) 4.1, 4.5, 9.1, 9.2, 9.4

This section attempts to introduce students to the mechanism of evolution through history. Inevitably much of the evidence is secondhand. It can be illustrated by pictures and film. The questions at the end of the section are based on Darwin's findings, and those of others such as Lack, who have followed him to the Galápagos Islands. This particular segment of biological history lends itself particularly well to teaching, since the ideas emerging in the late eighteenth and mid-nineteenth centuries provide a chronological sequence which is logical and relatively easy to follow. Moreover, it is possible to relate the changes in scientific outlook to corresponding changes in social and religious attitudes.

Practical problems

Pupils may well ask whether any situation comparable with the Galápagos is to be found nearer home. Perhaps the nearest is in the Isles of Scilly where variation in the meadow brown butterfly, *Maniola jurtina*, has been studied. Judging by the distribution of spot markings on the hind wings of the insects, different races occur on many of the smaller islands even though some are isolated from their nearest neighbours by no more than a quarter of a mile of sea.

Questions and answers

Suggest a hypothesis to account for the similarities and differences between the plants and animals of the Galápagos Islands and those of the mainland.

a Similarities suggest a common ancestral stock while differences indicate divergent evolution and adaptive radiation.

What would you consider to have been the most important factors responsible for bringing these differences about?

b Differences could have resulted from isolation, the diversity of ecological niches available which do not occur on the mainland, and a lack of other species competing for them. It seems doubtful if the woodpecker finch would have evolved in competition with a true woodpecker.

What selective agents are likely to have played a predominant part in causing the evolution of the woodpecker finch?

c Perhaps the need for food and intensive competition for other insectivore niches. Alternatively, this remarkable adaptation might have evolved in an animal with unusual manipulative ability and with a diet restricted to a particular range of insects only to be found under bark or in similar situations.

How could you account for the unequal distribution of the different species of finches, whereby some occur on one island but not on another?

d This might represent adjustment to ecological situations which vary somewhat from one island to another, favouring different species in different places.

9.1 Evolution in action

Principles

One of the reasons why Darwin's theory of evolution has come to be universally accepted is because unlike any of its predecessors, it is susceptible of scientific test. If evolution is going on all round us as he suggested, then it should be possible not only to observe changes taking place, but also to measure their rate for comparison with others of a similar kind occurring elsewhere. In Darwin's time and, indeed, until comparatively recently, it was believed that selective advantages were quite small (of the order of 1 per cent) and hence evolutionary changes were likely to take place so slowly as to be undetectable in a human lifetime. However, recent researches, such as those of Kettlewell on the peppered moth, have radically changed our views on the effect of selection and it is now clear that advantages of 30 per cent or even more may be quite common. Indeed, it has proved possible to detect the effects of selection on a wild population in a single generation.

All this is most heartening where the teaching of evolution is concerned. While it is unlikely that the process of evolution can actually be detected in a natural population during a sixth form course, cumulative records kept over a few years could achieve this quite easily. Moreover, polymorphic species, such as those of the genus *Cepaea*, provide excellent material for studying the products of selection and the diversity of stabilizations achieved by different phenotypes under varying environmental conditions.

Teaching procedure

Associated materials
S(P) 4.1, 4.4, 4.5, 9.2, 9.3, 9.4, 9.5
Film loop 'Selection by predation'
NBP–54

As mentioned earlier, cumulative records of changes in a polymorphic species such as *Cepaea*, inhabiting a particular area or range of localities, could quite easily be built up. Meanwhile, if facilities permitted, a study could be made of the way in which the morphs of a species (for instance, banded and unbanded shells in *Cepaea*) assume different values in different places. One rather striking finding which will almost certainly emerge from such studies is that one stabilization may suddenly be replaced by another in a matter of a few yards, in terrain that appears to be quite uniform. For instance, a population of snails with 5 per cent banded shells may be replaced by one with 50 per cent banded within a distance of a few yards and with no discernible barrier separating the two. Such a situation might well be regarded as only transient but this is often not so; it may remain unchanged for years, in spite of a considerable amount of movement by individuals of both populations across the intervening ground. Evidently, we are concerned here with some sort of powerful selection pressure, at present largely unknown. Birds act as selective agents on snails and it is an instructive study to compare the characteristics of shells of living snails with shells of those predated by thrushes and accumulated at nearby anvil stones. The birds will be found to select their prey not only for banding and background colour of shell, but also for size. Such an investigation could be closely linked to work in Chapter 1.

Practical problems

The chief practical problems are likely to arise through lack of sufficiently rural conditions. Possibly some of the work might be carried out at a field centre. Film can provide much good material for discussion. The work can be linked with that of Chapter 2. For those who are mathematically inclined, a model evolutionary situation could be set up using beads, such as was done for population genetics and selection in Chapter 4. This is certainly a most impressive way of illustrating the effects of selection and the rapidity with which a change in gene-frequency can be brought about by selective advantages of the order of 30 per cent, such as probably obtained during the period of evolution of the melanic form of the peppered moth in the industrial midlands.

Questions and answers

In the situation you have studied, what evidence was there of differential selection? What selective agents were involved?

What do you think might be the long-term effects of continual selection in this way?

a and *b* Answers will depend on the situation. Differential selection of snails by birds (judged by evidence from anvil stones) could give some idea of the possible direction of evolution both now and in the future.

In industrial areas, the melanic forms of moths are usually common (see figure 58) and the inherent melanic character is dominant. Occasionally, melanic forms of some species occur in rural areas. In this case the melanic character is recessive. Suggest a hypothesis to account for this situation.

c That dominance and recessiveness are themselves products of selection.

The black variety of the scalloped hazel moth, Gonodontis bidentata, *has almost completely replaced the lighter form in the Manchester area but has not yet appeared in Birmingham only 80 miles away. Can you suggest any possible reasons for this apparent anomaly?*

d Limited mobility of the species; do the melanic forms in Manchester not fly as far as Birmingham? Peculiar conditions in Birmingham unfavourable to melanic forms, possibly lower pollution? Perhaps a lack of food plants resulting in a smaller population of peppered moths and hence giving less opportunity for the spread of melanic forms? There are many other possibilities.

9.2 Evidence for evolution from geology

Principles

Darwin realized that fossils provide the only tangible evidence that evolution has occurred in the past. Today, we are less concerned than the Victorians were in establishing that evolution is universal, since the fact that it has occurred and we ourselves are products of it is almost everywhere accepted. Nonetheless, it is important that students should realize the contributions that a study of fossils can make to our understanding of the evolutionary process (and those it cannot). The incompleteness of the fossil record needs stressing.

Teaching procedure

Associated materials
S(P) 9.1, 9.4

Viewed from a historical angle, the study of geology in the early nineteenth century fits in exceedingly well with that of evolution since both were following parallel courses. The contributions of men such as Lyell, whose classic work, *Principles of geology*, was to have such an influence upon Darwin, paved the way for the evolutionists in throwing new light on the mode of formation of the sedimentary rocks and hence on the probable age of the Earth. Once such ideas had been established and scientists saw that there had been life on Earth far longer than had previously been supposed, the appeal of Darwin's theory of evolution became even more compelling.

The principal difficulty likely to arise in teaching this section is the obtaining of suitable material. Unfortunately, fossiliferous rocks are not always accessible and it may well be impossible to organize an expedition to a good area. Should this be at all possible, however, the value gained will far outweigh the extra trouble involved, for there is no doubt that pupils tend to be fascinated by fossils, particularly if they can collect them themselves. Local geologists or museum authorities will advise, especially on any need to conserve fossil supplies.

Practical problems

Should it prove impossible to pay a visit to an area of stratified rocks (preferably containing fossils), it may be possible to obtain some of the surplus stock which frequently accumulates in museums. Alas, this all too often lacks data about its origin, but it is better than nothing. In the absence of original fossils, plaster casts can be used. Some of these are most useful, particularly those relating to fossil horses which can be studied in chronological sequence and in relation to the changing environment in which the animals lived.

Questions and answers

What light does your investigation of fossils (or casts) throw on the evolution of the animal or plant groups concerned?

a The answer depends on circumstances. Casts of fossil horses would be good material to use in this context.

Does the examination of such material provide any indication of the ecological conditions in which the organisms must have lived?

b Only to a very limited extent. For instance, the conditions in which the early horses lived (e.g. 3-toed *Eohippus*) were probably more moist than those in which the modern *Equus* evolved. The difficulty in interpreting the fossil remains of many organisms is that we so often have little idea of their ecology.

The age of the earth is estimated to be around 4000 million years. Why, do you think, does the fossil record end at about 600 million years (see figure 62)?

c Because the organisms which existed before that time lacked hard parts. Also the very ancient rocks provide rather poor media for fossilization.

9.3 Evidence for evolution from comparative anatomy

Principles

This short section has been included to illustrate the relationship between the structure of organs, their function, and their evolutionary relationships. Here is a good opportunity to introduce the ideas of homology and analogy, and to discuss them in an evolutionary and classificatory context. While analogous structures may be of little interest to the evolutionist, their existence can be invaluable for making keys. For example, an effective key to the flowering plants has been built up by grouping the various species, as a start, according to the colour of their flowers.

Teaching procedure

Associated materials
S(P) 9.1, 9.4

There is nothing particularly original in the approach; the material is familiar enough and included in most standard textbooks. A danger is that classwork can degenerate rather easily into mere verification. For this reason it is important that the work should be made as exploratory as possible by introducing a wide range of material, not only the few vertebrates usually regarded as 'types'. Specimens could include skeletons, disarticulated bones, preserved and stuffed animals and, of course, living specimens if these are available.

Questions and answers

To what extent do the examples of homologous structures that you have chosen provide evidence of evolutionary relationships?

a The answer depends on the examples chosen. Pentadactyl limbs are good material for answering this sort of question.

Do the modifications of the basic pentadactyl plan provide any indication of the changing ecological environments in which the animals must have lived?

b Yes, to some extent. The splay toes of *Eohippus* suggest a moist terrain; the single toe of *Equus*, drier conditions.

Other evidence for evolution

Principles

Associated materials
S(M) 2.8, 2.9, 4.6
S(P) 1.1, 4.5, 4.7, 6.6, 9.1, 9.2, 9.4
S(D) 7.5
S(C) 2.7

As in 9.4, this is material that requires little comment as it is fully covered in the standard texts. How much is included must be a matter of opinion, but evidence from embryology and geographical distribution is certainly worth mentioning since this relates to earlier work, as indicated in the *Laboratory guide*.

Questions and answers

What additional evidence for evolution is provided by a study of:
1 *Embryology?*
2 *Geographical distribution? (Refer back to 9.1)*
3 *Classification?*
4 *Comparative physiology and biochemistry?*
5 *Comparative parasitology?*

In each instance, is there any evidence that might explain the reason for the evolutionary changes concerned?

a and *b* Answers will depend on the material used. See also the items in *Study guide (P)*, Chapter 9.

Additional bibliography

General reading

Barnett, S. A. (Ed.) (1958) *A century of Darwin*. Heinemann. (Symposium of contributions.)
Bell, P. R. *et al* (Eds.) (1959) *Darwin's biological work*. Cambridge University Press. (Symposium of contributions.)
Cain, A. J. (1954) *Animal species and their evolution*. Hutchinson. (Treatment of the species problem from the zoological standpoint.)
De Beer, Sir G. (1963) *Charles Darwin*. Nelson. (Biography.)
Ford, E. B. (1957) *Mendelism and evolution*. 6th edition. Methuen.
Ford, E. B. (1964) *Ecological genetics*. Methuen. (Modern experimental approach to evolution.)
Heslop-Harrison, J. (1960) *New concepts in flowering plant taxonomy*. Heinemann. (The species problem from the botanical standpoint.)
Mayr, E. (1964) *Systematics and the origin of species*. Dover. (Evolution viewed from the classificatory standpoint.)
Sheppard, P. M. (1958) *Natural selection and heredity*. Hutchinson.
Simpson, G. G. (1951) *Horses*. Harcourt, Brace & World. (Account of fossil forms.)
Simpson, G. G. (1953) *Life of the past*. Harcourt, Brace & World. (Introduction to palaeontology.)

References

Aston, J. L. and Bradshaw, A. D. (1966) 'Evolution in closely adjacent plant populations. II *Agrostis stolonifera* in maritime habitats.' *Heredity*, **21**, 649–664.
Cain, A. J. and Sheppard, P. M. (1950) 'Selection in the polymorphic land snail, *Cepaea nemoralis*.' *Heredity*, **4**, 275–294.

INDEX

Nuffield Foundation Science Teaching Project

Advanced Biological Science

Consultative Committee

Professor J. H. Burnett
Professor D. R. Newth
Dr D. H. Adams
Dr J. K. Brierley, H.M.I.
A. G. Clegg
R. J. Doolan, H.M.I.
Professor J. D. Gillett
Professor J. L. Harper
Professor K. W. Keohane
E. J. Machin
S. T. S. Skillen, H.M.I.
Professor M. M. Swann, F.R.S.
Miss M. Thomas
Miss M. Tilstone
Professor N. Tinbergen, F.R.S.
Professor J. M. Thoday

Area co-ordinators

J. A. Barker
M. S. Bridges
Professor J. H. Burnett
R. J. Doolan, H.M.I.
J. H. Gray
Professor J. L. Harper
H. F. King
E. J. Machin
S. T. S. Skillen, H.M.I.
C. F. Stoneman
Miss M. Thomas
D. Tomley
K. O. Turner

Evaluation Committee

P. J. Kelly
W. H. Dowdeswell
J. F. Eggleston
Professor J. F. Kerr
R. E. Lister
Dr R. Mayer
Mrs D. M. Penfold
Professor P. H. Taylor

Examinations Committee

R. E. Lister, Examinations Co-ordinator and Chief Examiner
Professor J. T. Allanson
Miss A. M. Almond
W. G. Bott
Dr R. F. S. Creed
R. J. Doolan, H.M.I.
W. H. Dowdeswell
J. F. Eggleston
W. A. L. Evans
Dr W. Gladwell
B. M. Hobby
P. J. Kelly
Professor J. F. Kerr
T. L. MacDonald
Mrs D. M. Penfold
A. R. Stephenson
Dr J. Webster

The Nuffield Foundation is grateful to the following for their help:

Professor M. Abercrombie, F.R.S.
Professor J. T. Allanson
Dr G. E. Anderson
Dr M. Ashby
Professor L. J. Audus
W. M. M. Baron
J. K. Barras
Dr E. W. Baxter
Professor J. N. Black
B. Bracegirdle
Professor A. D. Bradshaw
A. Brindle
Professor L. Broadbent
Miss H. Bruce
Dr R. V. Brunt
J. J. Bryant
Professor J. R. Busvine
R. A. Butler
Professor A. J. Cain
Dr J. D. Carthy
M. R. A. Chance
Dr J. M. Cherrett
A. G. Clegg
Dr J. Cohen
D. M. Cole
K. J. Connolly
W. O. Copland
Dr K. Cowan
Dr L. K. Crowe
Professor A. G. S. Curtiss
A. Darlington
A. Davies
Dr A. F. G. Dixon
R. B. Drysdale
A. Ellis
Wing Commander J. Ernsting
D. H. Evans
Dr S. M. Evans
Miss V. J. Evans
R. A. Faires
Dr P. Fleetwood-Walker
Dr W. W. Fletcher
Dr R. R. Folley
Dr C. P. Friedlander
Mrs V. C. Fyfe
Dr B. F. Gill
Dr R. Gliddon
Dr K. M. Goodway
Dr D. J. Griffiths
Dr J. P. Grime
B. J. F. Haller
J. Halcrow
Mrs E. Hambly
Dr J. Hannay
M. W. Hardisty
Professor J. L. Harper
Dr N. E. Hickin
Miss M. Hogg
Dr J. W. Hopton
Professor G. M. Hughes
S. W. Hurry
Dr D. A. Jones
Dr J. S. Kennedy
Dr M. Knight
Dr C. W. Lawrence
Dr R. M. Leech
Dr K. R. Lewis
Dr A. P. M. Lockwood
Dr R. Lowery
Dr F. G. H. Lupton
Professor A. Macfadyen
Dr A. D. McKelvie
Miss D. Manuel
Dr H. Heidner
Professor W. Melville Arnott
Professor D. E. W. Miles
Dr D. Moore
Dr D. H. Morgan
J. A. Moss
Dr R. A. Nilan
Dr T. G. Onions
D. W. Parry
Dr J. Philipson
Miss E. S. M. Phillips
Dr J. Pusey
Dr M. Pyke
J. Rendall
Dr M. Richardson
Professor C. M. Rick
Dr A. W. Robards
Dr M. B. V. Roberts
Miss A. Rogers
Dr A. Seaman
Dr C. Selby
Professor P. M. Sheppard
Dr N. W. Simmonds
Professor E. W. Simon
Dr K. Simpson
Dr R. Sladden
Dr J. Smith
W. S. Smith
Dr S. Spickett
Dr C. A. Suneson
Professor J. F. Sutcliffe
Professor J. M. Thoday
Miss J. Thurston
Dr R. A. E. Tilney-Bassett
Dr A. Upshall
C. G. Vosa
B. Vowles
Dr D. M. Vowles
Dr D. A. Walker
Dr M. A. Wallace
Dr F. L. Waterhouse
Dr U. Weidmann
Dr H. L. K. Whitehouse
Dr D. Wilkie
J. D. Wray
Dr H. V. Wyatt

Trial schools and teachers

Arnold County High School, Nottingham	B. W. Thompson
	Miss M. Nuttall
Ballyclare High School	P. A. Campbell
	J. L. Flemming
Bexley Grammar School	M. S. Bridges
	Mrs V. A. Bland
Bletchley Grammar School, Bucks.	R. Robinson
Brockenhurst Grammar School	W. I. Stopher
	Miss P. Emmett
	Miss B. A. Lewis
Bromsgrove County High School	D. Hobson
	H. R. Heywood
	R. Leedham
Bury Grammar School	Mrs E. James
Cambridge Grammar School for Boys	H. F. King
	M. P. Goldsborough
	Dr Boursnell
Cambridgeshire High School for Girls	Miss M. Salton
	Mrs Coleman
Cambridge House School	Miss G. E. Drennan
Campbell College, Belfast	R. J. Wells
	R. H. Pottage
Catford County School	Mrs N. Filtness
Cheadle Hulme School	A. Ellis
Chislehurst and Sidcup G.S. for Boys	W. H. Freeman
	R. O. Knight
Chorlton High School, Manchester	N. Crane
Christ's College, London	J. B. Quinn
	I. Barker
Coleraine Academical Institution	D. B. Jagoe
	A. Nichol
Colwyn High School	Miss M. E. Jones
Darlington Girls' High School	J. Dodds
Dauntsey's School, Wilts.	E. E. Hickford
	A. K. Thomas
Dulwich College	S. A. Cole
	C. F. Stoneman
	D. V. Hillier
Ecclesbourne School, Derbyshire	C. B. Johnson
	Mrs G. E. Garland
Edinburgh Academy	P. R. Booth
Eltham Hill School	Mrs E. R. Jefferis
	Miss I. Tozer
	Mrs J. E. C. Tickell
Fettes College	C. D. Pighills
	A. H. Tothill
George Dixon Grammar School, Birmingham	E. R. Robertson
Hinckley Grammar School	K. O. Turner
	K. W. Rogers

Holland Park School	Mrs R. S. Patterson
	C. Martin
Holloway School	D. Kay
	A. K. Massey
Holt County School, Berks.	Miss G. Monger
	Miss A. M. Dengate
	Mrs R. King
King Edward VI Camp Hill School for Girls, Birmingham	Miss M. K. Sands
	Miss J. Maudsley
King Edward VI High School for Girls, Birmingham	Miss B. Foxton
King's Norton Grammar School for Girls	Miss D. M. Evans
	Mrs Gallimore
Malvern College	A. Darlington
	P. D. Burke
	J. C. Weatherley
Malvern Girls' College	Miss M. Jago
	Miss M. Waters
Manchester Grammar School	J. H. Gray
	F. C. Minns
	D. Tomley
	A. D. Morgan
Market Harborough County Grammar School	G. Myton
	Miss M. E. John
Mayfield School, London	Mrs J. Cooper
	Mrs J. A. Godley
Methodist College, Belfast	Miss G. M. D. Gotto
	P. A. M. Paice
	Miss H. E. Wilson
Nuneaton High School for Girls	R. W. Bacon
	G. V. Davies
Perse School for Girls, Cambridge	Miss A. I. Taylor
Queen Elizabeth Grammar School, Penrith	H. T. C. Owen
St. Joseph's Grammar Technical School, Co. Durham	Miss M. McLevy
	J. McArdle
Stretford Grammar School for Boys	R. Kearns
	T. Kershaw
	J. Reed
Stretford Grammar School for Girls	Miss J. Macarthur
	Mrs B. S. Beech
Westminster City School	J. B. Hunt
	D. P. Marshall
	R. Snook
William Hulme's Grammar School, Manchester	R. A. Haynes
The College, Winchester	W. M. M. Baron
	Dr R. Gliddon
County High School for Girls, Winchester	Mrs C. Baldry
	Mrs M. Meredith
	Mrs J. Young